ALL SHOOK UP

Also by Glenn C. Altschuler

Rude Republic: Americans and Their Politics
in the Nineteenth Century (with Stuart M. Blumin)

Changing Channels: America in TV Guide
(with David I. Grossvogel)

Revivalism, Social Conscience, and Community
in the Burned-Over District
(with Jan Saltzgaber)

Better Than Second Best: Love and Work in the Life of Helen Magill

Race, Ethnicity, and Class in American Social Thought, 1865–1919

Andrew D. White—Educator, Historian, Diplomat

PIVOTAL MOMENTS
IN AMERICAN HISTORY

Series Editors
David Hackett Fischer
James M. McPherson

James T. Patterson
Brown v. Board of Education:
A Civil Rights Milestone and Its Troubled Legacy

Maury Klein
Rainbow's End:
The Crash of 1929

James M. McPherson
Crossroads of Freedom:
Antietam

GLENN C. ALTSCHULER

ALL
SHOOK
UP

HOW
ROCK 'N' ROLL
CHANGED AMERICA

OXFORD
UNIVERSITY PRESS

OXFORD

UNIVERSITY PRESS

Oxford   New York
Auckland   Bangkok   Buenos Aires   Cape Town   Chennai
Dar es Salaam   Delhi   Hong Kong   Istanbul   Karachi   Kolkata
Kuala Lumpur   Madrid   Melbourne   Mexico City   Mumbai   Nairobi
São Paulo   Shanghai   Taipei   Tokyo   Toronto

First published by Oxford University Press, Inc., 2003
198 Madison Avenue, New York, New York 10016

www.oup.com

First issued as an Oxford University Press paperback, 2004
ISBN-13 978-0-19-517749-7

Oxford is a registered trademark of Oxford University Press

The Library of Congress has cataloged the cloth edition as follows:
Altschuler, Glenn C.
All shook up : how rock 'n' roll changed America / Glenn C. Altschuler.
p. cm.— (Pivotal moments in American history)
Includes bibliographical references (p.) and index.
ISBN-13 978-0-19-513943-3

Rock music—Social aspects—United States.
Rock music—United States—History and criticism.
I. Title. II. Series.
ML3534 .A465 2003
781.66'0973–dc21
2003001214

22
Printed in Canada on acid-free paper

To Jed, voluntary brother,
and to Rob, ceremonial son

CONTENTS

EDITORS' NOTE

This volume is part of a series called Pivotal Moments in American History. Each book in this series examines a large historical event or process that changed the course of American development. These events were not the products of ineluctable forces outside the boundaries of human choice; they were the results of decisions and actions by people who had opportunities to choose and act otherwise. This element of contingency introduces a dynamic tension into the story of the past. Books in the Pivotal Moments series are written in a narrative format to capture that dynamic tension of contingency and choice.

The design of the series also reflects the current state of historical writing, which shows growing attention to the experiences of ordinary people and increasing sensitivity to issues of race, ethnicity, class, and gender in the context of large structures and processes. We seek to combine this new scholarship with old ideas of history as a narrative art and traditional standards of sound scholarship, mature judgment, and good writing.

The movie *Blackboard Jungle* with its theme song "Rock Around the Clock," released in 1955, surely marks a pivotal moment in American cultural history. Having evolved from the African-American musical genre of rhythm and blues, rock 'n' roll was here to stay. Denounced by the over-thirty generation, ridiculed by self-proclaimed arbiters of musical taste, deplored by guardians of sexual morality, attacked by whites who feared its breaking of racial barriers, blamed by the media for juvenile delinquency, rock 'n' roll was embraced by the young. For the baby boomers it was a music of liberation. Every generation tries to define its own identity by rebelling against its elders. For the teenage generation of the 1950s, which came of age in the next decade, rock 'n' roll was the catalyst of that rebellion. Without rock 'n' roll, writes Glenn Altschuler, "it is impossible to imagine the '60s in the United States." Initially apolitical, this cultural phenomenon helped generate the civil rights and antiwar movements that gave that decade its distinctive ethos. The "shook up generation," according to Altschuler, "transformed an inchoate sense of disaffection and dissatisfaction into a political and cultural movement."

As a musical genre, rock 'n' roll did not take a simple or single form. Its 2–4 beat has many variations: rhythm and blues, country rock, romantic rock, heavy metal, punk rock, grunge rock, Christian rock, and others. Music whose leading performers included Little Richard and Pat Boone, Jerry Lee Lewis and Ricky Nelson, Chuck Berry and Buddy Holly, Elvis Presley and the Beatles "frustrates anyone intent on giving it a rigorous, musical definition."

Glenn Altschuler avoids the trap of rigorous definition. All of these performers—and many others—are here in this book in all of the colorful variety of their musical styles and personalities. In a lucid, readable narrative that covers two decades but concentrates on the crucial years of 1955 to 1965, Altschuler brings to life the vivid human drama of this cultural revolution. All who lived through those tumultuous years will relive them in these pages; those born too late will discover the origins of the world they inherited.

David Hackett Fischer
James M. McPherson

ACKNOWLEDGMENTS

Born in 1950, I was a bit too young to get "all shook up" over rock 'n' roll in the 1950s, let alone think about it as a "pivotal moment" in American culture. Therefore for me the project has provided an opportunity not only to revisit a decade—but to discover some phenomenal music about which I have been only dimly aware. I am grateful to James McPherson for believing that this topic was a worthy addition to the series he and David Hackett Fischer are editing for Oxford University Press—and for signing me up (after my friend and colleague Joel Silbey introduced us) to write the volume.

Several students, former students, and friends helped with the research. As he combed through issues of *Seventeen* magazine, Michael Sharp carefully distinguished between the prescriptive and the descriptive. Rob Summers spent parts of several semesters and one summer in the Cornell archives and the Library of Congress ferreting out material on rock 'n' roll in newspapers, mass circulation magazines, and industry publications. An accomplished rock musician himself—and now a superb high school teacher—he turned out to be the most thorough and insightful research assistant I have ever worked with. Adam Lawrence took precious time from work and family to find many of the photographs.

Three fine historians and friends—Stuart Blumin, Ralph Janis, and Nick Salvatore—read the manuscript in its entirety. They made bibliographical suggestions, improved the prose and organization, and helped sharpen the themes. Finding just the right mix of encouragement and critical insight, they are everything one could want in colleagues. Jeff Cowie served as my guide to Springsteen.

James McPherson and David Hackett Fischer also provided careful readings of the manuscript, catching some errors and insisting always on a concise, precise presentation. The comments of Peter Ginna, editorial director at Oxford, were extraordinarily helpful. At every stage in the process, he has shown himself to be a consummate professional. India Cooper has been a thorough, skillful, and diplomatic copy editor.

As she has for years, Esther Tzivanis has been a jack of all trades and master of each one—tracking down books and articles, processing my words, managing the calendar of a dean who wants to continue writing books. I would not have agreed to write *All Shook Up* and could not have completed it without her help.

Jed Horwitt, Tom and Dottie Litwin, Isaac Kramnick, R. Laurence Moore, and my mother, May Altschuler, listened to me talk about rock 'n' roll—and talk and talk. On occasion, they even appeared to be interested in what I was saying. They probably will not agree to accept responsibility for any errors that might appear in this book. Nonetheless, I cherish their friendship and love.

ALL SHOOK UP

"ALL SHOOK UP"

1

Popular Music and American Culture, 1945–1955

"Rock 'n' Roll Fight Hospitalizes Youth," the *New York Times* announced on April 15, 1957. In a fracas between white and black boys and girls following a rock 'n' roll show attended by ten thousand fans, fifteen-year-old Kenneth Myers of Medford, Massachusetts, was stabbed and thrown onto the tracks at a subway station. Myers missed touching a live rail by inches and scrambled back onto the platform seconds before a train sped into the station. "The Negro youths were responsible for it," police lieutenant Francis Gannon told reporters. "The fight was senseless . . . but we expect difficulty every time a rock 'n' roll show comes in."[1]

For two years the *Times* printed dozens of articles linking destructive activities at, outside, or in the aftermath of concerts to "the beat and the booze" or the music alone.[2] Public interest in rock 'n' roll was so great, *Times* editors even viewed the absence of a riot as newsworthy. "Rock 'n' Rollers Collect Calmly," readers learned, following a concert at the Paramount Theater in New York City. The journalist attributed the good order on this occasion and several others that year to the police, who arrived early and in force, as many as three hundred strong, some of them on horseback, to set up wooden barriers along the sidewalk, separate the crowd from passersby on Times Square, and then station themselves in the aisles and at the rear of the theater to

3

keep the audience "under surveillance." During the performances, the fans "cheered, shrieked, applauded, and jumped up and down." A few dancers were escorted back to their seats, and the police ordered several excited fans who stood up to sit down. But no one had to be removed or arrested for "obstreperous" behavior. The implication was clear: teenage rock 'n' rollers should not be left on their own.[3]

Reports of riotous behavior convinced many public officials to ban live rock 'n' roll shows. After frenzied fans in San Jose, California, "routed" seventy-three policemen, neighboring Santa Cruz refused permits for concerts in public buildings. Mayor Bernard Berry and two commissioners in Jersey City, New Jersey, decided not to allow Bill Haley and the Comets to perform in the municipally owned Roosevelt Stadium. Following several fistfights at a dance attended by 2,700 teenagers that were broken up by twelve police officers, the city council of Asbury Park, New Jersey, ruled that "swing and blues harmonies" would no longer be permitted.

The epidemic even spread to the armed forces. In Newport, Rhode Island, Rear Admiral Ralph D. Earl Jr. declared rock 'n' roll off base, for a least a month and perhaps forever, at the enlisted men's club of the naval station. Earl issued his edict following an inspection of the club, which had been wrecked during a "beer-bottle throwing, chair swinging riot." The altercation began when someone turned out the lights, plunging the dance floor into darkness, as Fats Domino's band played on. Ten sailors were injured and nine arrested. Although white and African-American sailors and marines and their wives and dates were involved, the admiral ruled out racial friction as the cause of the melee, attributing it to the "frenzied tempo" of the music.[4]

Cities across the United States joined the "ban wagon." In Atlanta, Georgia, children under eighteen could not attend public dances unless a parent or guardian went with them or gave written permission. The city council of San Antonio, Texas, eliminated rock 'n' roll music from the jukeboxes at municipal swimming pools because the primitive beat attracted "undesirable elements" who practiced their "spastic gyrations" in abbreviated bathing suits. In Boston, as a grand jury indicted the sponsor of a rock 'n' roll concert for inciting the "unlawful destruction of property," Boston mayor John D. Hynes announced that the city would not rent public facilities to promoters. The shows they mounted, he claimed, invariably attracted "troublemakers."[5]

Rock-and-Roll Called 'Communicable Disease'

HARTFORD, Conn., March 27 (UP)—A noted psychiatrist described "rock-and-roll" music today as a 'communicable disease" and another sign of adolescent rebellion."

Dr. Francis J. Braceland, psychiatrist in chief of the Institute of Living, called rock-and-roll a "cannibalistic and tribalistic" form of music. He was commenting on the disturbances that led to eleven

ROCK 'N' ROLL STABBING

Teen-Agers Attack Sailor in Brawl After Boston Show

BOSTON, May 4 (UP)—Teen-aged b------ -t---b-- - -----

Segregationist Wants Ban on 'Rock and Roll'

BIRMINGHAM, Ala., March 29 (UP)—A segregation leader

BOSTON, NEW HAVEN BAN 'ROCK' SHOWS

BOSTON, May 5 (AP)—Rock 'n' roll musical shows in public auditoriums were banned in Boston and New Haven today.

Other New England cit braced for the same show t preceded violence in Boston Saturday night.

Fifteen persons were stabb beaten or robbed by gangs roving teen-agers and adu after an Alan Freed show en at the Boston Arena.

Albert Raggiani, 18-year-sailor from Stoughton, stabbed repeatedly in the che He was taken to Chelsea Na Hospital. His condition was ported satisfactory.

Mayor John B. Hynes of B ton said promoters for s shows in the future will not granted licenses.

"I am not against rock

roll as such," Mr. Hynes said, "and not when it is conducted under the auspices of an established organization. However, I am against rock 'n' roll dances when they are put on by a pro-

JERSEY CITY ORDERS ROCK-AND-ROLL BAN

Special to The New York Times.

JERSEY CITY, July 9—The phonograph record appeared today to be the last stand of rock-and-roll music here. City officials, for the second time this year, refused to allow an in-person performance of the latest teen-age musical craze.

Mayor Bernard J. Berry and City Commissioners Lawrence A. Whipple and Joshua Ringle announced they would not allow the use of municipally owned Roosevelt Stadium Friday night for a rock-and-roll "concert" by Bill Haley and his Comets.

The mass media spread the alarm about the dangers of rock 'n' roll, as in these newspaper headlines from the mid-1950s.

As the nation's elders fumed, fretted, and legislated over rock 'n' roll, they pondered its appeal to the youth of the United States. Adults agreed that "this hooby-doopy, oop-shoop, ootie ootie, boom boom de-addy boom, scoobledy goobledy dump" was trash. They differed only about its impact. Judge Hilda Schwartz, who presided over Adolescents' Court in New York City, believed that rock 'n' roll did not cause riots or juvenile delinquency. A few "bad eggs," looking for trouble and likely to find it wherever they went, and not the music, were responsible for the disturbances. Like the Charleston, rock 'n' roll evoked a physical response, but it allowed teenagers to discharge excess energy and was essentially harmless. While a tiny fraction of youngsters lining up around theaters were hostile or insecure, the vast majority were "wholesome boys and girls following an adolescent fad as only adolescents can."[6]

In the mass media, however, alarmists drowned out apologists. That pop singers would not like the competition might be expected, but their condemnations of rock 'n' roll were especially venomous. It "smells phony and false," said Frank Sinatra, at whose feet bobby-soxers had swooned and shrieked in the 1940s. "It is sung, played, and written for the most part by cretinous goons, and by means of its almost imbecilic reiteration and sly, lewd, in plain fact dirty, lyrics it manages to be the martial music of every side-burned delinquent on the face of the earth." Therapists weighed in as well. *Time* magazine informed readers that psychologists believed that teenagers embraced rock 'n' roll because of a deep-seated, abnormal need to belong. Allegiances to favorite performers, *Time* warned, "bear passing resemblance to Hitler's mass meetings." The *New York Times* provided a platform to psychiatrist Francis Braceland, who had a similar view. Branding rock 'n' roll "a cannibalistic and tribalistic" form of music that appealed to the insecurity and rebelliousness of youth, he thought it all the more dangerous because it was "a communicable disease."[7]

A few went further, declaring the music of teenagers a tool in a conspiracy to ruin the morals of a generation of Americans. In their best-seller *U.S.A. Confidential*, journalists Jack Lait and Lee Mortimer linked juvenile delinquency "with tom-toms and hot jive and ritualistic orgies of erotic dancing, weed-smoking and mass mania, with African jungle background. Many music shops purvey dope; assignations are made in them. White girls are recruited for colored lovers. . . . We know that many platter-spinners are hopheads. Many others are Reds, left-wingers, or hecklers of social convention. . . . Through disc jockeys, kids get to know colored and other musicians; they frequent places the radio oracles plug, which is done with design . . . to hook juves [juveniles] and guarantee a new generation subservient to the Mafia."[8]

Rock 'n' roll generated sound and fury. What, if anything, did it signify? The rise of rock 'n' roll and the reception of it, in fact, can tell us a lot about the culture and values of the United States in the 1950s. According to historian James Gilbert, there was a struggle throughout the decade "over the uses of popular culture to determine who would speak, to what audience, and for what purpose." At the center of that struggle, rock 'n' roll unsettled a nation that had been "living in an 'age of anxiety'" since 1945.[9]

The Cold War produced numerous foreign crises—the Berlin Airlift and the Korean War among them. A fear of internal subversion by Communists, stoked by the often irresponsible charges of Senator Joseph McCarthy, resulted in loyalty oaths, blacklists, and a more general suppression of dissent. In a national poll conducted in 1954, more than 50 percent of Americans agreed that all known Communists should be jailed; 58 percent favored finding and punishing all Communists, "even if some innocent people should be hurt"; and a whopping 78 percent thought reporting to the FBI neighbors or acquaintances they suspected of being Communists a good idea. Coinciding with the Cold War, of course, was the nuclear age, and the possibility of a war that would obliterate the human race. The construction of fallout shelters, and instructions to schoolchildren about how to survive an atomic attack ("Fall instantly face down, elbows out, forehead on arms, eyes shut . . . duck and cover"), probably alarmed as much as they reassured.[10]

The family seemed as vulnerable as the nation to internal subversion in the 1950s. "Not even the Communist conspiracy," U.S. Senator Robert Hendrickson asserted, "could devise a more effective way to demoralize, confuse, and destroy" the United States than the behavior of apathetic, absent, or permissive parents. Americans worried about working moms, emasculated dads, and especially about a growing army of teenage terrors, poised to seize control of the house, lock, stock, and living room. These fears, Gilbert has shown, crystallized in a decade-long crusade against juvenile delinquency, replete with dozens of congressional hearings and hundreds of pieces of legislation to regulate youth culture.[11]

Finally, a principled and persistent civil rights movement demanded in the 1950s that the commitment to equal rights for African Americans no longer be deferred. With the Supreme Court decision in *Brown v. Board of Education*, the Montgomery, Alabama, Bus Boycott, and the use of federal troops to escort black students into heretofore all-white Little Rock Central High School in Arkansas, a revolution in race relations was well under way. Americans in the North as well as the South were not at all sure where it was headed.

Rock 'n' roll entered indirectly into Cold War controversies, but in helping young Americans construct social identities, it did provide a discourse through which they could examine and contest the meanings adults ascribed to family, sexuality, and race. That discourse was not always verbal. Rock 'n' roll moved audiences as much with the body language of performers and the beat of the music as with its lyrics, perhaps more. When rock 'n' roll tries to criticize something, critic Greil Marcus believes, "it becomes hopelessly self-righteous and stupid." When the music is most exciting, "when the guitar is fighting for space in the clatter while voices yelp and wail as one man finishes another's lines or spins it off in a new direction—the lyrics are blind baggage, and they emerge only in snatches." Without a consistent or coherent critique, and never fully free from an attachment to traditional 1950s values, rock 'n' roll nonetheless provided a fresh perspective, celebrating leisure, romance, and sex, deriding deferred gratification and men in gray flannel suits stationed at their office desks, and delighting in the separate world of the teenager.[12]

According to media commentator Jeff Greenfield, by unleashing a perception that young bodies were "Joy Machines," rock 'n' roll set off "the first tremors along the Generational Fault," paving the way for the 1960s. "Nothing we see in the Counterculture," Greenfield claims, "not the clothes, the hair, the sexuality, the drugs, the rejection of reason, the resort to symbols and magic—none of it is separable from the coming to power in the 1950s of rock and roll music. Brewed in the hidden corners of black American cities, its rhythms infected white Americans, seducing them out of the kind of temperate bobby-sox passions out of which Andy Hardy films are spun. Rock and roll was elemental, savage, dripping with sex; it was just as our parents feared."[13]

Like Jack Lait and Lee Mortimer, to whom he sounds eerily similar, Greenfield almost certainly exaggerated the influence of rock 'n' roll. Nonetheless, the music did leave an indelible imprint on the society and culture of the United States. Listened to, sometimes furtively, in millions of bedrooms and bathrooms, and argued across the dinner table, rock 'n' roll seemed to be everywhere during the decade, exhilarating, influential, and even pivotal to some, and an outrage to Americans intent on ignoring, wishing away, or suppressing dissent and conflict.

Rock 'n' roll was especially unwelcome to those who asserted that "the Great Boom" that followed the Depression and World War II had ushered in a "dream era." If the decade of 1950s was an age of anxiety, it was also an era with a pervasive, powerful, public ideology proclaiming the United States a harmonious, homogeneous, and prosperous land. The American people, boasted Fred Vinson, director of mobilization and reconversion during the war and then Chief Justice of the U.S. Supreme Court, "are in the pleasant predicament of having to learn to live fifty percent better than they ever have before." Between 1940 and 1955 the personal income of Americans rose 293 percent. National wealth increased by 60 percent between 1947 and 1961. Six percent of the world's people, Americans consumed one-third of the world's goods and services by the middle of the 1950s.[14]

The "great expectations" Americans had for the future depended on stable, nuclear families with each member performing his or her assigned roles. Secure in his career, the father was "the meal ticket," leaving his wife in charge of the home to raise polite children, eager and well prepared to assume their responsibilities as adults. Such families seemed to be everywhere. In 1946, 2.2 million couples married, setting a record unequaled for thirty-three years. According to the 1950 census, the average age at marriage was 22.0 for men and 20.3 for women, a drop from the 1940 rate of 24.3 and 21.5. Young couples continued to marry throughout the decade. They began producing "baby boomers" almost immediately. An all-time high of 3.4 million children were born in 1946, 20 percent more than in 1945. As the teenage population began to expand in the '50s, and boys and girls needed rooms of their own, home ownership became a reality for millions of Americans. Of the thirteen million residences built between 1948 and 1958, eleven million were in the suburbs. More people moved to the suburbs each year during the decade than had come through Ellis Island. As they lounged on the back deck, many Americans smiled at their good fortune in reaching adulthood in the United States at mid-century. If there were juvenile delinquents, they lived somewhere else. If some were not yet prosperous, their time was coming because America rewarded anyone willing to work. If Negroes were discriminated against, that was in the South, and, anyway, the problem would soon be resolved. "It was the Zeitgeist," concluded psychologist Joseph Adelson, "the spirit of the times."[15]

The zeitgeist was evident on the new mass medium, television. Installed in nearly two-thirds of American households by 1955, television spread the gospel of prosperity, barely acknowledging the existence of poverty or conflict. Whether dramas were set in the Old West of Marshal Matt Dillon or the courtroom of Perry Mason, viewers had no difficulty distinguishing right from wrong or the good guys from the bad guys. In the end, justice was always done. Situation comedies, the reigning genre of the 1950s, presented a lily-white, suburban United States, full of happy housewives like June Cleaver, fathers like Jim Anderson, who knew best, and cute kids like the Beaver, whose biggest dilemma was the size of his allowance. TV commercials suggested that every viewer could easily afford the most modern appliance and the latest model automobile. When African Americans appeared on the small screen, they played chauffeurs, maids, and janitors or sang and danced. The small screen, then, was mainstream. Another America might be glimpsed occasionally on an Edward R. Murrow documentary, or *Playhouse 90*, or the Army–McCarthy hearings, but with the nightly network news limited to fifteen minutes, television rarely left viewers uncertain or scared.[16]

In the early '50s, popular music sent similar messages. Bing Crosby and Perry Como sang soothing, romantic ballads, while the orchestras of Mantovani, Hugo Winterhalter, Percy Faith, and George Cates created mood music for middle-of-the-road mid-lifers, who hummed and sang along in elevators and dental offices. Seeking to create a calm, warm environment for men and women who made love with the lights out, pop singers, according to Arnold Shaw, adhered to the following precepts: "Don't sing out—croon, hum, reflect, daydream. Wish on a star, wink at the moon, laze in the sun. . . . Accentuate the positive, eliminate the negative. . . . DO stick with Mister In-Between." Popular black singers—Nat King Cole and Johnny Mathis—harmonized with white tastes, in style, sound, and lyrics. As late as 1955, the top five on the pop charts were "Unchained Melody," "The Ballad of Davy

Crockett," "Cherry Pink and Apple-Blossom White," "The Yellow Rose of Texas," and "Melody of Love." Those who knew physical activity began after "I give my heart to you . . ." did not want to talk about it.[17]

Another sound, however, was available. Before it was supplanted by rock 'n' roll, rhythm and blues provided a dress rehearsal on a smaller stage for the agitation that reached the *New York Times* in the second half of the decade. After World War II, the industry substituted rhythm and blues for the harsher-sounding "race records" as the term for recordings by black artists that were not gospel or jazz. But R&B also emerged as a distinctive musical genre, drawing on the rich musical traditions of African Americans, including the blues' narratives of turbulent emotions, and the jubilation, steady beat, hand clapping, and call and response of gospel. Rhythm and blues tended to be "good time music," with an emphatic dance rhythm. Its vocalists shouted, growled, or falsettoed over guitars and pianos, bass drums stressing a 2–4 beat, and a honking tenor saxophone. "Body music rather than head or heart music," according to Arnold Shaw, appealing to the flesh more than the spirit, rhythm and blues "embodied the fervor of gospel music, the throbbing vigor of boogie woogie, the jump beat of swing, and the gutsiness and sexuality of life in the black ghetto."[18]

R&B responded to a massive migration of African Americans, from South to North and farm to city, that began early in the twentieth century and accelerated during and after World War II. Between 1940 and 1960, three million blacks left the states of the Old Confederacy. The percentage of blacks living on farms dropped from 35 to 8; the percentage living in cities grew from 49 to 73. Most of the migrants were young. During the '40s alone, more than one-third of all African Americans between the ages of twenty and twenty-four in Deep South states moved to the border states or farther north. They resettled in St. Louis, Kansas City, Memphis, and especially Chicago, where the black population surged 77 percent, from 278,000 to 492,000, between 1940 and 1950. They found work in a booming economy. By 1950, blacks in the United States earned four times the wages they took home in 1940. To be sure, the average paycheck was only 61 percent of the pay earned by whites. But with this migration, what had been a diffuse "race market" in the South became a more concentrated—and burgeoning—urban ghetto market.[19]

Three strains of rhythm and blues music appealed to that market. Louis Jordan was the premier exponent of "the jump blues." Born in Brinkley, Arkansas in 1908, Jordan played alto sax with the bands of Louis Armstrong and Chick Webb before forming his own combo, the Tympany Five, in 1938. A showman in the tradition of Cab Calloway, Jordan cut records that for a decade kept him at or near the top of the "Harlem Hit Parade," *Billboard* magazine's title for its black charts. But Jordan's exuberant hits, unlike those of Calloway, the Mills Brothers, or Nat King Cole, drew on the manners, mores, and hazards of life in the ghetto.

Jordan's earthy themes, vernacular language, and humorous, amorous, and amused tone are evident in the titles of his songs: "The Chicks I Pick Are Slender, Tender, and Tall," "Is You Is or Is You Ain't Ma Baby?," "Reet, Petite, and Gone," "Beans and Cornbread," "Saturday Night Fish Fry," and "What's the Use of Gettin' Sober (When You Gonna Get Drunk Again)?" Urban blacks may have felt they were laughing, from a distance, at their lower-class, hayseed cousins. Or, as Shaw suggests, Jordan may have communicated to his audience that he was self-confident enough to laugh at himself.[20]

More romantic and idealistic were the vocal or street-corner "doo-wop" groups, whose output resembled the standard juvenile fare of white pop music. These balladeers preferred the "preliminaries" and "hearts and kisses" to sweaty sex, in such songs as "Hopefully Yours" (the Larks), "I'm a Sentimental Fool" (the Marylanders), and "Golden Teardrops" (the Flamingoes). On occasion, as R&B historian Brian Ward suggests, the grain of the voices, the tone of the instruments, and the manipulation of harmonies and rhythms subverted the saccharine lyrics, hinting at "barely contained lust and sexual expectancy." The dominant theme of "doo-wop," though, was adolescent longing and loss.[21]

The third and most controversial strain dominated and defined rhythm and blues. It appealed to urban blacks who had fled from deference and demeaning employment in the South but remained powerless to control key aspects of their lives. Perhaps in compensation, R&B "shouters" proclaimed—and sometimes parodied—their independence and sexual potency with a pounding beat and lyrics that could be vulgar, raunchy, and misogynist. "Let me bang your box," shouted the Toppers; "Her machine is full of suds ... it will cost you

30 cents a pound," proclaimed the Five Royales. One of the most talented of the shouters was Nebraska native Wynonie Harris, a tall, dapper, handsome man who billed himself as the "hard-drinkin', hard-lovin', hard-shoutin' Mr. Blues." Harris's biggest hit, "Good Rockin' Tonight," recorded in 1947, was vintage jump blues, but he made a career bellowing songs about sex. Telling readers of *Tan* magazine that "deep down in their hearts" black women "wanted a hellion, a rascal," Harris sang of "cheatin' women" and men who were better off satisfying their needs with a mechanical "Lovin' Machine" in songs like "I Want My Fanny Brown" and "I Like My Baby's Pudding." Harris's idol and sometime partner in duets, Big Joe Turner, also found love "nothin' but a lot of misery," but in the macho tradition of R&B shouters, he refused to whine: "Turn off the water works," he tells his woman. "That don't move me no mo'."[22]

Shouters made good use of a new instrument, the electric guitar. The first mass-produced, solid-body electric guitar, the Fender Esquire, became available in 1950. By eliminating the diaphragm top of the acoustic guitar, Leo Fender helped musicians amplify each string cleanly, without feedback. Electricity, argues music historian Michael Lydon, provided "that intensity that made non-believers call it noisy when played low, but made believers know it had to be played loud." In the hands of a master, like bluesman Aaron "T-Bone" Walker, the electric guitar could also be a stage prop, held behind the head when he did the splits, and a phallic symbol, pressed against the body or pointed provocatively at the audience.[23]

In the '40s and early '50s, rhythm and blues fought its way onto the radio and records. As the Federal Communications Commission sifted through a backlog of applications for new radio stations at the end of World War II, white entrepreneurs founded independent stations aimed at urban African Americans, who in the aggregate had considerable disposable income—and nearly all of whom owned radios. In late 1948 and early 1949, WDIA in Memphis abandoned white pop to become the first radio station in the United States to program entirely for blacks, putting former schoolteacher Nat D. Williams on the air as its first black announcer. Its ratings began to climb. Within a few years, 70 percent of the African-Americans in Memphis turned to the station at some time during the day. When thousands in the mid-South joined them, national advertisers flocked to WDIA. Stations throughout the

T-Bone Walker, showman of the electric guitar, does the splits, part of rock 'n' roll's onstage "return to the body." *(Michael Ochs Archives)*

country began to expand "Negro appeal programming." In 1949, WWEZ in New Orleans hired a black DJ, Vernon Winslow ("Doctor Daddy-O"), for "Jivin' with Jax"; that same year, WEDR in Birmingham, Alabama, went all black, and WERD in Atlanta became black owned and operated. Farther west, in Flagstaff, Arizona, KGPH began to feature R&B in 1952. By the mid-'50s, twenty-one stations in the country were "all black"; according to a "Buyer's Guide" survey, more than six hundred stations in thirty-nine states, including WWRL in New York City, WWDC in Washington, D.C., and WDAS in Philadelphia, aired "Negro-slanted" shows. In 1953, *Variety* noted that the "strong upsurge in R&B" provided employment for black disc jockeys, with some five hundred of them "spotted on stations in every city where there is a sizable colored population."[24]

The dramatic shift toward television as the entertainment medium of choice for white adults helped convince executives to reorient radio toward young people's music, and particularly R&B. The kids stayed with radio throughout the '50s, as transistors replaced large, heat-generating vacuum tubes, and cheap portable radios and car radios became available. By 1959, 156 million radios were in working order in the United States, three times the number of TV sets.[25]

As R&B found a niche on radio, independent record producers established R&B labels. The major companies—Capitol, Columbia, Decca, Mercury, MGM, and RCA—stuck with pop music, leaving R&B to the "indies." The latter could compete because after 1948 they could acquire high-quality, low-cost recording equipment. Because producers paid composers and performers as little as $10 and a case of whiskey per song (Bo Diddley once referred to R&B as "Ripoffs and Bullshit"), they could break even with sales of only 1,500 units. Between 1948 and 1954, a thousand "indies" went into business. Unlike the majors, whose offices were in New York City, independents spread across the country. Founded by former jukebox operators, nightclub owners, music journalists, and record manufacturers, only some of whom (like Ahmet Ertegun and Jerry Wexler of Atlantic) knew a lot about music and almost all of whom were white, independent producers grossed $15 million in 1952, much of it on R&B. "I looked for an area neglected by the majors," confessed Art Rupe, founder of Specialty Records in Los Angeles, "and in essence took the crumbs off the table in the record industry."[26]

Bottom-line businessmen, independent producers, and radio station operators often exploited R&B artists, but many of them recognized and endorsed the role that the music industry was playing in the struggle for civil rights. Following World War II, which was in no small measure a war against racism, some progress had been made. When he broke the color barrier in baseball in 1947 Jackie Robinson had, in essence, put the nation on notice that the days of segregation were numbered. A year later, by executive order, President Harry Truman ended the practice in the army. But the hard battles had yet to be fought, let alone won. The laws in southern states separating the races in schools, buses, trains, and public swimming pools and bathrooms had been upheld by the U.S. Supreme Court in a decision, *Plessy v. Ferguson* (1896), that was still in force. Many southerners remained implacably racist. "The Negro is different," insisted Ross Barnett, governor of Mississippi, "because God made him different to punish him. His forehead slants back. His nose is different. His legs are different, and his color is sure different." Such attitudes made it impossible in 1955 to convict the murderers of black teenager Emmett Till, whose crime was daring to converse with (and perhaps whistle at) a young white woman. Race mixing of any kind, according to Barnett, was unnatural and unthinkable: "We will not drink from the cup of genocide."[27]

In the North, racial antipathy was often muted but no less real. Discrimination in employment in the public and private sectors was pervasive, and African Americans often had to take the most menial jobs. While segregation was not legal in any northern state, the races remained largely separate, with many white neighborhoods implacably opposed to black renters or owners of apartments or houses. The migration of blacks to the North made the situation more volatile. In 1951, Harvey Clark, a graduate of Fisk University, moved his family's furniture into an apartment they had leased in Cicero, Illinois. When the Clarks' van arrived, the police intervened and an officer struck him, advising the veteran of World War II to leave the area "or you'll get a bullet through you." When Clark persisted, four thousand whites trashed the apartment building, destroying furniture and plumbing while the police were "out of town." As the NAACP tried to raise funds to replace the Clarks' furniture, a grand jury investigated, only to return an indictment against an NAACP lawyer, the owner of the apartment, her lawyer, and the rental agent, for conspiring to reduce property values by causing "depreciation in the market selling price." Months later a federal grand jury did indict police and city officials for violating the civil rights of the Clarks, but even then three of the seven defendants were acquitted. Occurring in one of the most "southern" of northern cities, the Cicero riot was hardly a typical occurrence in the 1950s, but it served as a graphic reminder that "the Negro problem" was a national problem.[28]

The music business could not solve the problem, of course, but because it depended so heavily on African-American writers and performers, civil rights advocates pressed record producers and radio station owners to promote integration—and practice what they preached. In his monthly column on rhythm and blues in the music industry publication *Cash Box*, Sam Evans pushed for the employment of more African Americans in all phases of the business. When NBC's San Francisco outlet KNBC hired Wallace Ray in May 1952,

Evans detected a "fast growing trend." A qualified black, he suggested, is always available to fill the job: "In short course we expect to find a fair and equal representation, racially speaking, in the record manufacturing and distribution biz." Ernie and George Leaner became the agents for OKeh Records, a division of Columbia, in seven midwestern states, Evans informed readers a few months later, not because they "are Negroes, or because they are fat or skinny, or because they are tall or short. But just because the boys are good sound businessmen and know how to run a record distributing company." Evans took an entire column to sum up racial progress in the jukebox, recording, radio, and television businesses. "We have seen supposedly insurmountable barriers broken down," he claimed. In addition to "Negro talent" onstage, "many industry companies, and allied branches, are today employing young Negro people in positions of responsibility and trust. The day when the Negro was automatically delegated to the broom department is a thing of the past. Now we see typists, accountants, bookkeepers, receptionists, road managers, traveling representatives, A&R [artist and repertoire] men, publicity men, publishers, staff radio announcers, staff radio engineers, plus many other jobs, and all drawn from the huge Negro labor market." With praise came a plea that all applicants for employment be judged "only by personal qualifications rather than by skin pigmentation." In the next decade, as high schools and colleges turned out thousands of educated African-American men and women, Evans predicted, the clarion call would be "Give us jobs, and we will win the Freedom."[29]

Even if the music industry did not discriminate in hiring—and Evans's account was far too sanguine—its most important role was not behind the scenes. Mitch Miller, A&R man for Columbia Records and, it would turn out, no friend of rock 'n' roll, suggested that as whites listened to African-American music and cheered performers on the stage, they struck a blow for racial understanding and harmony. Since jazz and the blues reached relatively few whites, R&B probably had the greatest impact. "By their newfound attachment to rhythm and blues," Miller wrote, "young people might also be protesting the Southern tradition of not having anything to do with colored people. There is a steady—and healthy—breaking down of color barriers in the United States; perhaps the rhythm and blues rage—I am only theorizing—is another expression of it."[30]

In the short run, at least, Miller proved to be too sanguine, too. White teenagers were listening, but as they did a furor erupted over R&B. Good enough for blacks, apparently, the music seemed downright dangerous as it crossed the color line.

Actually buying R&B records required some effort. Most music stores in white neighborhoods did not stock them. Until 1954, New Yorkers usually went to 125th Street to buy best-selling R&B platters. Neither the stores on Broadway nor any Madison Avenue shop carried them. On radio, rhythm and blues got airtime primarily on small, independent stations, and even then, Sam Evans reported, "in the very early hours of the morning or late at night."[31]

In pursuit of R&B, however, white teenagers proved to be resolute and resourceful. At the Dolphin Record Store, located in an African-American neighborhood in Los Angeles, about 40 percent of the customers for rhythm and blues in 1952 were white. There, and in other stores in ethnic neighborhoods, in addition to R&B, the stock included the multicultural musical fare produced in the city. In 1948, for example, "Pachuco Boogie," a song blending Mexican speech patterns with African-American scat singing and blues harmonies, sold two million copies.[32]

Whites habituated black nightclubs throughout the country as well. Although some clubs, fearing trouble from the authorities, restricted them to "white spectator tickets," forbidding them to dance or even sit down, "the whites kept on coming," Chuck Berry remembered.[33]

In Memphis, Budgie Linder became aware of R&B in 1951 or 1952, when he heard "Mama, Don't Treat Your Daughter Mean." By watching blacks at his high school and at clubs, Linder learned "a slower, more sensuous, dance." He did not dance with black girls because "that wasn't allowed . . . that would have been bad manners." But he abandoned the jitterbug for the "dirty boogie," and "got booted out over at Sacred Heart [High School]," at a dance where his aunt served as one of the chaperones!

As Bettye Berger grew up in rural Tennessee, she turned to gospel music on the radio, then sat outside the window of a local black church "just to listen to them singing." As a teenager, she picked up R&B on WLAC, a white-owned station out of Nashville. When she listened, "it didn't make any difference what color they were, it just made me feel good." Berger went with some girls from her high school from a prom to the Plantation Inn, in West Memphis. They watched black musicians perform for white audiences, then take breaks outside or in the kitchen, since fraternizing with whites was forbidden. Berger and her girlfriends entered with corsages, white gloves, formal dresses, and "their little hair fixed just perfectly, beauty shop, you know, everything in place." They left carrying their hose, shoes, and corsages, having "perspired, and probably smooched, and you know, just had a great old time." Berger did not record the reaction of her parents when she returned home.[34]

Many white teens, like Berger, were introduced to R&B on radio. In Memphis they turned the dial to WDIA. Referred to by a white salesman as "We Done Integrated Already," the station actually refused to permit blacks to read the news, and hired no African Americans as program directors, station managers, or even receptionists until the 1960s. Aware that white parents were upset when their children listened to black disc jockeys, WDIA executives in 1949 hired white ex-serviceman Dewey Phillips, who had a southern drawl "as thick as a stack of Aunt Jemima's pancakes," as the host of the late-night "Red, Hot, and Blue Show." With his signature line, "Tell 'em Phillips sencha," the red-haired, freckle-faced DJ established a bond with black listeners, expressing "deep appreciation" on the air, after an automobile accident, to Negroes who had sent cards and made telephone calls. As he played the music of Muddy Waters, Howlin' Wolf, Little Richard, and Hank Ballard and the Midnighters, Phillips attracted young white listeners as well. By the early '50s, the audience for "Red, Hot, and Blue" approached one hundred thousand.[35]

The more attractive R&B became to white youth, the more controversial it became, no matter who spun the platters. It's easy to see why. Since whites, as Brian Ward argues, "had long reified black culture as the perpetually fascinating but feral, alluring but alarming, sensual but sordid antithesis to the dominant white one," rhythm and blues gave them nightmares that their teenagers would live out the fantasy described by Jack Kerouac in *On the Road*: "At lilac evening I walked with every muscle aching among the lights of 27th and Welton in the Denver colored section, wishing I were Negro, feeling that the best the white world had offered was not enough ecstasy for me, not enough life, joy, kicks, darkness, music, not enough night."[36]

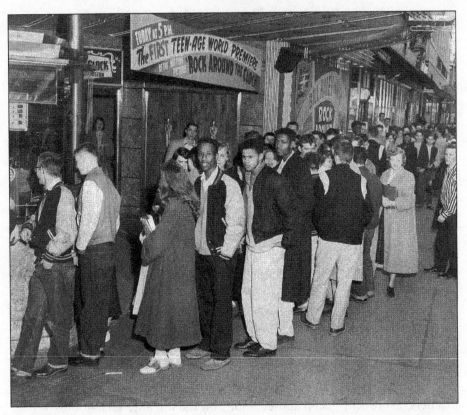

The interracial audiences for rock 'n' roll were welcome to some and un-settling to others. *(Movie Still Archives)*

The vast majority of R&B fans remained orderly, obedient, and buttoned down, but rhythm and blues did release inhibitions and reduce respect for authority in enough teenagers to give credibility to charges that the music promoted licentious behavior. "The first time I ever saw a guy put his hand down a girl's pants was at the Paramount," explained a white fan of Chuck Berry. As a teenager in Granite City, Illinois, Bonnie Bramlett went to the Harlem Club in East St. Louis, even though she knew it "was definitely the wrong neighborhood for white girls." She and her friends had a wonderful time, "sneakin' and smokin' and drinkin' and doin' damn near everything."[37]

By 1954, *Cash Box* was reporting that as R&B records received greater airplay, "the complaints are pouring in from parents." Unless record companies stopped producing all "suggestive and risqué" songs, the publication predicted, adults would prohibit their children from purchasing any R&B records, and the goose that had been laying golden eggs would perish.[38]

The call for self-regulation did not go unheeded. After 1954, R&B records were less raspy and raunchy, with more of the "sweet stylings" of vocal groups like Frankie Lymon and the Teenagers ("Why Do Fools Fall in Love?") and Little Anthony and the Imperials ("Tears on My Pillow"). By then, however, the battleground had shifted: rock 'n' roll had gotten its name.

Alan Freed is generally credited with using the phrase to describe rhythm and blues. Born in Windber, Pennsylvania, just south of Johnstown, in 1921, Freed got his first experience with radio broadcasting when he was a student at Ohio State. A successful disc jockey in Akron, he moved to Cleveland in 1950, first to introduce movies on WXEL-TV, and then as the host of "Request Review" on WJW radio. Freed learned about rhythm and blues from Leo Mintz, the owner of Record Rendezvous, located near Cleveland's black ghetto, and began to showcase R&B music on his show. Billing himself as "Alan Freed, King of the Moondoggers," the DJ rang a cowbell, banged a telephone book, and bellowed a Negro-inflected patter into the microphone as he spun the platters. Freed had a "teenager's mind funneled into 50,000 watts," wrote Clark Whelton of the *New York Times*. He "jumped into radio like a stripper into Swan Lake," giving listeners the musical equivalent of a front-row seat for the San Francisco earthquake: "Freed knocked down the buildings you hated and turned the rest into dance floors."[39]

Black and white listeners, in the city and the suburbs, responded enthusiastically to the music and Freed's showmanship and sincerity. "The Moondog House" became the hottest show in town. With a national reputation, Freed in 1953 took on the management of the Moonglows and the Coronets, organized a concert tour, "The Biggest Rhythm and Blues Show," that opened in Revere, Massachusetts, and closed in New Orleans, and reached an agreement with WNJR to rebroadcast "The Moondog House" in Newark, New Jersey. So great was Freed's perceived power that after he became the first white DJ in Cleveland to play "Crying in the Chapel," by the Orioles, he got the credit for the thirty thousand records of the song sold in the city the next day! In 1954 Freed moved to WINS and soon became the dominant nighttime personality on radio in New York City.[40]

Alan Freed gave rock 'n' roll its name—and was its most famous casualty.
(AlanFreed.com)

In November, he faced a crisis. Thomas Louis Hardin, a blind street musician, composer, and beggar, who set up shop outside Carnegie Hall, decked out in shabby Viking garb, playing triangular drums he called trimbas, claimed that he had used the name "Moondog" for many years. Charging that Freed had "infringed" on his name, Hardin sued. When it turned out that Freed had played Hardin's recording of "Moondog Symphony" on his program, Judge Carroll Walter awarded Hardin $5,700 and forbade Freed from using the name "Moondog."

Initially "very angry and shocked," Freed quickly decided to change the name of his show to "Rock 'n' Roll Party." He had, in fact, occasionally used the phrase in Cleveland to describe his program, though he did not apply it specifically to the music he played. A black euphemism for sexual intercourse, "rock 'n' roll" had appeared in a song title as early as 1922, when blues singer Trixie Smith recorded "My Daddy Rocks Me (With One Steady Roll)." In 1931, Duke Ellington cut "Rockin' Rhythm," and three years later the Boswell Sisters sang "Rock and Roll." After Wynonie Harris's hit "Good Rockin' Tonight," in 1948 so many songs mentioned rock or rockin' that *Billboard* complained Connie Jordan's "I'm Gonna Rock" was the "umpteenth variation" on Harris's title. In 1952, a Rockin' Records Company did a brisk business in Los Angeles.

"Rock 'n' roll," then, was not, as Freed later claimed, an "inspirational flash" that came to him as a "colorful and dynamic" description of the "rolling, surging beat of the music." Nor did he use the phrase to eliminate the racial stigma of "rhythm and blues." Whether or not Freed consciously sought "to cultivate a broader audience" for the music—that is precisely what happened. With a sale of forty thousand records in the late '40s an R&B hit might reach the Top Ten; a rock 'n' roll smash would sell over a million.

As it entered popular discourse, rock 'n' roll was a social construction and not a musical conception. It was, by and large, what DJs and record producers and performers said it was. In any event, the phrase caught on, and Freed and WINS secured a copyright for it. Louis Jordan might complain, with considerable justification, that "rock 'n' roll was just a white imitation, a white adaptation of Negro rhythm and blues." What's in a name? Alan Freed's choice allowed fans to affirm—without having to think about it—that rock 'n' roll was a distinctive, not a derivative, musical form.[41]

A few months before Freed started plugging his radio "Rock 'n' Roll Party," *Billboard* magazine welcomed a "potent new chanter who can sock over a tune for either the country or the R&B markets. . . . A strong new talent." By 1955, he would be hailed as a rock 'n' roll sensation.[42]

Elvis Aron Presley was born in 1935 in Tupelo, Mississippi. His father, Vernon, a drifter, worked sporadically as a farmer or truck driver; Gladys, his mother, kept the family together. She lavished love on her only child (a twin brother, Jessie Garon, was stillborn). In 1948, when Vernon got a job in a paint factory, the Presleys moved to Memphis. As a teenager, Elvis developed the unique and self-contradictory combination of rebelliousness and adherence to conventional values he would exhibit throughout his life—and bequeath to rock 'n' roll. At Humes High School, he joined ROTC, the Biology Club, the English Club, the History Club, and the Spanish Club. With his family, he attended the Pentecostal Assembly of God. He enjoyed the music of Bing Crosby, Perry Como, Eddie Fisher, and Dean Martin. At the same time, Elvis imagined himself the hero of comic books and movies and contrived to let everyone know he was different. He let his sideburns grow long and got kicked off the high school football team for refusing to cut his hair. He bought clothes at Lansky's on Beale Street, a store patronized by blacks, dressed often in his favorite colors, pink and black, and kept his shirt collar up in back and his hair pomaded in a wave. Elvis later remembered that when his classmates saw him walking down the street, they yelled, "Hot dang, let's get him, he's a squirrel, get him, he just come down outta the trees."[43]

A misfit and an outcast, Elvis was, in essence, a southern juvenile delinquent. Journalist Stanley Booth has described the type, "lounging on the hot concrete of a gas station on a Saturday afternoon, stopping for a second on the sidewalk as if they were looking for someone who was looking for a fight. You could even see their sullen faces, with a toughness lanky enough to just miss being delicate, looking back at you out of old photographs of the Confederate Army. . . . All outcasts with their contemporary costumes of duck-ass haircuts, greasy Levi's, motorcycle boots, T-shirts for day and black leather jackets for evening wear. Even their unfashionably long sideburns (Elvis' were furry) expressed contempt for the American Dream they were too poor to be part of." And yet, Booth concludes, Elvis was an especially daring delinquent, unwilling to become a mechanic, housepainter, bus driver, or cop, as so many "hoods" did. With volcanic ambition, he aspired to become a singer, and a star.[44]

Elvis taught himself chord progressions on the guitar his mother gave him, as he listened to WDIA or the phonograph. A regular at Ellis

Auditorium's All-Night Gospel Singings, he was mesmerized by the amplitude of some spirituals and the delicacy of others. Although his parents disapproved, Elvis kept listening to blues men Big Bill Broonzy and Arthur Crudup. African-American music, Greil Marcus speculates, gave him more excitement than he could get from the "twangs and laments" of country music. It provided "a beat, sex, celebration, the stunning nuances of the blues and the roar of horns and electric guitars."[45]

After he graduated from Humes, Elvis drove a truck and worked as a machinist and as an usher at the movies. He gave his paycheck to Gladys Presley but kept enough money for his clothes and accessories. In 1953, he appeared with his beat-up guitar in the office of Sun Studios in Memphis. He wanted to make a record to surprise his mother, he said, but "if you know anyone that wants a singer . . ." "Who do you sound like?" the receptionist asked. "I don't sound like nobody." Elvis recorded two Ink Spots songs, "My Happiness" and "That's When Your Heartaches Begin," with Sam Phillips, the owner of Sun, listening from the control room. The receptionist wrote down next to his name "Good ballad singer," and Presley left, with an acetate and an inkling that he was about to be discovered. He reappeared in January and cut another record. But Sam Phillips did not yet recognize that his ship had just come in.

A native of Florence, Alabama, Phillips had dropped out of school to begin working in radio, as an engineer and disc jockey. He came to Memphis in 1945, joining WREC, the CBS affiliate, to set up national hookups of big band music from the Skyway at the Peabody Hotel. Phillips found the pop songs he played dreadfully dull: "It seemed to me that the Negroes were the only ones who had any freshness left in their music; and there was no place in the South they could go to record." He told just about everyone he met that he was looking for "Negroes with field mud on their boots and patches in their overalls . . . battered instruments and unfettered techniques." In 1950 Phillips opened a small office, recording bar mitzvahs and political speeches to defray the expenses of making demos of new artists and sending them to independent producers around the country. Within a short time, he sold recordings of Howlin' Wolf and B. B. King to Chess in Chicago and Modern Records in Los Angeles. He retained his job at WREC, until he could no longer abide snide coworkers asking him "whether he had been hanging around those niggers." By 1953, Sun Studios was promoting and distributing as well as producing, out of a two-person office. Rufus Thomas's "Bear Cat" was the studio's first success; "Feeling Good," by Little Junior Parker, and "Just Walkin' in the Rain," by the Prisonaires, were in the can. Sun's label, an orange, yellow, and black image of a rooster crowing and the sun rising, looked to a new day, and to an open door for African-American artists.[46]

Sam Phillips's commitment to rhythm and blues never wavered; throughout his career he sought out and recorded black singers. He also realized that in the South, and in the North as well, whites were uneasy about listening to black music. In the '50s, as one jukebox operator noted, putting a "black blues record on a honky tonk machine" in a white establishment was a mistake, "because somebody would go over there and play it, just for devilment, and the whole place would explode." So Phillips kept his eyes open for white country boys who could sing the blues. Marion Keisker, Phillips's colleague at Sun, remembers him saying over and over, "If I could find a white man who had the Negro sound and the Negro feel, I could make a billion dollars."[47]

In the summer of 1954, Phillips received a demo of a song called "Without You" from a black performer he did not know. For some reason, he thought the polite young man with the sideburns should record it. At the Sun Studio, Elvis tried and tried but failed to find the ballad's essence. Phillips persevered, asking the youngster to practice with Scotty Moore, a twenty-two-year-old guitarist. After several rehearsals, Presley and Moore returned, with stand-up bass player Bill Black, and played "I Love You Because," a country ballad. This session, too, went badly. Out of anxiety, or perhaps absent-mindedly, Elvis picked up his guitar to strum and sing "That's All Right," a blues song recorded by Arthur Crudup in 1946. Moore and Black joined in, and suddenly Sam Phillips stuck his head out of the control booth and asked them to play it again. He felt "like someone stuck me in the rear end with a brand new supersharp pitchfork." It sounds pretty good, he said, but "what is it? I mean, who, who you going to give it [i.e., sell it] to?" Elvis did not have the ragged tone, irregular rhythms, and intonation most blues singers used, but he had found something. Instinctively, Greil Marcus argues, he had turned Crudup's lament for a lost love into a "satisfied declaration of independence. . . . His girl may have left him but nothing she can do can dent the pleasure that radiates from his heart. It's the blues, but free of all worry, all sin; a simple joy with no price to pay." When the trio finished the song, Phillips, by now very excited, realized that if he was to get a record out in a hurry he needed something for the flip side. Within a few days, Presley, Moore, and Black recorded the hillbilly classic "Blue Moon of Kentucky." Here, too, Elvis produced a distinctive tone and sound, transforming a country classic into that hybrid of country and R&B that became known as "rockabilly."[48]

Even before he chose "Blue Moon of Kentucky," Sam Phillips played the acetate for his friend Dewey Phillips, by then at WHBQ, but still the "man with the platinum ear." As they listened, Sam wondered "where you going to go with this, it's not black, it's not white, it's not pop, it's not country." He was delighted when Dewey offered to play the songs on his show. As if by magic, most of Memphis seemed to be listening. When Dewey Phillips played "That's All Right," the switchboard lit up with requests that he play it again—and again and again. Dewey complied, then called the Presley home and asked Gladys to get Elvis, who was out at the movies, to the station for an interview. Within minutes the singer arrived, "shaking all over." Dewey told him to cool it and make sure to say "nothing dirty." During the brief chat, Dewey got Elvis to say that he had been a student at (all-white) Humes High School: "I wanted to get that out, because a lot of people listening had thought he was colored."[49]

On July 19, 1954, Sun released Elvis Presley's first record. An instant hit in Memphis, it had to overcome initial resistance elsewhere in the South, because disc jockeys did not know how to categorize it. Some DJs told Phillips that Elvis was so "country he shouldn't be played after five A.M."; others said flatly he was too black for their tastes. If he played the record, T. Tommy Cutrer, the top country DJ in Shreveport, Louisiana, told Phillips, his white country audience would "run me out of town." In Houston, Paul Berlin, who was still getting mileage spinning the platters of Tennessee Ernie Ford and Patti Page, said, "Sam, your music is just so ragged, I just can't handle it right now. Maybe later on." Even in Tupelo, Elvis's hometown, Ernest Bowen, the sales manager at WELO, told him the record was "a bunch of crap."[50]

When Phillips prevailed, and disc jockeys played the record, listeners couldn't get enough of it. And they liked "Blue Moon of

Elvis Presley electrified teenage fans with his rockabilly tunes and his stage presence. *(Michael Ochs Archives)*

Kentucky" every bit as much as "That's All Right." A scout for RCA asked Sam Morrison, a record dealer in Knoxville, "It's just a normal rhythm and blues record, isn't it?" No, it isn't, Morrison replied, "it's selling to a country audience." Just then, according to Morrison, a man with "more hair growing out of his ears and nose than on his head" entered the store and in an easy Tennessee drawl said, "By granny, I want that record." By mid-August the record was number 3 on *Billboard* magazine's regional country and western best-sellers.[51]

By then, Elvis was a performer as well as a singer. After a shaky debut in front of a "pure redneck" crowd at the Bon Air Club in Memphis, he backed up Slim Whitman at a hillbilly hoedown in an outdoor amphitheater in Overton Park. Elvis approached the mike, with legs quivering and lips contorted into what looked like a sneer. "We were all scared to death," Scotty Moore recalled, "and Elvis, instead of just standing flat-footed and tapping his foot, well, he was kind of jiggling. . . . Plus I think with those old loose britches that we wore—they weren't pegged, they had lots of material and pleated

"I did a little more, and the more I did, the wilder they went," Elvis recalled. (*Robert W. Kelley/Timepix*)

fronts—you shook your leg, and it made it look like all hell was going on under there. During the instrumental parts he would back off from the mike and be playing and shaking, and the crowd would just go wild, but he thought they were actually making fun of him." By the encore, Elvis knew that the image he had projected, whether by accident or not, with his eyes shut and his legs shaking, was arousing the audience: "I did a little more, and the more I did, the wilder they went."[52]

Elvis was something new under the Sun. Although he did not invent "rockabilly," he introduced it to tens of thousands of teenagers. With loose rhythms, no saxophone or chorus, rockabilly was a "personal, confiding, confessing" sound, as Charlie Gillett has defined it, with instrumentalists responding "more violently to inflections in the singer's voice, shifting into double-time for a few bars to blend with a sudden acceleration in the vocalist's tempo." After Elvis's meteoric rise, Sam Phillips signed other rockabilly singers, including Carl Perkins, Roy Orbison, Johnny Cash, and Jerry Lee Lewis.[53]

Beyond his musical style, Elvis embodied some of the characteristics of his "low-down" social class and of many fellow teenagers. Angry at a world that had excluded him, yet eager for recognition and status, Elvis could be arrogant and prideful—and also emotionally vulnerable, insecure, and deferential. No one has captured Elvis's "authentic multiplicity" better than Greil Marcus, who imagines the singer introducing himself as a "house rocker, a boy steeped in mother love, a true son of the church, a matinee idol who's only kidding, a man with too many rough edges for anyone ever to smooth away," a balladeer yearning to settle affairs, a rock 'n' roller apt to "break away at any time."[54]

By instinct more than design, Elvis contributed to the agitation about race relations during the 1950s. In public, and in the South, he acknowledged his indebtedness to the music of African Americans. "The colored folks been singing and playing it [rock 'n' roll] just like I'm doing now, man, for more years than I know," he told the *Charlotte Observer* in 1956. "They played it like that in the shanties and in their juke joints and nobody paid it no mind until I goosed it up. I got it from them. Down in Tupelo, Mississippi, I used to hear Arthur Crudup bang his box the way I do now and I said that if I ever got to the place where I could feel all old Arthur felt, I'd be a music man like nobody ever saw." Sam Phillips believed that Elvis was without prejudice and that "sneaking around through" his music, but clearly discernible to his fans, was an "almost subversive" identification with and empathy for blacks. Phillips's claim that he and Elvis "went out into this no man's land" and "knocked the shit out of the color line" should be dismissed as retrospective fantasy. He was, perhaps, closer to the mark in asserting that, with respect to race, "we hit things a little bit, don't you think?"[55]

As Alan Freed provided a name, and Elvis an icon, Bill Haley gave rock 'n' roll its anthem. In almost all respects, Haley was an improbable '50s teen idol. Born in Highland Park, Michigan, in 1925, he received his first guitar at age seven and began to play hillbilly music, taking as his models country singer Hank Williams and cowboy star Gene Autry. Billed as the "Ramblin' Yodeler," Haley toiled in obscurity for years, performing at fairs, auction barns, and amusement parks in Delaware, Indiana, and Pennsylvania, decked out in cowboy boots and hat. In the late '40s, he formed his own band, first named the Four Aces of Western Swing, then the Saddlemen. Thwarted by the limited appeal of country music in the region, Haley began to experiment with rhythm and blues. In 1951, the Saddlemen recorded "Rocket 88," a stomping R&B song about an Oldsmobile. A year later came "Rock the Joint," a loud and lively jump blues hit, which sold well in Philadelphia and New Jersey. Haley was now ready to exchange his boots and hat for a Scotch plaid jacket or a tuxedo, shave his sideburns, and rename the Saddlemen "Bill Haley and the Comets." Composed of six or seven men, playing stringed instruments, drums, and a saxophone, with Haley as guitarist and lead singer, the Comets played driving and danceable music. Haley's own composition, "Crazy, Man, Crazy," reached the *Billboard*'s Top Twenty. The tune had a pop beat, *The Cash Box* reported; the lyrics "lend themselves to R&B treatment, and the instrumentalization is hillbilly."[56]

Signed by a major national label, Decca, Haley and the Comets recorded "(We're Gonna) Rock Around the Clock" early in 1954. Bursting with energy, the song used a snare drum to produce a heavy backbeat and featured an electric guitar solo. After just one week on *Billboard*'s pop charts, at number 23, it faded. Late that year, however, with "Shake, Rattle, and Roll," a "cover" of Joe Turner's R&B song, with sanitized lyrics, Haley had a huge hit, selling more than a million copies. In his version, Haley copied the basic R&B beat but did not use many other musical effects—the loosely pronounced words, complex and harmonious backing, the slurred "bluesy" notes. He added guitar work and his own thumping, shouting delivery. The success of this song, and the emergence of rock 'n' roll, convinced Hollywood producers to use "Rock Around the Clock" in the film *Blackboard Jungle.*

As the opening credits of *Blackboard Jungle* rolled across the screen, the soundtrack blared "One, two, three o'clock, four o'clock ROCK." An asphalt schoolyard appeared on the screen, visible through a chain-link fence, and students danced, with a few toughs hovering in the background, a saxophone and electric guitar blaring on. For two minutes and ten seconds, "Rock Around the Clock" issued a clarion call to students to break out of jail and have fun. Whereas *Rebel Without a Cause* and *The Wild Ones* belied their themes of youth rebellion with big band sound tracks, *Blackboard Jungle* found music appropriate to its melodramatic ad campaign: "A drama of teenage terror! They turned a school into a jungle." "It was the loudest sound kids ever heard at that time," Frank Zappa remembered. Bill Haley "was playing the Teenage National Anthem and he was LOUD. I was jumping up and down. *Blackboard Jungle*, not even considering that it had the old people winning in the end, represented a strange act of endorsement of the teenage cause."[57]

Despite a conclusion designed to reassure, with an alliance between a young black student, played by Sidney Poitier, and the teacher, played by Glenn Ford, *Blackboard Jungle* (and, by implication, "Rock Around the Clock") suggested that generational conflict was endemic in American culture.[58] In an unforgettable scene, the class fidgeted as a teacher at North Manual High tried to connect with them by playing his favorite jazz records. When the sound track countered with *their* music, the youths erupted, tossing his 78s across the room, then shattering them, as the hapless teacher dissolved in tears. As they watched the movie, observers noted, some teenagers sang along, danced in the aisles, and slashed their seats. *Blackboard Jungle*, music critic Lillian Roxon has written, had a "special, secret defiant meaning for teenagers only." It suggested to them that "they might be a force to be reckoned with, in numbers alone. If there could be one song, there could be others; there could be a whole world of songs, and then, a whole world." The movie reinforced the association between rock 'n' roll and anarchy in the minds of anxious adults.

Blackboard Jungle, Time magazine opined, undermined the American way of life, giving aid and comfort to Communists. If it were not withdrawn, predicted Clare Booth Luce, U.S. ambassador to Italy, the film would "cause the greatest scandal in motion picture history." "No matter what the outcome of the film," Senator Estes Kefauver's committee on juvenile delinquency concluded, a substantial number of teenagers would identify with Artie West, the sadistic teenager in *Blackboard Jungle*, who assaults Glenn Ford's young and pretty wife. "It was unfortunate," no less an authority than Alan Freed acknowledged, that Haley's song about having a good time had been used "in that hoodlum-infested movie," which "seemed to associate rock 'n' rollers with delinquents."[59]

Blackboard Jungle was denounced by teachers' organizations, the Daughters of the American Revolution, the American Legion, and the Girl Scouts. Banned in Memphis until MGM threatened an injunction, the film played in several cities with the sound track turned off during the opening and closing credits. Despite—and perhaps because of—these denunciations, *Blackboard Jungle* was a sensational hit. And, with a second chance, "Rock Around the Clock" climbed to the top of the charts. By the end of 1955, two million records had been sold, and by the end of the decade the song was gaining on Bing Crosby's "White Christmas" as the best-selling single in history. Bill Haley did not quite know what had hit him. Thirty years old in 1955, chunky, blind in one eye, with chipmunk cheeks and a spit curl plastered on his forehead, Haley found it difficult to compete with younger, sexier performers. Although he went on to make a short feature film, *Rock Around the Clock*, with Freed, in 1956, and had another gold record, "See You Later, Alligator," Haley seemed out of touch with the culture of rock 'n' roll. "He didn't even know what to call it, for the love of Christ," snorts critic Nick Tosches, citing Haley's comment that the Comets used country and western instruments to play rhythm and blues, "and the result is pop music." Haley was no rebel against the dominant values of the 1950s. While the Comets were on the road, he instituted bed checks and prohibited drinking and dating by members of the band. In 1957, the group recorded "Apple Blossom Time"; a year later, "Ida, Sweet as Apple Cider."[60]

Although Bill Haley was unable to take full advantage of it, rock 'n' roll had emerged as a mass culture phenomenon. At the end of

1956, 68 percent of the music played by disc jockeys was rock 'n' roll, an increase of two-thirds over the previous year. By December 1957 virtually every position on *Billboard*'s Top Ten was occupied by a rock 'n' roller. "Whatever emotional and psychological factors there are behind its acceptance," *Cash Box* editors asserted, "whatever spark it may have touched off in a teenager's makeup, the one fact that remains certain is that youngsters today find what they are looking for in the way of music in Rock 'n' Roll. It seems futile to try to deny this fact or pretend that it is a temporary thing."[61]

As Carl Perkins's "Blue Suede Shoes" and Elvis Presley's "Heartbreak Hotel" surged to the top of the pop, rhythm and blues, and country charts, *The Cash Box* exulted that rock 'n' roll was affecting "the lives of everyone in our country." Rock 'n' roll, the editors believed, provided evidence of and served as an impetus for greater cultural harmony and homogenization in the United States. "Greater mobility and more dynamic means of communication," they explained, "have brought the taste and mode of living of people in various areas of our country to the attention and knowledge of those in other areas." In a banner headline, they predicted that "Rock and Roll May Be the Great Unifying Force!"[62]

They were wrong. Although rock 'n' roll was a commodity, produced and distributed by a profit-making industry, and therefore subject to co-optation by the dominant culture, it continued to resist and unsettle "mainstream" values. For African Americans, rock 'n' roll was a mixed blessing. At times a force for integration and racial respect, rock 'n' roll was also an act of theft that in supplanting rhythm and blues deprived blacks of appropriate acknowledgment, rhetorical and financial, of their contributions to American culture. Rock 'n' roll deepened the divide between the generations, helped teenagers differentiate themselves from others, transformed popular culture in the United States, and rattled the reticent by pushing sexuality into the public arena. Anything but a "great unifying force," rock 'n' roll kept many Americans in the 1950s off balance, on guard, and uncertain about their families and the future of their country.

"BROWN-EYED HANDSOME MAN"   2

Rock 'n' Roll and Race

The emergence of rock 'n' roll as a cultural phenomenon coincided with great ferment in the movement to grant civil rights to African Americans. Enmeshed in the racial politics of the 1950s, rock 'n' roll was credited with and criticized for promoting integration and economic opportunity for blacks while bringing to "mainstream" culture black styles and values. In the South, rock 'n' roll became a lightning rod for die-hard segregationists who associated the music—and African Americans—with depraved beliefs and behavior. Rock 'n' roll was also big business, and therefore subject to the dictates of the white mass market, as interpreted by recording and broadcasting professionals. In pursuit of profit they shunned controversy, exploited black performers, bleached the music, and promoted white rock 'n' rollers. Subject to these pressures and counterpressures, rock 'n' roll remained a highly visible and contested arena for struggles over racial identity and cultural and economic empowerment in the United States.

The seminal event for proponents of black rights in the 1950s was the decision by the U.S. Supreme Court in five cases (from Kansas, Delaware, South Carolina, Virginia, and the District of Columbia) challenging segregation in public schools—usually cited by reference to the first, *Brown v. Board of Education of Topeka, Kansas*. The cases, which capped decades of work by the NAACP and other organizations, tested the doctrine, enunciated in 1896 in *Plessy v. Ferguson*, that public facilities for blacks and whites were constitutional if they were "separate but equal." The plaintiffs in *Brown* demonstrated that separate but equal in the South was a sham: southerners spent twice as much to educate white children as they did for blacks, four times as much for white school facilities, and more than ten times as much for white colleges. In its brief to the Court, the NAACP also introduced psychological findings (based on Kenneth Clark's experiments with the responses of children to black and white dolls) that separating people by race engendered feelings of inferiority. On May 17, 1954, Chief Justice Earl Warren read the opinion for a unanimous Court: "We conclude that in the field of public opinion the doctrine of 'separate but equal' has no place. Separate educational facilities are inherently unequal." A year later, the Court mandated that compliance with the ruling in *Brown* should proceed "with all deliberate speed."

The decision emboldened African Americans to take to the streets in search of racial equality. On December 1, 1955, in Montgomery, Alabama, a black seamstress, Rosa Parks, was arrested for refusing to comply with a municipal ordinance requiring her to yield her seat on a bus to a white passenger. The next night community leaders met and organized the Montgomery Improvement Association, with Martin Luther King Jr., the twenty-six-year-old minister of the Dexter Avenue Baptist Church, as its president. The association launched a boycott of the city buses. Smart, courageous, and eloquent, King brought to the civil rights movement a philosophy (and strategy) of nonviolent, passive resistance. He hoped to attract the attention of the media, win adherents, and wear down antagonists by appeals to the heart, the conscience, and "our capacity to suffer." Blacks in Montgomery, who constituted three-quarters of the passengers on city buses, King pledged, were determined to "work and fight until justice runs down like water and righteousness like a mighty stream." Withstanding threats, arrests, and bombings, they did just that, forming car pools, hitchhiking, or walking to work and school for several months. On December 20, 1956, the Supreme Court gave the civil rights movement another victory, striking down segregation in public transportation.

The following September, Orval Faubus, governor of Arkansas, called out the National Guard to thwart a court order mandating that Little Rock Central High School admit nine black students. With John

Chancellor, a junior reporter for NBC, on the scene, millions of Americans saw bayonets raised to keep the students from entering the school. They heard Chancellor's account, with the expletives deleted, of a mob shouting at fifteen-year-old Elizabeth Eckford, "Go home, you bastard of a black bitch." The coverage forced President Dwight Eisenhower, who did not believe "you can change the hearts of men with laws or decisions," to act. Although two months earlier he could not "imagine any set of circumstances that would ever induce me to send federal troops," Eisenhower federalized the Arkansas National Guard and sent a thousand paratroopers from the 101st Airborne to escort the students to school and protect them. Soldiers stayed in Little Rock for the entire school year. The students faced constant harassment; they were kicked, tripped, their lockers broken into, their books stolen. But Central High School had been integrated.[1]

By 1956, then, white southerners understood that the entire edifice of Jim Crow segregation was under assault. Senator James Eastland of Mississippi promised that the region would neither "abide by nor obey" the decisions of "a political court."[2] Legislators in several states introduced "freedom of choice" school bills designed to avoid compliance with the Supreme Court by providing public funding for "private" schools. Even more ominously, the Ku Klux Klan reemerged. The Klan was responsible for at least 530 incidents of racial violence across the South between 1955 and 1959. White Citizens Councils were formed as well, dedicated to take any measure necessary to oppose integration. Virginia Senator Harry F. Byrd supplied a rallying cry for militant segregationists: "Massive Resistance." In 1956, 101 members of Congress signed a "Southern Manifesto." Branding the Supreme Court's *Brown* decision a "clear abuse of judicial power," they pledged not to obey it. At the end of the year six southern states had not yet allowed a single black child into a school attended by whites.

Rock 'n' roll became a target of southern segregationists, who believed that race mixing led, inevitably, to miscegenation and that exposure to black culture promoted juvenile delinquency and sexual immorality. Asa Carter, former radio commentator, soft-drink salesman, and member of Ku Klux Klan Klavern No. 31, used the threat of rock 'n' roll to enhance his status as a leader of the White Councils in Alabama. Lumping together rock 'n' roll, bebop, blues, "congo rhythms," and "jungle music," Carter got the attention of *Newsweek*

Though he was not a rock 'n' roll performer, Nat King Cole was assaulted in Birmingham, Alabama, by racist thugs who feared "the savagery" of black music. *(Frank Driggs Collection)*

and the *New York Times* with an assault on the "basic, heavy-beat music of the Negroes. It appeals to the base in man; brings out animalism and vulgarity." The roots of rock 'n' roll, according to Carter, were in "the heart of Africa, where it was used to incite warriors to such frenzy that by nightfall neighbors were cooked in carnage pots! The music is a designed reversion to savagery!" Part of an NAACP plot "to mongrelize America," rock 'n' roll music should be purged from jukeboxes and record shops throughout the South. Action committees of White Citizens Councils, Carter announced, had been formed "to see the people who sponsor the music, and the people who promote Negro bands to play for teenagers."[3]

This rhetoric helps explain the assault on Nat King Cole, hardly a rock 'n' roll performer, at a whites-only concert in Birmingham on April 10, 1956. As Cole sang the Tin Pan Alley standard "Little Girl," someone shouted, "Let's go get that coon," and several whites jumped onto the stage to wrestle the singer to the floor. A stunned Ted Heath Orchestra switched, incongruously, to "God Save the Queen" until the police rescued Cole. The plot, it turned out, had been conceived four days earlier at a gas station by members of the Alabama Citizens Council, one of whom was an editor of Carter's newspaper, *The Southerner*. In their cars, the assailants had brass knuckles, blackjacks, and .22-caliber rifles. They had hoped that the white men in the audience would join them when they stormed the stage.[4]

Asa Carter, who attended the concert, denied that he had any role in the assault. At the same time, he insisted it was only "a short step ... from the sly, nightclub technique vulgarity of Cole, to the openly animalistic obscenity of the horde of Negro rock 'n' rollers." In the pages of *The Southerner*, the motive for the attack emerged. The paper printed pictures of Cole and white fans, with captions such as "Cole and His White Women" and "Cole and Your Daughter." In an article accompanying a photograph of Cole at the piano with white singer June Christy behind him, her hands touching his shoulders, Carter asked, "How many negroes have been encouraged to make advances to white girls and women, by the constant strumming of such propaganda in their minds? ... You have seen it, the fleeting leer, the look that stays an instant longer, ... the savagery, now, almost to the surface."[5]

Carter then put the pressure on rock 'n' roll. His North Alabama Citizens Council picketed a concert featuring the Platters, LaVern Baker, Bo Diddley, Clyde McPhatter, and white performer Bill Haley, with placards proclaiming, "NAACP says integration, rock & roll, rock & roll." The city commissioners of Birmingham responded quickly, instructing the manager of the Municipal Auditorium "not to book any shows, basketball games, or any other type of event that had mixed races in the personnel." Other southern states acted as well. In the

summer of 1956 the legislature of Louisiana banned interracial dancing. A few months later, the school board of Little Rock, Arkansas,
declared that "social functions which involve racial mixing will not be
held." In Norfolk, Virginia, singer Larry Williams, who had recorded
the hits "Bony Maronie" and "Dizzy Miss Lizzy," was arrested after
he took off his shirt and leaped off the stage—and across the color
line—to dance with his white fans. Elvis had reportedly "cracked"
Memphis segregation laws in June 1956 by attending an amusement
park during what was designated as "colored night"; he found a judge
in Jacksonville, Florida, in August, waiting in the wings to arrest him
if there was a "vulgar performance."[6]

Outside the South as well, a racialized discourse accompanied
denunciations of rock 'n' roll. White supremacists in Inglewood, California, showed pictures of black men and women dancing, with the
captions "Boy meets girl . . . be-bop style" and "Total mongrelization."
"Rock and roll enflames and excites youth like jungle tom-toms," the
Reverend John Carroll told the Teachers Institute of the Archdiocese
of Boston. Worried about alienating listeners and advertisers, owners
of radio stations hesitated before "contaminating" previously lily-white
stations. Television was even more skittish: rock 'n' roll was rarely performed on variety shows until late in the decade, except on Dick
Clark's *American Bandstand*. Officially integrated in 1957, *Bandstand*,
Julian Bond remembered, "always had a black couple. Usually a black
couple, never more than one. A couple because they always had to
have someone to dance with. Each other."[7]

Attacks on Negro performers and rock 'n' roll tended to polarize;
in many quarters they evoked more vocal support for the civil rights
movement. When NAACP official Walter White asked the rhythm and
blues group the Dominoes to perform at a fund-raiser, Billy Ward
lauded "the great work the organization is doing for mankind," declaring it an "honor and a privilege to place my group at your disposal."[8]
Even more instructive was the response in African-American communities to Nat King Cole's self-professed political indifference in the
aftermath of the attack on him in Birmingham. "I can't understand it,"
Cole told reporters. "I have not taken part in any protests. Nor have I
joined an organization fighting segregation. Why should they attack
me?" A native of Alabama, Cole seemed eager to assure southern
whites that he would not challenge the customs and traditions of the

region. A few would keep the protests going for a while, he claimed, but "I'd just like to forget about the whole thing." Cole had no intention of altering his practice of playing to segregated audiences in the South. He did not condone the practice but was not a politician and believed "I can't change the situation in a day."

Denunciations of the singer by African Americans were immediate, harsh, and virtually unanimous, unaffected by Cole's revelations that he had contributed money to the Montgomery Bus Boycott and had sued several northern hotels that had hired but refused to serve him. Thurgood Marshall, chief legal counsel of the NAACP, reportedly suggested that since he was an Uncle Tom, Cole ought to perform with a banjo. Roy Wilkins, the executive secretary of the organization, challenged Cole in a telegram: "You have not been a crusader or engaged in an effort to change the customs or laws of the South. That responsibility, newspapers quote you as saying, you 'leave to the other guys.' That attack upon you clearly indicates that organized bigotry makes no distinction between those who do not actively challenge racial discrimination and those who do. This is a fight which none of us can escape. We invite you to join us in a crusade against racism. . . ."

Cole's appearances before all-white audiences, the *Chicago Defender* charged, were "an insult to his race." As boycotts of his records and shows were organized, the *Amsterdam News* claimed that "thousands of Harlem blacks who have worshiped at the shrine of singer Nat King Cole turned their backs on him this week as the noted crooner turned his back on the NAACP and said that he will continue to play to Jim Crow audiences." To play "Uncle Nat's" discs, wrote a commentator in *The American Negro*, "would be supporting his 'traitor' ideas and narrow way of thinking."

Deeply hurt by the criticism of the black press, Cole was also suitably chastened. Emphasizing his opposition to racial segregation "in any form," he agreed to join other entertainers in boycotting segregated venues. He quickly and conspicuously paid $500 to become a life member of the Detroit branch of the NAACP. Until his death in 1965 Cole was an active and visible participant in the civil rights movement, playing an important role in planning the March on Washington in 1963.[9]

The criticism of Cole reflected African Americans' enthusiasm for and rising expectations about integration and racial justice in the

1950s. "Negroes don't want to be Negroes anymore," a reader wrote
to *Ebony*. "We want to be Americans whose skins are incidentally
dark." The editors of the magazine agreed: "The faulty walls of prejudice are crumbling. . . . The Negro is at last being assimilated into the
great melting pot that is America . . . as his acceptance as an American becomes a reality, his role as a full-time Negro should diminish."
In a poll conducted by *Ebony*, a majority of teenagers indicated that
current discrimination in employment would not dissuade them from
preparing for careers of their choice. "By the time we are ready for
the jobs," said Alfred Arnold, an honor student at Lincoln High
School in Kansas City, Missouri, "the doors will be open." Along
with white supporters of civil rights, blacks looked to entertainment,
especially rock 'n' roll, as a weapon in the struggle against Jim Crow.
The "campaign against 'crazy music,'" the *Pittsburgh Courier* recognized, "is an indirect attack against Negroes, of course, because they
invented rock 'n' roll (as they did all other distinctive U.S. music)
and because it has so captivated the younger generation of whites
that they are breaking down dance floors and gutting night clubs
here and abroad. As between rock 'n' roll . . . and the chill austerities
of white supremacy, we think the young white Americans will choose
the former with all of its implications." Herbert Reed of the Platters
put a more positive spin on the same point. "Wherever we go," he
claimed, "white kids beg us for autographs." In Austin, Texas, "a rope
was put up to separate Negroes and whites in the audience. When
we started singing, the kids broke the rope and started dancing
together. That rock 'n' roll beat gets them all."[10]

Convinced that the music promoted racial harmony, African
Americans also embraced rock 'n' roll as a vehicle for social mobility
for talented blacks. Reaching out to readers interested in joining the
mainstream material-and-money-accumulating middle class in the
United States, black newspapers and magazines zeroed in on rock 'n'
rollers' income. "Never before in show business," *Ebony* crowed, "has
Negro youth asserted itself so profitably and in such numbers." They
made up 80 percent of the teenage-age "doo-wop" groups "riding the
Cadillac path of the multi-million dollar rock 'n' roll business."
Twenty-seven-year-old LaVern Baker also rode rock 'n' roll from
rags to riches. Before she recorded "Tweedle Dee," Baker was a little-
known blues singer earning $125 a week—when she worked. Now,

the "chunky bundle of musical fire" with the husky voice, "sexy gestures and daring body movements" was "the high priestess of rock 'n' roll, taking home more than $75,000 a year."[11]

In Antoine "Fats" Domino, *Ebony* found an ideal role model for its readers. Born in 1928 in New Orleans, Domino (his real name) learned to play the piano as a youngster. He expanded into his nickname (bestowed in homage to his idol, jazz pianist Fats Waller), growing out more than up, to five-foot-two and 224 pounds. Good humored, with a Creole patois and a style reminiscent of the R&B showman Louis Jordan, Fats closed his shows by shoving the piano across the stage as the band played "When the Saints Go Marching In." By the early '50s, he had three million-selling records to his credit: "The Fat Man," "Goin' Home," and "Goin' to the River." In 1955, he became a rock 'n' roll star, with "Ain't That a Shame," which he cowrote with his arranger and producer, Dave Bartholomew.

Released three months after Domino had performed at Alan Freed's first "Rock 'n' Roll Ball" in New York City—and while *Blackboard Jungle* and "Rock Around the Clock" were sweeping the nation— "Ain't That a Shame" shot to the top of the R&B charts and reached number 10 on *Billboard*'s pop best-sellers. For the remainder of the decade, Domino was one of the most popular recording stars in the United States, striking gold with one genial good-time hit after another, including "Blueberry Hill," "Whole Lotta Loving," and "I'm Walkin'."[12]

Ebony hailed Domino as the "King of Rock 'n' Roll." When Elvis performed, according to the magazine, teenagers swooned. Pat Boone made them "flop around like headless chickens." But when Fats Domino "builds to a climax, riding along on the locomotive-like beat of his seven-man combo, pandemonium erupts. Teen-agers shriek and contort their bodies; their limbs jerk in spastic rhythms; their eyes roll" and they shake "like leaves." On at least three occasions in 1956, the mass hysteria at his concerts required riot police to restore order. The singer neither caused nor condoned the violence, *Ebony* hastened to add, attributing the disturbances in Newport, Rhode Island, and Fayetteville, North Carolina, to an inadvertent "dousing of lights" during the performances. "I don't know why music should make anybody fight," Fats agreed. "It makes me happy even when I'm feeling bad."

Photo captions underscored Domino's appeal to a broad cross-section of Americans. One showed him at a gallery, where "teen-agers

With "Ain't That a Shame," Antoine "Fats" Domino became the first black rock 'n' roll millionaire. *(Frank Driggs Collection)*

rub shoulders with older fans." Another affirmed that he cut "through age and race barriers," providing pictures of conversations with "screaming teen-agers, an elderly woman in Massachusetts and a matronly fan in California."

According to *Ebony*, Domino was likely to become the first black rock 'n' roll millionaire. Already making as much as $2,500 a night, he had been paid $7,500 for an hour's work in the movie *The Girl Can't Help It*. But success had not gone to his head. On the road some 340 days a year, Domino called his wife, Rosemary, every day, running up a telephone bill of $200 each month. A devoted mate and mother, Rosemary enjoyed her husband's music and watched him on TV but never attended any of his concerts. "I don't like clubs and parties and all those people," she confessed. Rosemary had gotten used to her husband's absences, though she often wished he had "a plain job." Like him, she had not succumbed to conspicuous consumption. "I don't own a fur coat," she told *Ebony*, because the weather in New Orleans "did not get cold enough" for her to wear one very often.13

In this portrait, pride alternates with defensiveness. Many blacks were delighted that rhythm and blues was having a tremendous influence on the popular music of the nation and that African-American artists like Fats Domino, as *Cash Box* put it, were "accepted for themselves alone." They relished the rush by white pop singers to record rhythm and blues songs. Most of all, they were pleased that as they danced, in pink and black peg pants, toreadors and pin curls, those incorrigible rock 'n' roll fans were, at least for a few moments, integrated Americans. Nonetheless, as products of an unsettled 1950s, they worried as much as white adults about rock 'n' roll's tendency to release economic and emotional inhibitions and undermine the authority of the family, the church, and the state. For blacks in (or poised to enter) the middle class there was an added concern: the possibility that, thanks to rock 'n' roll, Negro culture would be defined and disdained as vulgar and licentious, the contributions of its intellectuals, politicians, and professionals ignored. With its animal gyrations, said Congressman Emmanuel Cellar, rock 'n' roll violated good taste, but it had its place, at least "among the colored people." African Americans did not have to read Norman Mailer's essay "The White Negro" (1957) to know that for some whites Negroes represented an ethic of "immoderation, childlike in its adoration of the present," and of Saturday night kicks where the pleasures of the mind were surrendered "for the more obligatory pleasures of the body." Even when delivered in a "laundered popular way," the music gave voice to the rage of the white male "and the infinite variations of joy, lust, languor, growl, cramp, pinch, and despair of his orgasm."[14]

These concerns reached into—and divided—many churchgoing African-American families, who were otherwise attracted by the prospect of lives of material comfort that seemed, finally, to be within their grasp. In 1958, fourteen-year-old Alleasie Titus confessed in a letter to Martin Luther King Jr. that she enjoyed rock 'n' roll but assured him she did not dance. "Can a person be a Christian and interested in those things?" she asked. "I know I can't combine the work of the Devil and the Lord. Should I quit listening to them?" King had answered this question earlier in the year, in an "Advice for Living" column in *Ebony*. Gospel music and rock 'n' roll, he asserted, were "totally incompatible" because the latter "often plunges men's minds into degrading and immoral depths."[15]

Swimming in the mainstream might also weaken the attachment of African Americans to their own cultural—and musical—heritage. Langston Hughes, the eminent black poet, thought rock 'n' roll an unsophisticated musical genre, less satisfactory, in theme and form, than jazz, blues, and gospel. Rock 'n' roll, he recognized, borrowed the "gut-bucket heartache" of the blues, the "I'm gonna be happy anyhow in spite of the world kind of hope" of the spirituals, and the "steady beat of Congo square—that going on beat—and the Marching Bands' loud and blatant yes!" But it combined them in a "teenage 'Heartbreak Hotel,'" appealing to juveniles because "you are never too young to know how bad it is to love and not have love come back to you." Rock 'n' roll, Hughes concluded, with less than fulsome praise, "makes a music so basic it's like the meat cleaver the butcher uses— before the cook uses the knife—before you use the sterling silver at the table on the meat that by then has been rolled up into a commercial fillet mignon."[16]

Most blacks were eager to end the oppressive conditions in the United States that caused this "gut-bucket heartache," even if it meant they would be less motivated to sing the blues. A few intellectuals in the '50s, however, worried that Negroes were getting "too close to white ways." "Embarrassed about, angry at, or ashamed of" the blues and jazz, charged white music critic Berta Wood, black youngsters listened to Liberace, Jo Stafford, Joni James, and rock 'n' rollers "in a careless, popular way," indistinguishable from whites. Even worse, they were "eaten up" by the "diseases that spring from psychological inhibitions" that once were "exclusive to white civilization." If they tried to think and act like white people, Wood concluded, Negroes would lose their creativity, their physical grace, and their "soft, flowing voices."[17]

The concerns raised by Wood would resurface, with greater intensity, in the 1960s. In the '50s, an awareness that integration might make African-American culture less distinctive and reduce the special affinity of blacks for music tended to be subordinated to an endorsement of its social, political, and economic impact. That some ambivalence remained is apparent in the assessment of rock 'n' roll by black jazz pianist Billy Taylor. "It's musically trite," Taylor told *Down Beat* magazine. "The kind of beat it brought back would have been better discarded." Taylor attributed the popularity of rock 'n' roll to the tenacity of its promoters: "They'll tie the disc jockey's shoelaces, shave him, baby sit for him." But when asked whether rock 'n' roll promoted integration or produced riots, the normally articulate musician grew tongue-tied, his answer the non sequitur of a man reluctant to give rock 'n' roll credit for anything but unwilling to criticize any phenomenon that might be good for African Americans: "The social aspects of rhythm and blues [as he insisted on calling it] have nothing whatsoever to do with the quality or lack of it in the music. I would say that teenagers obviously are neither children nor are they grown. They have to have something completely their own—a manner of dress, favorite movie stars, and now, rhythm and blues. Bop doesn't make it with them because it was useless for their social purposes—they couldn't sing or dance to it."[18]

Whether Billy Taylor, Berta Wood, and Langston Hughes liked it or not, rock 'n' roll was here to stay—and pay. Echoing *Ebony*, white liberals viewed it as a barometer of, and to some extent a vehicle for, progress in race relations in the United States. Rock 'n' roll, *Cash Box* exulted, was "Breaking Down the Barriers." Noting that R&B hits were routinely appearing at the top of the pop charts, the editors published article after article applauding the industry for opening doors for African-American artists and promoting understanding between blacks and whites. With white acceptance of Fats Domino, Little Richard, and Clyde McPhatter, the "buying of records according to the color of the artist was shattered beyond recognition." *Cash Box* revealed that every song Bob Lloyd of WAVZ in New Haven, Connecticut, played on his morning program on the first day of Brotherhood Week was performed by a black artist. Not one person called the station to take note of or complain about the disc jockey's choices. Lloyd was ready to draw a moral to his story: "Let's, therefore, all judge people as fairly as we do the records on a radio show—individually and on the merits of each."[19]

Rock 'n' roll was also breaking down parochial tastes and promoting a national culture, a phenomenon that seemed entirely salutary to most Americans in the 1950s, because they linked an embrace of universal values to racial tolerance and integration. The music opened minds and helped people appreciate "qualities which they never could see before," *Cash Box* claimed, a change "which in the ordinary course of events might have taken untold amounts of time" to accomplish. "How better to understand what is known to you than by appreciation of the emotional experience of other people. And how better are the emotions portrayed than by music?"[20]

Anecdotal evidence supported the view that rock 'n' roll challenged racial stereotypes as it brought white and black youth together. Industry publications noted, at almost every concert, a "mixed audience," conversing with one another as they waited on line to get in, then "cheering themselves hoarse." Harry Weinger, bass singer of the Platters, saw white kids venture into African-American neighborhoods, in search of rock 'n' roll. The experience gave them "a sense of fair play," he thought, that made them receptive to the civil rights movement. These kids invited the Platters into their homes, even though their "fathers looked at us like we were going to steal the goddammed refrigerator." Chairman Johnson of the group Chairmen of the Board observed the same phenomenon in South Carolina: "It was at the beach that racial segregation began to break down, white kids could listen to R&B behind their folks' backs."[21]

Many whites in the music industry recognized that rock 'n' roll was a metaphor for integration. In Buffalo, New York, white disc jockey George "Hound Dog" Lorenz played rhythm and blues on WKBW, used slang adapted from black language patterns, and sponsored concerts where black and white kids sat side by side watching black and white performers. Radio, records, and television, to be sure, permitted rock 'n' roll fans to listen to the music without venturing into black neighborhoods or rubbing shoulders with African Americans. Rock 'n' roll surely did not do more for integration than *Brown v. Board of Education*, as Herbie Cox of the Cleftones claimed, but it may have created a climate that supported desegregation and voting rights for blacks.[22]

White teenagers occasionally courted physical danger to confront racists. Shortly before he began his record hop for an all-white audience at Don's Teen Town, in Bessemer, Alabama, in 1960, disc jockey Shelley Stewart learned that eighty Ku Klux Klansman intended to assault him. When the club manager announced that he was canceling the show because the Klan did not think that that "nigger, Shelley the Playboy," should spin platters or dance with white girls, the audience erupted and set upon the Klansmen, permitting Stewart and three black colleagues to sneak out and escape in his 1959 Impala. Pursued by a white trooper, who evidently was more worried about a black man exceeding the speed limit than a white mob bent on violence, Stewart got away. He was convinced that the white teenagers had saved his life.[23]

Although such incidents transformed those who experienced them, they were rare. Rock 'n' roll did not always raise the racial or political consciousness of fans. Some listeners remained blissfully ignorant of the racial connotations of rock 'n' roll. Nineteen-year-old Virginia Lemon of Little Rock, Arkansas, idolized Elvis Presley and James Dean but chose to be photographed in *Look* magazine wearing a Confederate cap and waving a Confederate flag. In the North, many high school and college students saw no conflict between listening to rock 'n' roll, disapproving of segregation in the South, and joining fraternities and sororities that were segregated by race and religion.[24]

Did rock 'n' roll provide unprecedented opportunities for African-American performers, as the black media suggested? Before 1954, as Arnold Shaw has pointed out, the walls of musical segregation were high enough to keep most black performers out of the mass market controlled by the major record companies but low enough to allow white artists access to black audiences. Until then, as one observer put it, "you couldn't make it unless you were white, sleek, nicely spoken, and phoney to your toenails." Thus, the hits of Howlin' Wolf and of

Ivory Joe Hunter and Ruth Brown's "Teardrops from My Eyes," and "Mama, He Treats Your Daughter Mean" reached the R&B charts but were nowhere on the pop radar screen. By contrast, Johnnie Ray, a white man who fashioned his style of singing by listening to Joe Williams, Bessie Smith, and Billy Daniels, rocketed to the top of both charts in 1951 with "Cry."[25]

Among the black artists ignored by the majors and most radio stations was Arthur Crudup, a big man with a high-pitched voice, who sang the blues like a shouter in a plantation field. Having achieved a minor reputation with the songs "Mean Old Frisco Blues" and "That's All Right," Crudup jumped from label to label while working day jobs in Indianapolis, in Chicago, and on the Mississippi River to support a family of four children and nine stepchildren. In 1952, billed as Elmer James, he left Bluebird for Trumpet Records. He then signed with another "indie," Checker, as Perry Lee Crudup, before joining Ace Records as Big Boy Crudup. Although he did record again in the mid-'60s, Crudup's heyday ended in 1954. When Elvis was recording "That's All Right," Crudup was a migrant laborer en route to Florida.[26]

As R&B performers "crossed over" to the pop charts with rock 'n' roll hits, and pop singers scrambled to "cover rhythm and blues songs as soon as they showed any sign at all of making noise," blacks hoped music would become color-blind. *Billboard* announced in February 1957 that it was ending its "Rhythm and Blues Notes" column and inaugurating "On the Beat—Rhythm and Blues—Rock and Roll." The new format covered the "musical areas that have developed in the past few years under the inspiration of the unusually wide acceptance of the R&B idiom," including rock 'n' roll and rockabilly. "No abstract categories prevent the teenagers of today from buying records of Fats Domino, Elvis Presley, Bill Haley, Carl Perkins, or Little Richard at one and the same time. The trade, therefore, must revise and perhaps abandon some of its old boundary lines." R&B artists, columnist Gary Kramer observed in "On the Beat," now regularly reached white and black audiences, "an interesting case of the integration of the tastes of the majority into the tastes of the minority."[27]

Rock 'n' roll did open doors for African Americans. Of the 730 Top Ten hits on the *Billboard* charts between 1957 and 1964, black artists recorded 204, the largest percentage they ever registered. But the record of the music industry was mixed. In the phenomenon of "cover" versions of hit songs, one can see both racial progress and the pervasiveness and tenacity of racism.[28]

Assessing the impact of the cover phenomenon on African Americans is more difficult than many music critics and historians have acknowledged. Although covers "whitened" rhythm and blues, and many black singers were exploited by record producers, covers also helped develop a mass market for R&B and provided opportunities for black writers and musicians. Many rhythm and blues performers, no doubt, were as eager to "cross over" to that mass market as Ray Charles: "My people made me what I am, because you have to become big in your own community first, but as far as leaving that black audience exclusively, I never even thought twice about it."[29]

Moreover, learning from, borrowing, and copying came with the territory in music. Black as well as white musicians covered one another all the time. "Musically, at least," wrote Ralph Ellison, the great novelist and aficionado of jazz and blues, "each child in our town was an heir of all the ages." Ellison did not doubt that the blues, spirituals, and jazz were influenced by classical music: "This is a pluralistic society and culturally the melting pot really melts." Ray Charles, too, was untroubled that Carl Perkins, Pat Boone, and Elvis recorded rhythm and blues songs. "It was just one of those American things," he concluded. "I believe in mixed musical marriages, and there's no way to copyright a feeling or a rhythm or a style of singing. Besides, it meant that White America was getting hipper." Charles was flattered that some singers sounded so much like him they must have slept with his records beneath their pillows. After all, he had done much the same thing as a young performer, never thinking twice about imitating Nat King Cole or feeling bad "about copying the cat's licks."[30]

Black songwriters occasionally profited from covers by white artists, either by selling the rights to their music or by earning royalties from record sales. When Georgia Gibbs, "a nice Jewish girl," copied (and Cloroxed) LaVern Baker's "Tweedle Dee," songwriter Winfield Scott "was torn. I had to think two ways.... As a writer, you think, 'Gee, I have another record,' so here's a chance to secure a bigger income. And again, I had to feel, 'Wow, this must be devastating to LaVern,' because her record came out first, now here comes the cover, and all of a sudden she fades into obscurity. And I didn't know how to deal with that."[31]

Many black artists covered songs, sometimes reaching back into the 1920s and '30s for material. Fats Domino's "Blueberry Hill" was introduced by Gene Autry and made a hit by the Glenn Miller Orchestra; Domino's "Corinna Corrina" covered a black artist, Cab Calloway, who recorded the song in 1933; "My Blue Heaven" was written by Walter Donaldson in 1927. "In the Still of the Night," a Five Satins hit, was written by Cole Porter and first sung by Nelson Eddy; the Orioles' "Crying in the Chapel," an R&B and pop smash in 1953, was a cover of a country song by Darrell Glenn. In 1956, the Cadets covered Elvis Presley's "Heartbreak Hotel," as the flip side of "Church Bells May Ring."[32]

Sometimes, it was difficult to determine who was covering whom. "Hound Dog" was written by Jerry Leiber and Mike Stoller, two whites with a passion for black culture, who hung out in black neighborhoods in the late '40s, listening to R&B. They showed the song to Johnny Otis, the son of a Greek immigrant grocer, who played drums in several black bands in Watts and West Oakland, California. Married to a black woman, Otis had rock 'n' roll shows on three Los Angeles television stations in the '50s. White, Asian, black, and Hispanic kids attended the dances he promoted. In fact, some fans thought he was black. Otis showed the song to Willie Mae ("Big Mama") Thornton, who recorded it, with Otis taking composing credit. Elvis made substantial changes to the tempo and lyrics of "Hound Dog," and his version made it to number 1 on both the country and R&B charts. Although Leiber and Stoller wrote the song, Greil Marcus insists that it is a black tune, "probably a rewrite of an old piece of juke joint fury."[33]

At least once a cover advanced the fortunes of a black rock 'n' roll singer. In 1951, Randy Wood, owner of a record store in Gallatin, Tennessee that specialized in country music and rhythm and blues, established an independent label, Dot Records. Dot featured white pop singers covering R&B songs. In 1955, the company produced two big hits: a cover of "Hearts of Stone," by the Fontane Sisters, who had appeared frequently with Perry Como, reached number 1 on the pop charts; and Gale Storm, star of the TV sitcom *My Little Margie*, made it to number 2 with "I Hear You Knockin'," an R&B song, first recorded by Smiley Lewis and Dave Bartholomew. In search of the trifecta for '55, Wood asked Pat Boone to record "Ain't That a Shame," Fats Domino's new hit.

Willie Mae "Big Mama" Thornton recorded "Hound Dog" before Elvis did. *(Michael Ochs Archives)*

At twenty-one, Boone was already a veteran of *Ted Mack's Original Amateur Hour*, Arthur Godfrey's *Talent Scouts*, and a radio show of his own in Nashville. Boone was a clean-cut crooner who sported argyle socks, white buck shoes, and a bachelor's degree from Columbia University. Although he was a native of the South, Boone knew little about rhythm and blues. When Wood got him to listen to "Two Hearts," by the Charms, Boone wondered whether the phonograph was running at the right speed. Nonetheless, with the help of a polished arrangement, a big band background, and a chorus scat of "bop-a-do-do-wop" during instrumental interludes, Boone turned "Ain't That a Shame"—and himself—"into a "coast to coast rock and roll sensation."

The cover also breathed new life into Fats Domino's version. While "Ain't That a Shame" (Boone wanted to make the title "Isn't That a Shame"), reached number 1 on *Billboard*'s pop chart, Domino's "Ain't

That a Shame" climbed to 10. Years later, as he sat in the audience at a concert in New Orleans, Boone was invited on the stage by the Fat Man, who pointed to the diamond rings on each of his fingers and said, "This man bought me this ring with this song." Domino and Boone then performed "Ain't That a Shame" together.[34]

Fats Domino was not the only African-American singer to consciously court the crossover market. Clyde McPhatter, the Platters, and Sam Cooke, among others, attracted white audiences, using melodic, highly orchestrated styles and old standards to do so. Sometimes, the strategy worked. In 1956, with only one exception, original rhythm and blues songs outsold covers. Four of nine Top Ten hits, including "Blueberry Hill," were not covered in that year. The lesser hits confirm the pattern. With thirteen of them, the original either outperformed the cover or was not covered. Only two covers did better than the originals. During the rest of the decade, as the majors began to exploit rock 'n' roll, covers surged back, though a few black performers held their own with original versions.[35]

Although some resourceful and talented African Americans enriched themselves through rock 'n' roll, the music industry in the 1950s remained, as LeRoi Jones (later Amiri Baraka) put it, "the harnessing of Black energy for dollars by white folks." Broadcast Music Incorporated (BMI) gave black artists far better copyright protection than its Tin Pan Alley–dominated rival, the American Society of Composers and Performers (ASCAP), but many were tricked or pressured into signing exploitative contracts. In the 1940s and '50s, lawyer Howard Begle discovered that most contracts to blacks paid royalties at the rock bottom rate of between 1 and 4 percent of the retail price of the record or, even worse, provided a one-time payment of $200 for records that generated hundreds of thousands or millions of dollars in sales.[36]

In 1955, for example, Leonard Chess told Chuck Berry to sign what he called "a standard contract." Berry did not understand such phrases as "residuals from mechanical rights," "writer's and producer's percentages," and "performance royalties and publisher fees." When he saw the word "copyright" several times, Berry was reassured "that it was connected with the United States government, it was legitimate, and I was likely protected." After all, his father had frequently told him that no one could "take your achievements from you when they're

patented and copyrighted." When he received his first royalty statement for "Maybellene," Berry noticed that Alan Freed and a disc
jockey named Russ Fratto were listed as co-composers of the song.
Chess told him that the song would get more attention if big names in
the industry had an interest in it. "With me being unknown," Berry
recalled, "this made sense to me, especially since he failed to mention
that there was a split in the royalties as well."[37]

Berry's experience was by no means an anomaly, even among successful black artists. Colonel Tom Parker, Elvis Presley's manager, insisted that Otis Blackwell share songwriting credits with Elvis for "All
Shook Up" and "Don't Be Cruel." Blackwell was angry but then "realized that songwriters who'd been in the business much longer than I
had, and who were much better off financially, were going along with
this. Some people would even have paid to have a song done by Elvis.
So I figured what the hell. And I can't complain about how I made out."
The payola hearings at the end of the decade would demonstrate that
assigning copyrights in this manner was "established practice" in the industry. Dick Clark, for example, held copyrights on more than 150
songs, ranging from "Let's Go to the Hop," by Danny and the Juniors, to
the flip side of Paul Anka's gold record "Diana" to the Crests' "Sixteen
Candles." African Americans were by no means the only victims of
these practices, but they suffered disproportionately from them.[38]

At their worst, covers involved outright theft, with whole arrangements lifted from black records. Ruth Brown "wasn't so upset about
other singers copying my songs because that was their privilege, and
they had to pay the writers of the song," but when they copied "the
style, the whole idea," Brown felt violated. With the help of BMI,
artists did fight back. They pressured WINS, a music radio station in
New York City, to distinguish between "copy" and "cover" records and
stop playing those that lifted without alteration distinctive vocal or
instrumental styles. "Imitation may be the sincerest form of flattery,"
LaVern Baker quipped, "but that kind of flattery I can do without."
After Baker complained that Georgia Gibbs had copied her rendition
of "Tweedlee Dee," including the "odd rhythm beat," Congressman
Charles Diggs Jr. introduced a bill to prevent performers from duplicating arrangements on original releases of records.[39]

African Americans lacked the clout, however, to curtail the cover
trade, which was particularly threatening to them because most disc

jockeys and owners of radio stations, in the North as well as the South, preferred to play the music of white performers and major record labels. When a record was covered, *Cash Box* claimed, "many jockeys immediately switch as soon as it is available." Dependent on radio exposure, black performers were at a competitive disadvantage throughout the decade.[40]

Music historian Jonathan Kamin has documented the disproportionate airplay bestowed on white covers. Between 1952 and 1956, for example, whenever radio gatekeepers had a choice, they played a cover more and an R&B original less than their relative positions on the charts merited. Although "Earth Angel," by the black vocal group the Penguins, was on the *Billboard* pop Top Ten for a month in 1955, it was never higher than thirteenth among the most frequently played records in the United States. At the same time, the Crew Cuts cover of the song, which was fourteenth on the charts, was one of the ten most frequently aired records. Johnny Ace's "Pledging My Love" suffered the same fate. Although it was seventeenth on *Billboard*'s list when Teresa Brewer's cover was released in March 1955, ten places higher than Brewer's, radio stations stopped playing the original. One final example should suffice. In 1956, "Why Do Fools Fall In Love?," by Frankie Lymon and the Teenagers, spent a month on the charts, rising to number 9, before it appeared on radio's most-played list. Gale Storm's cover got a big boost from radio, becoming the ninth most played record when it was number nineteen on *Billboard*'s pop listing.[41]

To retain and regain their hold on the white pop market, many black rock 'n' rollers utilized a sweeter sound, a smoother look, and more soothing lyrics. The phenomenon *Cash Box* called "rhythm and happies" helps explain the success of African-American performers in 1956; it was used by virtually every black singer who reached the charts during the rest of the decade. Glittering in their tuxedos, crooning "whitened" ballads like "Only You" and "Twilight Time" that resembled pop hits from the 1930s, the "doo-wop" group the Platters, for example, connected again and again with millions of fans.[42]

The African-American rock 'n' rollers who crossed over to the pop mainstream did not sing songs that were explicitly about black life or the social, economic, and political realities of the 1950s. In 1956, *Cash Box* boasted that when the ballad "The Death of Emmett Till" was played on WGES radio, the telephone company in Chicago reported 8,394 busy signals, virtually all of them listeners trying to contact the station. There was no rock 'n' roll equivalent of "The Death of Emmett Till." Nor did any rock 'n' roll headliner publicly condemn President Eisenhower for his halfhearted attempts to desegregate Little Rock Central High School, as jazz man Louis Armstrong did. Moreover, rock 'n' roll songs occasionally presented stereotypes of blacks, as comic figures ("Charlie Brown"), superstitious ("Witch Doctor"), without sexual restraint ("Shimmy Shimmy Ko Ko Bop"), and, as late as 1963, addicted to watermelon ("Watermelon Man").[43]

As happened so often in African-American culture, racial references in rock 'n' roll were below the surface, confined to subtexts, in coded language. As slaves, blacks had learned that they might be able to sing what they could not say. The venerable Negro refrain set forth the strategy: "Got one mind for folks to see / 'Nother for what I know is me; / He don't know, he don't know my mind." With their 1955 hit "The Great Pretender," for example, the Platters used lyrics reminiscent of Ralph Ellison's great novel *Invisible Man*. In the white world, they implied, blacks wore masks: "Oh yes, I'm the great pretender / Just laughing and gay like a clown / I seem to be what I'm not, you see / I'm wearing my heart like a crown."[44]

Although the race of the protagonist is never identified, some black listeners may have responded to "The Great Pretender" as the story of the double lives of African Americans. But as they slow-danced to the song, white teenagers, with few exceptions, probably thought it the sad reflection of a lovesick young man, putting up a brave front ("pretending that you're still around"), and then feeling what his "heart can't conceal:" his girl has left him "to dream all alone."

Perhaps the best way to assess how rock 'n' roll both accommodated to and challenged the status quo in race relations is through an examination of the careers of Little Richard Penniman and Chuck Berry, who, along with Fats Domino, were the most successful African-American rock 'n' rollers. In distinctly different ways, Berry and Little Richard struggled with black identity and culture, onstage and in their music, as they consciously adopted styles and subject matters that appealed to a predominantly white audience.

Born in Macon, Georgia, in 1932, Richard Penniman sang in a Baptist church choir as a youngster and traveled with his family's gospel troupe, the Penniman Family. Little Richard claimed that his family did not like rhythm and blues, preferring Bing Crosby, "Pennies from Heaven," and Ella Fitzgerald. Even as a kid, he "knew there was something that could be louder than that, but I didn't know where to find it. And I found it was me." According to one of his brothers, Richard hollered all the time: "I thought he couldn't sing, anyway, just a noise, and he would get on our nerves hollerin' and beating on tin cans and things of that nature. People around would get angry and upset with him yelling and screaming."

Ostracized by his friends and family, probably because they suspected that he was a homosexual, Penniman left home when he was fourteen to join Dr. Hudson's Medicine Show. He then signed on to sing with B. Brown and His Orchestra and also performed in drag in a minstrel show, "Sugar Foot Sam from Alabam." Using rhythm and blues singer Billy Wright as his model, he designed the look that would become his signature style: "I copied him as far as dressing, the hairdo and the makeup, 'cause he was the only man I ever seen wearing makeup before." At the same time, he worked as a dishwasher at the Greyhound bus station. In the South in the 1940s, a black knew that it was most unwise to talk back to his boss, so when insulted Penniman masked his anger with the nonsense response "Wop Bop a Loo Bop a Lop Bam Boom."

By the early '50s Little Richard had recorded several records, including a modest hit, "Every Hour." He had his own band, the Upsetters, and made "a darned good living" on the road in Georgia, Tennessee, and Kentucky. One of his most successful numbers, especially with white audiences, was "Tutti Frutti," a wild, gay song, whose raunchy lyrics included the lines "Tutti Frutti, good booty / If it don't fit, don't force it / You can grease it, / make it easy."

In 1955, hoping to break through to a national audience, Little Richard went to New Orleans to record for Specialty Records. With hair a foot high, according to Robert "Bumps" Blackwell, Specialty's artists and repertoire man, Richard wore a shirt that "was so loud it looked as though he had drunk raspberry juice, cherryade, malt, and greens, and then thrown up all over himself." But when he auditioned for Blackwell, the shouter who had attracted Specialty's attention did not shout. Since "Tutti Frutti" did not strike him as suitable for the session, Richard spent two days, much to Blackwell's consternation, singing desultory arrangements of the slow song "Lonesome and Blue" and Leiber and Stoller's "Kansas City." During a lunch break at a local establishment, the Dew Drop Inn, Little Richard jumped onto the bandstand and launched into "Tutti Frutti," yelling, "Awop-bop-a-Loo-Mop a-good Goddam." Blackwell thought the song might be a hit but also knew that the lyrics had to be changed, and quickly, because the musicians and the studio were booked only for the remainder of the day.

Blackwell contacted Dorothy La Bostrie, a young African-American songwriter, to rewrite. At first, Little Richard balked, claiming he was too embarrassed to sing the song to a woman. La Bostrie seemed equally uncomfortable. With time running out, Blackwell asked Little Richard "if he had a grudge against making money" and reminded La Bostrie that she was twenty-one, had several kids, and needed the

"Little Richard" Penniman was a brash, flamboyant rock 'n' roll shouter whose songs "Tutti Frutti" and "Long Tall Sally" became hits even though their lyrics were sanitized. *(Michael Ochs Archives)*

income: "Richard turned to face the wall and sang the song two or three times and Dorothy listened." A few hours later, the lyrics had been changed to "I got a gal named Sue / She knows just what to do / She rocks me to the east / She rocks me to the west / She's the gal I love best." While a sax-packed band pulsated with energy, Little Richard embellished the words of "Tutti Frutti" with screams, squeals, rasps, or sirens, in effect exhorting listeners to get loose and go crazy. The only performer Blackwell knew "who would beat the piano so hard he'd break an eighty-gauge piano string," Richard accompanied himself for what turned out to be two and a half minutes that made rock 'n' roll history.

Art Rupe, the owner of Specialty, did not like the song. He expected Little Richard to produce the "big band sound expressed in a churchy way," characteristic of mid-'50s black rock 'n' rollers. With little enthusiasm, Rupe finally agreed to distribute "Tutti Frutti." Little Richard was also convinced that the song would not be a hit, even with sanitized lyrics. They miscalculated. Little Richard became an exception to the "rule" that whites would not accept a black shouter. Within weeks, "Tutti Frutti" reached number 2 on the R&B charts. Despite almost no radio airplay, the song also climbed to number 18 on the pop charts. Over the next three years, Little Richard gave Specialty eleven more hits, including "Long Tall Sally" (1956), "Keep a Knockin'" (1957) and "Good Golly, Miss Molly" (1958).[45]

Little Richard brought manic energy and showmanship to live performances and records. He was brash and bombastic, telling audiences, "I'm just the same as ever—loud, electrifying, and full of personal magnetism" and "That piano was talkin' and the drums was walkin'. It made my big toe shoot up in my boot." Before Liberace went campy, Little Richard appeared with a puffed-up pompadour, heavy makeup, capes, and blousy shirts, prancing across the stage and letting loose a "Woooo" that Paul McCartney heard across the Atlantic and adapted to the music of the Beatles.[46]

There was, he subsequently recalled, a racially motivated method to his madness. In the 1950s, a terrible fate awaited a black man who was seen as sexually attractive to white women. To appear safe, Little Richard donned "eyelashes longer than Josephine Baker's" and his way-out platform persona. "By wearing this makeup," he claimed, "I could work and play white clubs, and the white people didn't mind the white girls screaming over me. . . . They was willing to accept me, 'cause they figured I wouldn't be no harm."[47]

Although Little Richard's explanation may have been designed, in part, to hide his ambivalence about his homosexuality, black rock 'n' rollers in the 1950s knew the dangers of appearing to be sexually threatening to whites. Part of the appeal of the juvenile "doo-wop" groups, no doubt, was that they were romantic but presexual. Even so, when fourteen-year-old Frankie Lymon, whose hit "Why Do Fools Fall in Love?" (with the Teenagers) was typical of the genre, impulsively grabbed a white girl as a dance partner at the end of Alan Freed's *Rock 'n' Roll Dance Party* on ABC-TV in 1957, thirteen affiliates, not all of them in the South, canceled the program, which was soon dropped by the network. That Fats Domino resembled Santa Claus more than he did a sexual predator also accounts in no small measure for his popularity with some white audiences. Still, according to Russ Sanjek, later vice president of BMI, "it was a time when many a mother ripped pictures of Fats Domino off her daughter's bedroom wall. She remembered what she felt toward her Bing Crosby pinup, and she didn't want her daughter creaming for Fats."[48]

Perhaps because of his presentation of self, Little Richard was not, at least in the mainstream press, perceived as a sexually threatening black or a homosexual. In *Billboard*, for example, Ben Walstein, the author of *Transference in Psychoanalytic Therapy*, pronounced rock 'n' roll an essentially harmless response to teenagers' sometimes frustrating search for an identity. Acknowledging that he had difficulty making "out what the words are" in Little Richard's song "Long Tall Sally," Walstein opined that the singer's "use of falsetto is significant because here we have an expression of a kind of problem all adolescents have, and that is the attempt to struggle through the period where all males, for instance, are trying to achieve some kind of masculine identification, and I think that this falsetto expression is it."[49]

Nonetheless, the sexual energy exuded by Little Richard made many Americans in the '50s anxious or angry. "Long Tall Sally," after all, was banned in Houston. So Specialty Records tried hard to assure white adults that Little Richard was harmless. In the liner notes for his second LP, Specialty announced that the singer had included some old pop tunes along with his rock 'n' roll hits "especially for his fans'

parents who may still not 'dig the beat.' He feels that if only they'll
listen to songs they remember like 'Baby Face,' and 'By the Light of
the Silvery Moon,' done up in the Little Richard style, they'll enjoy this
new album, too."[50]

As Little Richard shaped his public persona to accommodate a mass
audience, Chuck Berry considered whether (and how) to express musically the antiauthoritarianism he shared with some '50s teenagers. An
ambitious performer, Berry, like Little Richard, was willing to adapt his
music to reach white listeners, but beneath his endorsements of happiness, success, and fun, and his portrait of school as jail, he looked for
ways to give voice to black culture and social aspiration. Born in San
Jose, California, in 1926, and raised in St. Louis, Missouri, in a pleasant
one-family brick home in a black middle-class neighborhood, Berry
sang in the Antioch Baptist Church choir and in the glee club of his
high school, where a music teacher encouraged him to play the guitar.
He listened at home on the radio to a range of musical styles, from
gospel to country to ballads. In the 1980s, Berry rewrote history to
stress the formative influence of white singers on his sound: "I never
heard Muddy Waters. I never heard Elmore James, Howling Wolf, I
never heard 'em. I heard Frank Sinatra, I heard Pat Boone, you know
Pat Boone doing Muddy Waters or whoever's numbers. . . . And I said
now can I do as Pat Boone does and play good music for the white people and sell as well there as I could in the neighborhood. And that's
what I shot for." In fact, Boone did not cover any Muddy Waters song
and did not have his first hit until 1955, long after Berry's career had
been launched. On other occasions, and more accurately, Berry acknowledged his debt to Louis Jordan: "I have a lot of flighty things, like
Louis had, comical things and natural things, not too heavy."[51]

Despite a supportive home environment, Berry was a troubled
young man who was convicted of armed robbery and spent some time
in a reformatory. After his release, he worked on a factory assembly
line and then as a hairdresser. In 1951, he bought an electric guitar,
the "first really good looking instrument" he owned. He found it
"much easier to finger the frets" and was delighted that, with an
amplifier, it could be easily heard. A year later, Berry began his career
as a professional musician, forming a trio with the great boogie-
woogie pianist Johnnie Johnson and drummer Ebby Harding. At the
Cosmopolitan Club in East St. Louis, Berry worked country music

into his repertoire. The audience response, especially from whites, was extremely enthusiastic. "Salt and pepper mixed together" at the club, with whites constituting almost half of the clientele. To please the crowd, Berry changed the way he sang: "I stressed my diction so that it was harder and whiter.... It was my intention to hold both the black and white clientele by voicing the different songs in their customary tongues."[52]

The most popular song at the Cosmo was Berry's improvised version of "Ida Red," an up-tempo dance number recorded by country singer Roy Acuff in 1939. With encouragement from Muddy Waters, Berry in 1955 brought to Chess Records a tape of the tune he now called "Ida May" and a blues song he had written, "Wee Wee Hours," inspired by Joe Turner's "Wee Baby Blue." To Berry's surprise, Leonard Chess showed little interest in the blues material but waxed enthusiastic about the commercial possibilities in a hillbilly song "written and sung by a black guy." Chess wanted a bigger beat for the song and added a bass and maraca player to the trio at the recording session. He also thought Berry's title, "Ida May," "too rural." Spotting a mascara box on the floor of the studio, according to Johnnie Johnson, Chess said, "Well, hell, let's name the damn thing Maybellene," altering the spelling to avoid a suit by the cosmetics company. "The kids wanted the big beat, cars, and young love," Chess recalled. "It was a trend and we jumped on it."

With Alan Freed (to whom Chess assigned one-third of the songwriting credits and royalties) promoting the song on his radio program, "Maybellene" became one of the first records to reach number one on the rhythm and blues, country and western, and pop charts. Featuring some inimitable Chuck Berry riffs, some blues-style picking on a country guitar, and Johnson's piano, which added a hummable rhythm to the steady backbeat, "Maybellene" constituted a defining moment in the emergence of rock 'n' roll. As Chess had predicted, the song struck a chord with teenagers fascinated by cars, speed, and sexuality. Berry thought that because everybody had a car "or dreams about one," they might well identify with the narrator of "Maybellene": "As I was motorvatin' over the hill, / I saw Maybellene in a Coupe de Ville. / Cadillac rollin' on the open road, / Tryin' to outrun my V-8 Ford."[53]

Recipient of the *Cash Box* and *Billboard* awards for the most promising artist of 1955, Berry began to understand how well he had

Chuck Berry's lyrics to songs like "Brown-Eyed Handsome Man" played slyly with racial attitudes and even fears. *(Michael Ochs Archives)*

connected with whites. At an appearance before a "solid white audience" at the Brooklyn Paramount Theater in September 1955, he was
moved by the ecstatic response he received: "I doubt that many Cau-
casian persons would come into a situation that would cause them to
know the feeling a black person experiences after being reared under
old-time southern traditions and then finally being welcomed by an
entirely unbiased and friendly audience, applauding without apparent
regard for racial difference."[54]

Berry became one of rock 'n' roll's first and greatest superstars. His
hits included such classics as "Roll Over Beethoven" (1956), "Rock 'n'
Roll Music" (1957), "School Days" (1957), "Sweet Little Sixteen" (1958),
and "Johnny B. Goode" (1958). Berry's trademark "duck walk," in
which he glided across the stage with knees bent, his guitar held in
front of him, made him one of the most sought-after performers on
the live concert circuit. As they celebrated material things, while blam-
ing work or school for preventing people from pursuing pleasure, his
hits were the perfect vehicle for the aspiring but unsettled generation
of the 1950s.

Yet Berry crafted his songs to carry other meanings as well. The language he used in "School Days," for example, consciously invoked the
black gospel tradition. As they celebrate the liberating power of music
("Hail! Hail! Rock and Roll, / Deliver me from the days of old / The
feeling is there, body and soul") the lyrics hint at oppression and
deliverance, with a race consciousness recognizable to anyone familiar with African-American religion. The opening lines of "Brown-Eyed
Handsome Man" (1956) seem to promise a racialized discussion as
well, this time of economic oppression and sexual power: "Arrested
on charges of unemployment / he was sitting in the witness stand / the
judge's wife called up the district attorney / said free that brown-eyed
man." In the remainder of the song, Berry moves across time and con-
tinents, touching on Bombay and baseball, myth and love, but never
again on joblessness or justice in the United States. Nonetheless,
"Brown-Eyed Handsome Man" celebrates the sexual allure of black
men "ever since the world began." In the narrative, even the Venus de
Milo, exemplar of the beautiful white woman, "lost both her arms in
a wrestling match / to win a brown-eyed handsome man." At the end
of the song, as a young woman tries to "make up her mind / between

a doctor and a lawyer man," her mother has only one piece of advice: "go out and find yourself a brown-eyed handsome man."[55]

Berry intended to be more explicit with "Johnny B. Goode," the story of an illiterate, impoverished man, living "deep down in Louisiana" and dreaming of wealth and fame. Unlike John Henry or Stack O'Lee, mythic black heroes of another era, Johnny does not defy an oppressive system. He can win recognition from whites as well as blacks, Berry optimistically suggests, simply by demonstrating his genius with a guitar. But Berry did not make Johnny "a little colored boy," as he had in the original version of the song. Concerned that "it would seem biased to white fans," he made him a "little country boy" and, in a sense, invited listeners to see the song as a paean to careers open to talent in the United States, unrelated to race.[56]

Chuck Berry's experiences illuminate the opportunities for and complications with conducting a conversation about race through rock 'n' roll in the 1950s. As they made him a star, millions of Americans proved that they were ready to idolize an African American. And in Berry's live concerts, "salt and pepper" did mix together. At the same time, record producers and concert promoters robbed the performer of a substantial amount of the fruits of his labor, continuing a pattern of exploitation of blacks that spanned the century after "emancipation." For good reason, Berry remained an angry and suspicious man, insisting that he be paid in cash. He had, after all, been burned before, and his confidence that hard-working, talented blacks would, eventually, win the respect of whites was tempered by the recognition that racial discrimination was far more difficult to eradicate than segregation. Unwilling to risk losing his white audience by confronting racial issues directly, he persisted in exploring black identity, but only with those ready to face the music. Like many of his contemporaries in the 1950s, like rock 'n' roll as a whole, Berry advanced a racial agenda but moved forward with "all deliberate speed."[57]

"GREAT BALLS OF FIRE"

3

Rock 'n' Roll and Sexuality

In the '50s, rock 'n' roll became the focal point for anxiety that cultural life in the United States had become sexualized and teenagers addicted to the pleasures of the body. An ideology of abstinence, strenuously and sometimes stridently asserted, and the banishing of bedrooms from television underscored the depth and pervasiveness of that concern. Many adults feared that the weakening of traditional morality, diminished authority of parents, clergymen, and teachers, and availability of condoms and penicillin were making promiscuity safe, accepted, and universal to the post–World War II generation. Over the course of the decade, for example, all but two states dropped laws prohibiting the dissemination of contraceptive information or devices. At the same time, rock 'n' roll was demonstrating the power of the libido, as the music pulsated, the guitarist fondled his instrument, and the singer undulated sensuously. Rock 'n' roll seemed to be an anti-inhibitor, provoking erotic vandalism.[1]

In several ways, '50s rock 'n' roll was less than its critics feared. The music rarely endorsed sex outside of established relationships. Rock 'n' roll was also quite traditional with respect to the sexual roles of males and females. While weighing in against sexual repression and prudery, rock 'n' roll set sexuality in a context of love and marriage. Thus, as Simon Frith and Angela McRobbie have argued, rock 'n' roll operated as a form of sexual control as well as a form of sexual expression. Nonetheless, parents made no mistake in identifying the subversive sexual charge in the music. Although it was criticized, softened, and censored in the service of the status quo, rock 'n' roll was pivotal in a reassessment of sexual attitudes and behavior that only seemed to spring out of nowhere in the 1960s.[2]

Throughout the '50s, parents, politicians, and professionals were preoccupied with nonmarital sexual behavior. Convinced that teenagers who engaged in intercourse were likely to remain emotionally unstable and irresponsible, they struggled to find mechanisms of sexual containment. The old method, parental cautions and prohibitions, no longer seemed to work. Young people, "in whom the fear psychology has been built up," wrote therapist Frances Strain, "are in much greater danger morally than those who have been left free to build up their own standards and their own set of ethics." When their "normal sexual endowments" overcame parental sanctions, these young men and women were left with "no safeguard." Permissiveness, however, was even more problematic. Indeed, critics laid many of the ills of the postwar generation at the feet of weak and inattentive parents. Left to their own devices, they claimed, teenagers began to experiment sexually. In one national poll, 80 percent of high school students indicated that they had petted or necked while on a date or planned to, even though 50 percent of them acknowledged that their parents opposed such activities. In another survey, 60 percent deemed it appropriate for a couple who were going steady to "do anything they want."[3]

More than ever before, teenagers had the means, the motive, and the opportunity to transgress. Only a few years earlier, lamented Frederick Gelder, chairman of the Pennsylvania State Liquor Control Board, they "didn't get more than a block or two away from home at night. Today even a 16-year-old can borrow his father's car and if he has a license to drive he takes his girl 20 or 30 miles away." Benjamin Karpman, chief psychotherapist at St. Elizabeth's Hospital in Washington, D.C., told a subcommittee of the U.S. Senate investigating juvenile delinquency that boys were "under a great deal of sexual tension.... Tension is tension. It must break through." Ralph Banay, a psychiatrist at Columbia University, agreed: "A healthy boy or girl is a torrent of often chaotic energy. Without purpose or direction that plethora of priceless vigor can go astray in any number of chance channels, and many of these can be deleterious, destructive, and even vicious."[4]

What direction might adults provide? And how might they overcome the resistance of young men and women to taking direction from adults? Experts suggested providing outlets at home and school that might drain excess energy. Physical contact in group games and dances, athletics, and "various other types of legitimate touch experiences," Frances Strain believed, reduced "much of the drive toward excess love-making." Through these wholesome activities the needs and desires of teenagers could be acknowledged, institutionalized, and rechanneled.[5]

Even more important, adults sought ways to get young men and women to internalize norms of sexual behavior. They found hints on how to do it in *Parents' Magazine*, whose circulation jumped from 750,000 to 1.5 million in the decade following World War II. Some parents endorsed high school courses in sex education, as long as the material stayed "above the belt." Others encouraged their children to subscribe to teen magazines, which prescribed elaborate rules for dating, often putting them in the mouths of the youngsters themselves.[6]

Many parents encouraged dating. In doing so, they were bowing to the inevitable but also trying to endorse a stable relationship—or even a series of them—that would help couples "hold the line" until marriage. During the '50s, females learned to view restraint during courtship as their special responsibility. In a discussion of sex among six high school seniors, featured in *Seventeen* magazine, Sue defended the double standard: "I don't see how two people can get together on their wedding night and both be virgins." Convinced that "the greatest thing a girl can give her husband is her chastity," she thought it helpful that the boy be sexually active before marriage, "not with the whole world," of course, "but I want him to have experience." Necking and petting, especially "in front of people," repelled Valery; and Linda acknowledged, proudly, that her nicknames were "Frigid," "Snowberg," and "Iceberg." All the girls except Leslie believed that the sex drive was stronger in males than in females, and even Leslie recognized that a sexually active "girl has so much more to lose than a boy. . . . I think a lot of it is unfair, but that's the way it is; you can't fight it." There were many little things females could do to keep boyfriends from getting aroused, Leslie had learned, "like keeping your hand out of the

way" if you were at the movies and did not want it held. "Exactly,"
Linda added. "You put it in your popcorn bag."[7]

For teenagers who complied with the codes of courtship, sex
delayed felt like sex denied. Early marriage became a reward (and a
release) for them, a way to reconcile taboos against premarital intercourse with heightened pressure for intercourse. Premarital sex and
illegitimate births did not increase dramatically during the '50s, it
appears, because young people were told to say "no"—then promised
that they could pass "go" with a wedding certificate. With so many
kids exchanging vows, teen birth rates soared to levels not equaled in
any other decade in the twentieth century. In 1957, for example, 97 of
every 1,000 girls between fifteen and nineteen had a child; in 1983, only
52 out of every 1,000 were moms.[8]

The ideology of sexual containment was powerful and pervasive,
but in two studies of the sexual behavior of thousands of men and
women, Alfred Kinsey documented the existence of a huge gap
between private behavior and public morality. *Sexual Behavior in the
Human Male* (1948) and *Sexual Behavior in the Human Female*
(1953) were the first comprehensive surveys of the range, frequency,
distribution, and variety of sexual activity in the United States. Kinsey
found necking, petting, and other forms of noncoital intimacy almost
universal among dating couples. Fifty percent of women and almost
two-thirds of all men indicated that they had had premarital intercourse, often but not always with a partner who had made a
commitment to marriage in the near future (that commitment often
helped overcome the last vestiges of resistance). Most men did not
think premarital sex morally wrong for them and acknowledged sexual
encounters with women from a lower social class. Nearly half of the
men Kinsey interviewed wanted to marry a virgin. Eighty percent of
women branded coitus during courtship unethical, but 50 percent had
experienced premarital intercourse. Kinsey implied that the double
standard behind these responses produced sexual confusion and guilt.
He was convinced that the differences in sexual response between
men and women revealed in his study were socially determined and
not based in physiology. Finally, and most controversially, Kinsey
believed that premarital sex had proven useful in preparing couples
for a happy marriage.[9]

Sexual Behavior in the Human Female leaped onto the best-seller lists, with six printings and 185,000 copies sold within ten days of the book's release. That the book was reaching so many readers disturbed those already livid at its contents. The renowned anthropologist Margaret Mead explained why Kinsey's work was so dangerous. By removing a "previously guaranteed reticence" about sex, she observed, Kinsey had inadvertently "left many young people singularly defenseless in just those areas where their desire to conform was protected by a lack of knowledge of the extent of nonconformity." To many Americans in the 1950s, reticence, and even ignorance, about sex was bliss. Kinsey might have expected a denunciation by evangelist Billy Graham. But he was shocked when the president of Princeton compared the "rather trivial graphs with which the reports are loaded" to the work "of small boys writing dirty words on fences." And he was devastated by congressional investigations into the tax-exempt foundations that had funded his research and by the decision of the Rockefeller Foundation to withdraw support from him in favor of a grant to the Union Theological Seminary. Suffering from insomnia and heart trouble, Kinsey died in 1956. The messenger was dead, but the Maginot Line behind which Americans hid their sexual selves—and protected their children—had been breached.[10]

To many Americans, rhythm and blues was the Kinsey Report set to music, a manifesto in the movement to repeal sexual reticence. Before R&B, popular songs used clichés and euphemisms to hint at sexual passion. Occasionally commented on but rarely criticized, the approach was similar to that employed by film directors when they showed a couple kissing, then faded out to a scene of the surf pounding on some rocks near the shore. The musical equivalent, "If I Knew You Were Coming I'd've Baked a Cake," Eileen Barton's hit in 1951, may or may not have reminded listeners of more than Sara Lee. That year, Rosemary Clooney was probably not thinking of a Hershey bar when she invited her boyfriend to "Come on-a my house / I'm gonna give you candy."[11]

R&B lyrics, as we have seen, left rather less to the imagination. As long as the music was confined to the "black specialty market," late-night spots, and "out and out barrel houses," objections were few and far between, but as R&B entered the pop culture mainstream, a campaign against crudity was launched. Several songs were singled out. Recorded in 1951, "Sixty Minute Man," by the Dominoes, reached number 1 on the R&B charts and remained a best-seller for thirty weeks. Lead singer Clyde McPhatter made clear how the protagonist of the song spent his time: "If your man ain't treatin' you right, / Come up and see your Dan / I rock 'em, roll 'em all night long; / I'm a sixty minute man." In a provocative bass voice, Bill Brown added the chorus: "There'll be fifteen minutes of kissin' / Then you'll holler, please don't stop / There'll be fifteen minutes of teasin', / And fifteen minutes of squeezin' / And fifteen minutes of blowin' my top." In the background, as Brown sang, McPhatter sighed, more than once, "Don't stop."[12]

Equally provocative were three hits by lead singer and songwriter Hank Ballard and the Midnighters in 1954. The group had scored modestly with a recording of Johnny Otis's "Every Beat of My Heart" and the erotic "Get It" in 1953. Drawing on the latter in a song tentatively titled "Sock it To Me, Mary," Ballard got a new idea when Annie Smith, the pregnant wife of the Midnighters' sound engineer, visited the studio. "Work with Me, Annie" leaped to number 1 on the R&B charts. In a high-pitched tenor voice, somewhat reminiscent of Clyde McPhatter, Ballard delivered the raunchy lyric: "Annie, please don't cheat, / Gimme all my meat, / Oo-oo-wee, so good to me; / Work with me, Annie." The group followed with "Sexy Ways": "Wiggle, wiggle, wiggle, wiggle / I just love your sexy ways; / Upside down, all around, / Any old way, just pound, pound, pound." Then, exploiting the success of "Work with Me, Annie," the Midnighters put an exclamation point on an extraordinary year with another R&B number 1, "Annie Had a Baby." According to Syd Nathan, president of King Records, the distributor of "Annie Had a Baby," the response to the song was so great, sixteen presses worked twelve hours a day for weeks to produce platters.[13]

With evidence that the "Annies" and other "smutty" songs were "being listened to and purchased by impressionable teen-agers almost exclusively," a campaign to "clean up filth wax" swept the country in 1954 and 1955. The crusaders focused most of their attention on distributors, record stores, and radio stations. They asked voluntary compliance with a ban on producing, selling, or playing dirty records. The initial response was mixed. A group of disc jockeys in the East, *Billboard* reported with evident approval, formed a club pledged to keep filthy records off the air, thereby signaling the independents and the major record companies not to manufacture more of them. Spokesmen for the group singled out records in which "rock," "roll," or "ride" did not "deal with the rhythmic meter of the tune." Although the club was "not an association in any formal sense," *Billboard* expected it "to have considerable influence in the R&B field." On the other hand, *Billboard* editors acknowledged that many in the industry "wondered what all the fuss is about" and declined to take any action.[14]

The would-be censors did not trust the market. Recognizing that the very publication of the Top Ten gave a boost to every song on it, regardless of content, *Billboard* defended as a service to the industry its practice of showing what records were selling and what records were played in jukeboxes. But, the editors cautioned, "records on the chart should be listened to before they are played on the air, and if any of them are offensive, they should not be used." Any song denied airtime, they predicted, "will soon be a thing of the past."[15]

The editors of *Cash Box* pondered the perils of popularity as well. "Naturally you can market smut," they agreed. "No one denies that." For this reason, R&B record companies, which "had claimed repugnance at the thought of dirty records, disclaimed any intention of ever releasing such filth, and shedding tears at the hurt and degradation it causes the Negro people, now vie for the 'filth' market." And jukebox operators, "without full consideration and study," were placing discs, "some of which feature double entendre lyrics," in locations frequented by teenagers. Although R&B records were gaining popularity throughout the nation, *Cash Box* warned, "every word in them is being carefully scrutinized, every phrase searched for subtle meanings." These were ominous signs for the long-term profitability of rhythm and blues.

Cash Box promised dire consequences if the industry continued to turn out dirty records to make "the quick buck." Negroes would be the first and worst casualties. After decades, rhythm and blues was making inroads into pop music so that the "buyer of 1954 recognizes and desires its beat, melody and artists. But this is only the beginning. Complete acceptance is not here yet." In fact, several jukebox operators were now refusing to place R&B tunes in their machines, while others warned that they would close down establishments transformed into "instruments of an immoral character by smutty recordings." Because of the onus attached to it, "the entire Rhythm and Blues field" faced ruin.

Ruin might come in many forms, and *Cash Box* counted the ways. As complaints from parents poured in, amidst almost "universal condemnation by schools, churches and crusading newspapers," pressure was building for the industry to censor itself as comic book manufacturers recently had, with a "hurriedly appointed czar at a huge salary," or, even worse, for each state to set up its own censorship board. Either approach would burst the bubble of prosperity the industry currently enjoyed. *Cash Box* also invoked "a sociological problem," juvenile delinquency. Until recently, the editors claimed, the music business had fought delinquency by gathering kids in wholesome places and letting them have fun under the proper supervision: "What a disaster it would be if suddenly the idea were implanted in the minds of educators and parents that records, instead of ameliorating delinquency conditions, were actually contributing to them."

Fortunately, a solution was at hand. While dirty records ultimately killed off the market for themselves and all R&B music, "R&B records can be hits without being dirty—as a majority of them have shown." As they achieved widespread acceptance among pop audiences, clean records would regain respect throughout American society for the industry as a whole.[16]

Organized by groups as diverse as the National Piano Tuners Association, the National Ballroom Operators Association, and the Catholic Church, the censorship movement picked up steam. In the Midwest, Catholic high schools organized a "Crusade for Decent Disks," bombarding radio stations with tens of thousands of letters listing objectionable rhythm and blues songs. Chicago's WGN responded by establishing a board to review the lyrics of every song before permitting a DJ to play it. In New England, representatives from six radio stations formed a record censorship board, inviting religious leaders and journalists to join it. A Crime Prevention Committee in Somerville, Massachusetts, supervised by the police department, banned several R&B tunes, including the "Annie" discs, from jukeboxes. Radio stations in the South responded in a similar way to complaints about "off-color songs." WDIA in Memphis prepared a tape for callers requesting songs that had been banned: "WDIA, your goodwill station, in the interest of good citizenship, for the protection of morals and the American way of life, does not consider this record fit for broadcast...."[17]

The U.S. Senate and House of Representatives got into the act as well. Senator Pat McCarren, Democrat of Nevada, and Representative Ruth Thompson, Republican of Michigan, drafted bills forbidding the transportation or mailing in interstate commerce of any "obscene, lewd, lascivious, or filthy publication, picture, disc, transcription or other article capable of producing sound." Violators were subject to a fine of as much as $5,000, a prison term of up to five years, or both.[18]

The bills did not become law, but the furor over "smutty songs" had a significant impact on popular music. Although critics continued to complain, often vociferously, about "leerics," 1954 marked the end, at least for a time, of sexually explicit R&B songs. "Annie," Arnold Shaw quipped, got a makeover and lessons in deportment. While the Midnighters's "Annie's Aunt Fannie" flopped, Georgia Gibbs's "Dance with Me, Henry," a desexualized white cover of "Work with Me, Annie," became a Top Ten hit of 1955. The Midnighters tried again, this time with "Henry's Got Flat Feet," a tame, lame response to "Dance with Me, Henry." Neither critics nor fans noticed or cared.

Determined to be safe rather than sorry, record companies commissioned new lyrics for dozens of R&B songs. The transformation of "Shake, Rattle, and Roll" illustrates their thoroughness. Written by Charles Calhoun and originally recorded by Joe Turner, the song was sexually suggestive: "Well, you wear low dresses, / The sun comes shinin' through / I can't believe my eyes, / That all of this belongs to you." The version released by Decca in 1954 was dramatically different, as Bill Haley explained: "We take a lot of care with lyrics because we don't want to offend anybody. The music is the main thing, and it's just as easy to write acceptable words." Apparently concluding, as had the producers of TV sitcoms in the '50s, that if you can't stand the heat, you should get out of the bedroom, Decca scrubbed the song until it was squeaky clean: "You wear those dresses, / Your hair done up so nice / You look so warm, / But your heart is cold as ice." Omitted entirely was the steamy refrain: "I said over the hill, / And way down underneath / You make me roll my eyes, / And then you make me grit my teeth."[19]

By early 1955, *Billboard* was reporting that "most of the R&B discs are comparatively dirt free." *Cash Box* changed its tune as well, expressing consternation at the continuing castigation of rhythm and blues and rock 'n' roll by "sensation-seeking" newspapers uninterested in the fact that "rhythm and blues tunes are just another form of music and no more off color than a lot of pop tunes." Dismayed by efforts in Boston and Chicago to intimidate disc jockeys through organized letter-writing campaigns, *Cash Box* editors pleaded with station managers not to "knuckle down and take the easy way out" because they feared a loss of prestige, listening audience, and advertisers.[20]

The about-face of industry insiders was due, to a great extent, to the sanitizing of songs, but it was a response as well to the emergence of rock 'n' roll as a mass culture phenomenon. Whiter than R&B, rock 'n' roll could also be marketed as more wholesome. *Cash Box* took its name for a reason. "What the record industry needs," its editors claimed, with dollar signs dancing in their eyes, "is a change of attitude to coincide with its change of stature. . . . The point is, let's stop being unfair to ourselves. Let's stop knocking the products we create. An Elvis Presley, whether you like his style or don't, is a great thing for the record industry. Let's devote the energy we would spend in hating the guy to trying to develop several more who will sell records at the pace that he does." During the second half of the '50s, publicists labored to do just that, by "discarding improper material immediately" and associating performers and performances with good, clean fun. Examples abound. To combat the negative connotations associated with rock 'n' roll, Mercury Records sent the Platters on tour under the banner "Buck Ram Presents Happy Music" with a "Happy Beat for Happy Feet." Several disc jockeys invited listeners to phone in "Negative Requests," promising not to play any of the records they vetoed. To win over adults concerned that rock 'n' roll encouraged sexual liaisons, the owners of radio stations and record companies helped organize, fund, and supply performers for "canteens" for teenagers who might otherwise meet "on the corner in the light of a dim street lamp," a place that "lends itself to brooding. To dangerous thoughts. To sudden, sorrowful acts." These rock 'n' roll canteens allowed youths to vent their "energies, enthusiasms, emotions," providing places for dancing, under appropriate supervision, sipping cool soft drinks, and talking and laughing with other boys and girls.[21]

Efforts to gain acceptance for rock 'n' roll among adults reached into the style and content of the music itself. There were at least two streams of rock 'n' roll. Some performers encouraged an association between rock 'n' roll, foreplay, and intercourse. This stream did not disappear. But rock 'n' roll aimed a second, more mainstream musical fare at young teens who were, presumably, less interested in earthy, graphic, coital connections. "Work with Me, Annie" and "Shake, Rattle, and Roll" to the contrary notwithstanding, Bruce Pollock has recalled, at most Friday night school dances the boys stood on one side of the gym, staring at their shoelaces, while the girls peeked across the hall, then kicked off their shoes and danced with each other. These thirteen- and fourteen-year-olds, experiencing for the first time a crush, an awkward approach, a betrayal, or a breakup, were fascinated by music that spoke to their feelings. Smitten with the idea of eternal love, as they experienced impermanent, even fleeting relationships, young teens encountered immortality, bliss, and loss in songs with the titles "Earth Angel," "Teen Angel," "Altar of Love," "The Book of Love," "The Chapel of Love," and "Heaven and Paradise."[22]

Although he was a bit too old to be a rock 'n' roll pinup, Chuck Berry found in "Sweet Little Sixteen" (1958) an apt and funny way to describe these boys and girls, impatient to be adults: "Sweet little sixteen, she's got the grown-up blues / Tight dresses and lipstick, she's sportin' high-heeled shoes. / Oh, but tomorrow morning she'll have to change her trend / And be sweet sixteen and back in class again." Tommy Sands had the looks as well as the lyrics. Along with Pat Boone, he became the paradigmatic idol of wholesome young teens. "As uncomplicated as most of the songs he sings," according to *Time* magazine, Sands did not smoke or drink, lived with his mother in a four-room apartment, and confessed, with "his brown eyes watering," that in his opinion "all religions are the greatest." Recorded for Capitol Records, Sands's "Teenage Crush" climbed to number 3 in 1957, when the singer was twenty years old. Like its sequel, "Goin' Steady," released that same year, "Teenage Crush" captured the uncertainty, fragility, and demand for autonomy of youngsters uninitiated in the ways of love: "They call it a teenage crush, / They don't know how I feel. . . . They've forgotten when they were young, / And the way they tried to be free."[23]

Much to the dismay of performers and industry executives, this tender, teenybopper music did not escape scrutiny and censorship. Anxious about challenges to their authority and suspicious that their own children might be ticking sexual time bombs, many adults in the '50s found *all* rock 'n' roll music dangerous. In 1958, the Catholic Youth Center in Minneapolis demanded that DJs stop playing Elvis's

"Wear My Ring Around Your Neck" and Jimmie Rodgers's "Secretly." The lyrics, CYC officials pointed out, sanctioned going steady without parental approval. As these songs reached twelve- and thirteen-year-olds, they might accelerate the process of establishing permanent relationships between boys and girls who were not emotionally or physically prepared for them.[24]

The same concerns motivated Bostonians to ban "Wake Up, Little Susie." Featuring a soft, harmonic country rock, the Everly Brothers song reached the top of the charts in 1957. It concerned Susie and her boyfriend, who fall asleep as they watch a dull movie in a neighborhood theater and then awake to realize that Susie has stayed out well past her curfew. What should she say to her irate parents, who will not be inclined to believe the innocent truth? In "Wake Up, Little Susie," as in "Bye Bye Love," Don and Phil Everly's other smash hit in '57, parents heard the narcissism and even petulance of teenagers. They also heard themselves stigmatized as suspicious and unreasonable, their rules undermined. When boyfriends woke up their little Susies, parents believed, sexual innocence was at risk.[25]

To blunt these attacks, marquee rock 'n' rollers took to the offensive. Pat Boone became the principal spokesman for the music as wholesome entertainment. Clean-shaven, dressed in white sweaters and white bucks, a family man and a Christian, Boone came out of central casting as the model teenager. One look at him, and no parent could read sex into his songs. Onstage and in his films, fan magazines revealed, Boone refused to kiss any woman other than his wife, Shirley. No wonder one magazine called him "the first teen-age idol that grandma can dig too." With considerably more acid, Frank Sinatra made the same point. "I'd like my son to be like Pat," Sinatra quipped, "until he was three years old."[26]

If not for the "vanilla versions" of R&B songs that he and others recorded, Boone would assert, "rock 'n' roll, as we think of it, never would have happened." In the dozens of songs he covered, Boone excised even the most mildly offensive lyrics. His version of T-Bone Walker's "Stormy Monday" dropped "drinkin' wine" and added "drinkin' Coca-Cola." When covering Little Richard's "Tutti Frutti," Boone "had to change some words, because they seemed too raw for me." So "Boys, you don't know what she do to me" became "Pretty little Susie is the girl for me."[27]

Although he claimed to be a catalyst, "unwittingly and unintentionally," for rock 'n' roll's acceptance, Boone worked hard to
associate himself and his music with middle-class values. *The Pat
Boone Press Guide* enumerated the guideposts to maturity he thought
most important: the Bible, the Golden Rule, the maxim "cleanliness
is next to godliness," and sound financial practices. In his 1959 book,

With his white bucks, argyle socks, and Christian sentiments, Pat Boone
associated his brand of rock 'n' roll with middle-class values. *(National
Archives)*

'Twixt Twelve and Twenty, Boone shared his philosophy of life with the baby boomer generation.[28]

A nonfiction best-seller, *'Twixt Twelve and Twenty* was an advice manual for teenagers that was a godsend to their parents. As we shall see in chapter 4, Boone sought in this book to bridge the generation gap. In doing so, he commented extensively on courtship, marriage, and sexuality. Boone began by associating himself with his teenage readers: "I know what we feel like sometimes. We feel that we're set apart, shooed off together, accused as a group until we get on the defensive." Teenagers must recognize that they are insecure, restless, inconsistent, and indecisive. "If we just let these symptoms run riot," the singer observed, "we will find we are out of balance." Again and again, Boone suggested that teenagers not be seduced by the advice of the White Queen to Alice—"The rule is jam tomorrow and jam yesterday." Instead of trying to act or be treated like adults, teenagers should enjoy the security and relative innocence of adolescence. Apparently unaware of the multiple meanings behind his call to teenagers to "jam today," Boone predicted that the "tomorrow habit" ruined the lives of girls and sent boys to juvenile court.

Boone's message to teenagers about sex was simple: go slowly, very, very slowly. To control youngsters' bodies, so that their minds were ready to follow what was being said, he endorsed the administration of discipline by adults, including spanking. Noting that it "worked wonders in my case," Boone confessed that until he was seventeen his mother had hit him with a sewing-machine belt as he leaned over the bathtub. With or without corporal punishment, of course, the bodies of boys and girls would begin speaking to them when they reached their teens. Boone told them not to listen, and certainly not to give in to physical impulse. "We all know that indiscriminate kissing, dancing in the dark, hanging around in cars, late dates at this early stage can lead to trouble," he wrote. "Kissing for fun is like playing with a beautiful candle in a room full of dynamite! . . . I really think it's better to amuse ourselves in some other way." Adolescents would really enjoy themselves, the singer suggested, if they joined "the nicer play-by-the-rules crowd." To guarantee a better tomorrow, "I say go bowling or to a basketball game, or watch a good TV program (like the 'Pat Boone Chevy Show'!), at least for a while."

'Twixt Twelve and Twenty was silent about when, if at all, a teenager

might kiss, discriminately or indiscriminately. Nor did Boone provide advice about dating, going steady, getting engaged, or any activities between the time spent with "the nicer play-by-the-rules crowd" and a wedding day. Like many adults, Boone seemed to sense how easily the elaborate courtship rituals of the '50s could proceed to promiscuity. When he was nineteen, Boone admitted (without connecting his behavior to the strict discipline of his parents), he eloped with Shirley. His readers, he hoped, would learn from his mistakes. The elopement "shocked, disappointed, and hurt" Mr. and Mrs. Boone. On these grounds alone, Pat and Shirley should not have done it. Equally important, teenage marriage "is a time–money problem." Newlyweds 'twixt twelve and twenty, Boone told his readers, rarely have the education, the maturity, or the financial wherewithal to make a go of it.

Having, in essence, skipped the teenage years, Boone concluded his discussion of love and marriage with reflections on the division of labor and authority within the household. The husband, he believed, should have the final say. Because she was a "normal female," Shirley enjoyed her role as "vice president in charge of housekeeping." She wanted Pat to "take care of her and our family. All right, she has to let me do it."[29]

Pat Boone was enormously popular in the 1950s. In a survey of high school students in the pseudonymous "Elmtown, U.S.A.," sociologist James Coleman found that 45.2 percent of the girls and 43.5 percent of the boys named him their favorite singer. The comparable figures for Elvis Presley were 17.5 percent and 21.5 percent, while Tommy Sands was a distant third at 10.7 percent and 7.8 percent. Elites at the high school were much less inclined than other students to swoon over Elvis, whose appeal was greatest in "the rough crowd," most of whom smoked or drank and wore "rock 'n' roll jackets" as symbols of good times and a lack of concern with their academic work. Teenagers with high aspirations and achievements gravitated to Boone, Coleman concluded, because he "dispenses rock and roll without the implicit deviance and rebellion in Presley's image." Since 48.1 percent of high school females and 51.6 percent of males enjoyed rock 'n' roll more than any other kind of music, far more than any other popular genre, Coleman implied, parents were fortunate that Boone had made rock 'n' roll safe for tender ears, hearts, and other organs.[30]

Dick Clark was even more influential than Pat Boone in the struggle over the cultural content of rock 'n' roll. Like Boone, Clark was squeaky-clean-cut, with not a hair out of place, a Dentyne smile, and a calm, detached demeanor. An aggressive entrepreneur, Clark had little personal enthusiasm for the music of teenagers and did not have an extensive record collection of his own. To build a multimedia empire, he promoted rock 'n' roll as a universal form of music, sexually unthreatening, "within which almost all tastes can be satisfied." Through his television show, *American Bandstand*, an official in the police department of New York City proclaimed, Clark supplied "a tranquilizing pill" for teenagers.[31]

Born in 1929 in Bronxville, just north of New York City, Clark grew up in Westchester, an affluent suburban community. Educated at Syracuse University, with a major in advertising and a minor in radio, Clark landed a job in 1952 with WFIL, which owned radio and television stations in Philadelphia. Before long, he had his own radio show, "Dick Clark's Caravan of Music," and served as the announcer on Paul Whiteman's *TV-Teen Club*, the first television program to feature boys and girls dancing. Clark's big break came in 1956. Bob Horn, host of the successful TV show *Bandstand*, was arrested for drunk driving amidst rumors that he had slept with one of the young teenagers who danced on the show. A married man with three young daughters, Horn was fired by WFIL as an "embarrassment to the station." Dick Clark replaced him. Terrified by the sex scandal, he retained the show's format, including the popular "Rate-A-Record." He was also "150 percent deliberate" in cultivating a wholesome image. Donning a coat and tie on the theory that "if we looked presentable, normal, the way they [adults] think we oughta look, they'll leave us alone," Clark established on the air that he had "the most platonic of friendships" with the teenage dancers on *Bandstand*. Although, as a colleague put it, Clark "didn't know Chuck Berry from a huckleberry," he learned quickly and began booking prominent rock 'n' rollers for the show. By 1957, the ratings of Clark's *Bandstand* surpassed those of his predecessor.[32]

That same year, when ABC provided an afternoon slot, the show got a new name, *American Bandstand*, and a national audience. At 3:00 P.M. on August 5, Clark introduced himself, read congratulatory telegrams from Pat Boone and Frank Sinatra, watched performances by Kitty Kallen, the Chordettes, and Billy Williams, and invited viewers to enter a contest, "Why I'd Like a Date with Sal Mineo." Although reviews were mixed, the national media recognized that *American*

On *American Bandstand,* Dick Clark recruited clean-cut, well-dressed kids between fourteen and eighteen. He forbade any talk of sex beyond puppy love. *(Urban Archives, Temple University)*

Bandstand was an alternative to the less controlled atmosphere of Alan Freed's TV program, *Big Beat.* Viewers over twenty-one might find the show "something of an ordeal" to sit through, the *New York Times* opined, but *Bandstand*'s dancers were "an attractive group of youngsters ... [with] no motorcycle jackets and hardly a sideburn in the crowd," and Clark "a well-groomed young man richly endowed with self-assurance." *Billboard* was even less enthusiastic, acknowledging but not endorsing the mainstreaming strategy the show employed: "If this is the wholesome answer to the 'detractors' of rock 'n' roll, bring on the rotating pelvises." Almost immediately, however, *American Bandstand* became a hit, reaching more viewers than any other program on daytime television. Dick Clark's fortunes rose with those of the show: he became a television producer, record label and song copyright owner, promoter, distributor, discoverer and manager of performers—a force to be reckoned with in rock 'n' roll.[33]

To "set a good example for the people watching at home," Clark promulgated a strict code of conduct for the "regulars" he recruited to dance on *American Bandstand*. Boys wore sweaters, or jackets and ties. Girls wore skirts and blouses, or sweaters over their parochial school uniforms, with white dickies sticking out of the top in what became known as "the Philadelphia collar." Girls were not permitted to wear slacks or tight sweaters. Shorts were verboten for both sexes. Dancers risked expulsion if they behaved demonstrably or impulsively, waved to the camera, or chewed gum. Clark permitted no one under fourteen or above eighteen to dance on the show: thirteen-year-olds were "too giddy and difficult to control," he thought; eighteen-year-olds might be too blasé, and the upper limit enabled Clark to keep soldiers and sailors off the set. Most important, in his on-air conversations Clark eliminated any suggestions of sexuality beyond puppy love. While he asked teenagers, "Are you going with anyone?," he never used the phrase "going steady." When a cameraman wrote a love letter to one of the dancers in 1958, Clark fired him.[34]

Eliminated as well were controversial body movements from the dances featured on *Bandstand*. Although a writer for the *New York Herald Tribune* thought the furious pace made it "inconceivable that any dancer would have an ounce of energy left over to invest in any kind of hanky-panky whatsoever," Clark knew that many parents believed that dancing could be a form of sexual foreplay. When kids "slow-danced," he later recalled, "they could 'cop a feel.' Really sensuous girls threw the lower part of their bodies in the guy's groin; the girls would sort of backbend and chuck it right out." Such displays, of course, were out of bounds on *American Bandstand*, which preferred free-form dances, where the partners did not touch one another. Clark proved adept at introducing new dances (often adapted from African-American originals), including the Bop, the Stroll, and the Twist, accompanied by upbeat tunes, sung by cute, young, winsome performers.[35]

American Bandstand became a weekday afternoon habit for millions of American teenagers. The show was especially popular among high school freshmen and sophomores, George Gallup reported, with three times as many girls as boys attracted. Teenagers tuned in to learn the newest dance step, and watch the latest heart-throb lip-synch his latest hit, be it Paul Anka, Frankie Avalon, Bobby Rydell, Fabian, Dion DiMucci, or Bobby Darin. They tuned in as well to check out the latest trends in grooming and fashion. Viewers wanted to know what dancer Justine Carelli used to wash her hair and how she rolled it. When Carmen and Yvette Jiminez dyed blond streaks in their bangs, so did many of their female fans; the bells and pom-poms dancers hung on their double-layered, rolled bobby sox to divert attention from the saddle shoes they wore in Catholic school became a national fad as well.[36]

Many moms, it turned out, encouraged their teenagers to watch *American Bandstand* and, in Philadelphia, to try out for the show as dancers. When Justine was turned down because she was twelve years old, Mrs. Carelli sent her back to the studio with the birth certificate of an older sister. To the surprise of the producers of *Bandstand*, many mothers became devoted fans of the program themselves, preferring it to soaps and game shows. They wanted to see what young people looked like and what they wore. For the most part, the younger generation on *American Bandstand* pleased them. Some mothers danced to the music, with pillows named after their husbands as their partners. Clark quickly exploited this unanticipated bonanza, issuing press releases to affiliate stations boasting "Age No Barrier to *Bandstand* Beat." On the air, he addressed the "housewives" directly, inviting them to "roll up the ironing board and join us when you can."[37]

From his position as arbiter of the cultural and social mores of teenagers, Dick Clark published his own advice book. *The Happiest Years* was almost identical to *'Twixt Twelve and Twenty* in the behavior prescribed and the topics avoided, but unlike Pat Boone, Clark assumed the tone of a knowing, sympathetic authority, rather than a peer. No one would be critical of your musical tastes, he predicted, with his own program in mind, "if you turned the volume down to normal.... Who knows, maybe Dad and Mom might hear some discs they enjoy, too." As had Boone, Clark addressed the initiation into sex with a message that was concise and conventional. Girls who allowed boys to "go farther than they should have while petting," he wrote, acquired a bad reputation and therefore failed to find Mr. Right. Even boys who took advantage of girls began after a while to avoid them at school and at dances. More often than not, boys who treated their teenage girlfriends "loosely" carried "this selfish attitude along with them into a disturbed and many times turbulent adult life." *The Happiest Years* was the kind of book parents—and perhaps only parents—could love. It put Dick Clark and his brand of rock 'n' roll on their side, promising to protect the kids entrusted to them by teaching them emotional maturity and sexual responsibility.[38]

More sexually expressive brands of rock 'n' roll remained available, however, long after R&B "leerics" were scrubbed, simonized, and sanitized. Even *American Bandstand*, as we shall see, sometimes supplied a showcase for them. "There is no denying that rock and roll evokes a physical response from even its most reluctant listeners," *Time* magazine asserted, "for that giant pulse matches the rhythmical operations of the human body." *Life* magazine traced "rock 'n' roll rapture" to the "carefully calculated antics of the performer," whose bumps and grinds, glances, and gyrations triggered the emotions of "susceptible fans," setting off "a gale of screams and moans."[39]

Whether it was expressed as puppy love, in a teenage idiom, or brought to a hot, wet climax, rock 'n' roll was masculine and macho. Women were the subjects of songs, and the objects of affection, jealousy, or betrayal. They did not sing rock 'n' roll songs; men sang about them. In the 1950s, Pete Daniel has observed, Americans would not countenance a female performer grinding against her instrument. When Cordell Jackson performed in Pontotoc, Mississippi, she recalled, "men would just walk off," muttering, "Little girls don't play guitars." Early in the decade, before rock 'n' roll, about one-third of the best-selling songs were recorded by females. By 1957, only two women reached the Top Twenty-Five, Debbie Reynolds ("Tammy") and Jane Morgan ("Fascination"), neither of them a rock 'n' roller. The result was the same in 1958, unless Connie Francis's "Who's Sorry Now" is classified as rock 'n' roll as well as pop.[40]

Referred to in songs as "baby" or "angel," women were often idealized and invariably treated as dependent on men, as their property. "I know you're mine by the ring around your neck," Elvis sang in a typical rock 'n' roll expression of female subservience. In an interview in Amarillo, Texas, he was even more cocky. Asked if he intended to marry, Elvis reportedly asked, "Why buy a cow when you can get milk through the fence?" In "Thirteen Women (And Only One Man in Town)," the flip side of "Rock Around the Clock," Bill Haley fantasized about having female bombshells at his beck and call in the wake of a nuclear attack on the United States: "I had three gals dancin' the mambo, / Three gals ballin' the jack / And all of the rest really did their best / Boy, they sure were a lively pack."[41]

As they projected masculine prerogatives, rock 'n' roll performers sometimes revealed an emotional vulnerability, acknowledging that women could touch or hurt them. The needs and desires of the male, however, remained paramount. Elvis might plead "Love Me Tender" (1956) and "Don't Be Cruel"(1956), but not far from the romantic lyricism was a threat. In "Baby, Let's Play House" (1955), he expressed it: "You may go to college," but "I'd rather see you dead little girl than to be with another man."[42]

Women had a place in rock 'n' roll—in the audience. At concerts, rock 'n' rollers would have it no other way: the teenage heroes of the era were born, Thomas Morgan wrote in *Esquire*, "in the presence and at the pleasure of screaming young women." When females shook and sobbed at the seductive spectacles onstage, they in a sense endorsed the sexual status quo, reassuring their dates that they wanted only those things boys already assumed they wanted.[43]

Although a few observers, like Morgan, concluded that rock 'n' roll singers were "safe-sex" heroes, offering vicarious thrills at no risk, many others insisted that the music impaired the morals of minors. Although he protested, "I don't do no dirty body movements," Elvis remained Exhibit A for the prosecution. After all, Ann Fulchino, the publicist for Elvis's record label, acknowledged that Presley was "the equivalent of a male strip teaser, with the exception that he doesn't take his clothes off." All across America, *Time* reported, Elvis packed theaters and fought off shrieking admirers, "disturbing parents, puckering the brows of psychologists, and filling letters-to-the-editor columns with cries of alarm." It was easy to see why. "He isn't afraid to express himself," a fifteen-year-old girl told *Life* magazine. When he performs, "I get down on the floor and scream." Thirteen-year-old Steve Shad hoped some of Elvis's sexual magnetism would rub off on him. Like other teenagers in Jacksonville, Florida, Steve had little interest in Presley's singing style but mastered his motions and gestures as a good way to attract the attention of pretty girls.[44]

Using unintentionally phallic prose, *Time* averred that Elvis's appeal was more anatomical than musical: "Is it a sausage? It is certainly smooth and damp looking, but who ever heard of a 172 pound sausage.... Is it a corpse? The face just hangs there, limp and white with its little drop-seat mouth, rather like Lord Byron in a wax museum. But suddenly the figure comes to life. The lips part, the eyes half close, the clutched guitar begins to undulate back and forth in an uncomfortably suggestive manner. And wham! The mid-section of the body jolts forward to bump and grind and beat out a low-down rhythm.... As the belly dance gets wilder, a peculiar sound emerges.

Thirteen-year-old Steve Shad of Jacksonville, Florida, was one of millions of Elvis wannabes. *(Timepix)*

A rusty foghorn? A voice? Or merely a noise produced, like the voice of a cricket, by the violent stridulation of the legs?" If he read *Time* magazine, Steve Shad was probably taking notes.[45]

Like the clash over lyrics, the battle for Elvis's body aroused advocates of sexual containment and control. That it spread from radios, records, and concert halls to television, the bastion of traditional values, suggests that rock 'n' roll's commercial appeal provided leverage, even for its more controversial products. The contest between Elvis and his enemies ended inconclusively, an indication, perhaps, that the sexual genie was climbing out of the bottle, with the cork nowhere in sight.

On January 28, 1956, the day after RCA released "Heartbreak Hotel," Elvis made the first of six appearances on *Stage Show*, a variety program on CBS, hosted by Tommy and Jimmy Dorsey. Motivated by low ratings (*Stage Show* would be dropped after a single season), the producers were willing to book Presley when their competitors deemed rock 'n' roll too hot to handle. Although the Dorsey Orchestra had difficulty accompanying him, Elvis performed creditably, without attracting much attention from the media. As the sales of "Heartbreak Hotel" soared, Milton Berle, the original "Mr. Television," whose popularity was waning, signed Presley up for his show on NBC. In two appearances, Elvis sang "Heartbreak Hotel" and "Hound Dog," delivering the latter with a bump and grind and an erotic quiver of emotion. He also mixed it up with Uncle Miltie in comedy sketches, one of which cast Berle as Elvis's twin brother, Melvin. For the first time all season, *The Milton Berle Show* posted higher ratings than its competition, Phil Silvers's *Sergeant Bilko*. But if the NBC brass was pleased, commentators in the nation's newspapers screamed with moral outrage. Presley's "caterwauling," wrote Jack O'Brian in the *New York Journal-American*, "has caused the most heated reaction since the stone-age days of TV when Dagmar and Faysie's necklines were plunging to oblivion." "Elvis's grunt and groin antics," agreed Ben Gross of the *New York Daily News*, were "suggestive and vulgar, tinged with the kind of animalism that should be confined to dives and bordellos." Gross was amazed that Berle and NBC had "permitted this affront."[46]

Because Elvis was scheduled to appear on July 1 on Steve Allen's new Sunday night variety program, NBC took note of the criticism, but the network did not cancel. Recognizing that nothing boosted ratings better than a raging controversy, Allen found a way to have his guest and appear to satisfy the puritans. He assured viewers that he would not allow Presley "to do anything that will offend anyone." NBC announced that a "revamped, purified, and somewhat abridged Presley" had agreed to sing while standing reasonably still, dressed in black tie. On the air, Allen referred to the "great deal of attention" stimulated by the singer's television appearances. Interrupted by a barking sound from backstage, Allen continued, with a self-conscious laugh: "We want to do a show the whole family can watch and enjoy," so tonight, "we're presenting Elvis Presley in what you might call his first comeback. . . . Here he is." Elvis ambled out in his tux, tugging at his white gloves, and wiping his nose on his top hat. As he completed "I Want You, I Need You, I Love You," Allen appeared again, this time accompanied by a basset hound, the ostensible object of affection for "Hound Dog," a song about sex ("You can wag your tail, but I ain't gon' feed you no more"), originally recorded by Willie Mae "Big Mama" Thornton. To occasional giggles from the audience, Presley soldiered on, taking the dog in his arms, and kissing her once or twice as he sang. He completed his evening's work as "Tumbleweed Presley," in a cowboy sketch with Allen, Andy Griffith, and Imogene Coca.

The next day, as Elvis entered the RCA studios to record "Hound Dog," fans greeted him with signs that declared, "We Want the Real Elvis" and "We Want the Gyrating Elvis." In the press, critics were no kinder to the singer than they had ever been, this time pronouncing him a "cowed kid" who had demonstrated, once again, that he "couldn't sing or act a lick." But peeking through the predictable pans was some sympathy. Presley had a right to be distraught, according to John Lardner in a column in *Newsweek*: "Like Huckleberry Finn, when the widow put him in a store suit and told him not to gap or scratch," he had been "fouled" by NBC's attempt to "civilize him . . . for the good of mankind." The most important reviews, of course, came from the public. *The Steve Allen Show* annihilated CBS's powerhouse, Ed Sullivan's *Toast of the Town*, in the ratings. And "Hound Dog" became a runaway hit, eventually overtaking "The Tennessee Waltz" and "Rock Around the Clock" as the best-selling record of the '50s, with a sale of over seven million copies.

In another blow to the self-appointed arbiters of taste, Sullivan, who had vowed that he would not book Presley at any price ("He is not my cup of tea") announced that Elvis would make three appearances on his program in 1956 at an unprecedented fee of $50,000. On September 9, the season premiere of Sullivan's show, Elvis opened with "Don't Be Cruel" and then introduced "Love Me Tender," the title song from his new movie. At each movement of his body, however slight, the audience erupted in paroxysms of emotion. Later in the show, as he sang Little Richard's "Reddy Teddy" and began to move and dance, the camera pulled in, so that the television audience saw him from the waist up only. The studio audience screamed just the same, and unleashed another torrent when Elvis delivered two verses of "Hound Dog."

The show received a sensational Trendex rating of 43.7, which meant that it reached 82.6 percent of the television audience. Disc jockeys around the country began playing tapes they had made of Elvis's Sullivan-show rendition of "Love Me Tender," helping boost prerelease orders of the single to almost a million. As he wished Presley well following his third appearance on *Toast of the Town*, Ed Sullivan gave him a ringing endorsement: "I wanted to say to Elvis Presley and the country that this is a real decent, fine boy, and wherever you go, Elvis . . . we want to say that we've never had a pleasanter experience on our show with a big name than we've had with you." Sullivan had legitimized the singer with an adult audience, without in any way diminishing his standing with teenagers. Keeping Elvis's pelvis out of sight for a moment or two, moreover, was evidence not of the dominance of sexual censors but of the fact that they had been put on the defensive. In the *New York Times*, for example, Jack Gould began his review indignantly: Elvis Presley had "injected movements of the tongue and indulged in wordless singing that were singularly distasteful." Overstimulating the physical impulses of teenagers was "a gross national disservice." Gould supported common sense, not censorship, he hastened to add: "It is no blue-nosed suppression of the proper way of depicting life in the theater to expect stage manners somewhat above the level of the carnival sideshow." But Gould was discouraged by "the willingness and indeed eagerness" of businessmen to exploit teenagers. He concluded with an admission of defeat: "In the long run, perhaps Presley will do everyone a favor by pointing up the need for earlier sex education so that neither his successors nor T.V. can capitalize on the idea that his type of routine is somehow highly tempting yet forbidden fruit." Soon after this column appeared,

Elvis's manager, Colonel Tom Parker, put an exclamation point on Gould's suggestion that, like it or not, television now welcomed rock 'n' roll. Two guest appearances and an hourlong TV special by Presley, he announced, would now cost the networks $300,000.[47]

To be sure, later in his career, Elvis was often rather subdued. Intelligent and ambitious, he reached out, quite consciously, to adults as well as teenagers. Elvis's musical repertoire came to include ballads, classics, and Christmas songs, as well as rock 'n' roll, and he dutifully delivered his lines in a succession of mediocre Hollywood action romances. Nonetheless, even when he tried, the man once denounced as a "wreck and ruin artist" never lost his erotic appeal. Like Mae West, when Elvis was good, he was very good, but when he was bad, he was better. When he sneered, "If you're looking for trouble, you've come to the right place," teenage girls screamed, while bluenoses could only simmer and sigh.[48]

Elvis was by no means the only R-rated rock 'n' roller. While the Dick Clarks and Pat Boones labored to keep the lid on, Little Richard provided a surfeit of steam to blow it off. He put an erotic charge into "Tutti Frutti," despite its buttoned-down lyrics, and, somehow, he slipped the sexually incorrigible "Long Tall Sally" past the censors. Little Richard was pretty wild. Jerry Lee Lewis was ferocious. If the music of some of his contemporaries was sexy, journalist Andy Wickham subsequently observed, "his was promiscuous. Presley shook his hips; Lewis raped his piano. He would play it with his feet, he would sit on it, he would stand on it, he would crawl under it, and he would leap over it." At one concert, when he was given second billing to Chuck Berry, Lewis brought his audience to a frenzy and set his piano on fire, taunting Berry as he walked off, "Follow that, nigger."[49]

Torn between the hellfire-and-damnation fundamentalist Christian values of his family and the temptations of the flesh, Lewis earned his nickname, "the Killer," in a turbulent personal life. Anger, guilt, and self-hatred followed every transgression, but they were never enough to stop him. With his insatiable sexual appetite, Lewis was a poster boy for the cycle of repression and release ascribed by therapists in the 1950s to young people "in whom the fear psychology has been built up." On the stage, of course, Lewis was all release and no repression, displaying in every performance a sexual explosiveness that mocked the restraint censors sought to impose.

Lewis was born in Ferriday, Louisiana, in 1935 and grew up in a farmhouse without indoor plumbing or electricity. His father, Elmo Sr., was a cotton farmer, laid low by the Great Depression, who worked hard and drank harder, spending several years in a federal penitentiary for making moonshine. Elmo and his wife, Mamie, were devout Christians. Members of the Baptist church, they joined the Assemblies of God in the 1930s. A popular Pentecostal sect, the Assemblies of God preached the values of "old-time" religion, denouncing as sinful, drinking, smoking, gambling, picture shows, dance halls, swimming in public, and even life insurance. Pentecostals prohibited women from cutting their hair, applying cosmetics to their faces, or wearing trousers. Like other Assemblies of God congregants, the Lewises believed in ecstasy through glossolalia (speaking in tongues). They taught their son to resist the temptations of the world, especially sexual temptations.

Happily, the Assemblies of God did not discourage devotion to music. Elmo Sr. played the guitar and enjoyed country and western songs. As soon as he could scrape up a few dollars, Elmo bought a secondhand crank-up Victrola so that he could listen to his idol, Jimmie Rodgers. Mamie sang and danced in church, and when she noticed Jerry Lee singing to his daddy's records and with the black sharecroppers who lived nearby, she encouraged him to use his musical talent to serve the Lord. Before he was ten, Jerry Lee began to play the piano, practicing at a neighbor's house and on the keyboard in church. When he mastered "Silent Night," his proud parents purchased a Starck upright piano for him, "the sort of piano you'd have trouble giving away," a friend later recalled. They did not know that he was sneaking off to listen to African-American music and asking the inebriated black men huddled around the jukebox if they had ever seen the Devil.

To please his parents, Jerry Lee performed sacred songs at church, but his versions of "Silent Night" became increasingly rambunctious and boogie-woogified, as he learned to play a fast, heavy rhythm with his left hand and a wild melody with his right. From his father's Jimmie Rodgers and Al Jolson records, Jerry Lee taught himself yodeling and the audacious vocal style that became his trademark. In 1946, he discovered Freddie Slack's "The House of Blue Lights," a song about an establishment of ill repute. By this time, it was clear that Jerry Lee had no interest in or aptitude for schoolwork. In third grade alone, he compiled more than twenty F's. Instead of studying, he caroused with his cousin Jimmy Lee Swaggart (whose sexual peccadilloes as a minister in the 1980s would command the national stage), hung out in nightclubs, and broke into and robbed a few stores.

In 1949, Lewis performed a version of Stick McGhee's "Drinkin' Wine, Spo-Dee-O-Dee" at the local Ford dealership. A hat was passed around; Jerry Lee collected thirteen dollars and decided on a career as an entertainer. He quit school and hit the road, loading the Starck upright on the bed of his father's pickup. Mamie was not pleased that he was making the Devil's music, but the family needed the money, and Jerry Lee promised to remain a member of the church. Within a year, Jerry Lee had secured a twenty-minute slot every Saturday on a Natchez radio station. But doubts remained, stoked certainly by Mamie Lewis and, in a different way, by the pretty girls who caught Jerry Lee's attention as he sang. To cleanse himself and serve God, he enrolled in the Southwestern Bible Institute in Waxahachie, Texas, in 1950, to become a minister.

He was expelled after just three months. While his classmates studied or slept, Jerry Lee crawled out of his dormitory window and hitchhiked to Dallas, where he hit the amusement parks, nightclubs, and movie theaters. His teachers were not amused when he played "My God Is Real" boogie-woogie style at services, putting a this-worldly kind of feeling into the final lyric: "My God is real, for I can feel Him in my soul!" True religion, Jerry Lee told himself, as he boarded the bus back to Ferriday, does not come from "all the silly books y'all got here."

Jerry Lee returned to his mother's taunts and his own self-doubts. Like so many teenagers in the 1950s, he entered into an early marriage, tying the knot with Dorothy Barton, a preacher's daughter, in 1952, despite the protests of her parents. On his wedding night he lost his virginity and unlocked an insatiable sexual appetite. Still interested in the ministry, he delivered sermons in local churches, filled with allusions to the Pentateuch and the blood of Christ, but as his marriage faltered, he returned to the stage, with gigs in Ferriday and Natchez. In 1954, without informing or involving his wife or the state of Louisiana, Lewis married seventeen-year-old Jane Mitcham (the second of his six wives). They had met at a roller-skating rink, and he had gotten her pregnant. When Jane's brothers arrived in Ferriday with horsewhips and pistols, Jerry Lee decided to become a bigamist.

Although Lewis still aspired to "live for the Lord," he began to reach for the big time in show business. He auditioned unsuccessfully to be a backup for Slim Whitman at the Louisiana Hayride in Shreveport, a regional competitor of Nashville's Grand Old Opry. Then he heard Elvis Presley and used Elmo's egg money to travel to Memphis and the Sun Studios of Sam Phillips. "I'm gonna cut me a record," he told a friend. "If I don't make it, I'll never hit another lick as long as I live." Lewis's first session at Sun in November 1956 was a modest success. Phillips decided to release "End of the Road," a song Jerry Lee wrote for himself, and "Crazy Arms," a country tune Ray Price had turned into a big hit a few months earlier. Sun billed its new singer as Jerry Lee Lewis and His Pumping Piano. Although neither song reached the charts, Phillips invited Lewis back for several more sessions, including a now legendary date at the studio where Jerry Lee, Elvis, Carl Perkins, and Johnny Cash met accidentally. After Cash left to go shopping, the other three harmonized together on the church songs "When God Dips His Love in My Heart" and "Blessed Jesus Hold My Hand," as well as Charlie Singleton's profane single "Don't Forbid Me."

At another session, Lewis and Jack Clement, an engineer and creative consultant at Sun, decided to try "Whole Lotta Shakin' Going On" as the flip side of "It'll Be Me." Jerry Lee first heard the song in 1955, when Roy Hall recorded a pianoless version of it for Decca. Lewis's unrelenting rendition of the song's lecherous lyrics added layers of lasciviousness to them. "We got kickin' in the barn," he boasted. "Whose barn? What barn? My barn! . . . We ain't fakin', Whole lot of shakin' goin' on." Then the singer coached his woman on her sexual technique: "All you gotta do, honey, is just kinda stand in one spot. / Wiggle around just a little bit. / That's what you gotta do, yeah."

The song exploded onto the charts in 1957, reaching the top spot in country and western and R&B and rising to number 3 in pop. Lewis's live performances quickened the libidos of his listeners: Lewis leered at his audience, rolled his tongue, and, as he sang, slowly and sensually ran his fingers through his thick, blond hair. Sometimes he banged at the piano with his feet or his fists; sometimes he climbed on top of it. When he finished a number, Jerry Lee combed his hair, then blew at the crowd through the comb's teeth.

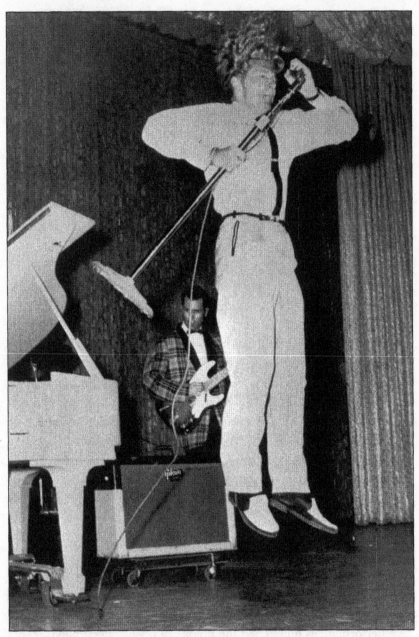

Jerry Lee Lewis "raped his piano. He would play it with his feet, he would sit on it, he would stand on it, he would crawl under it, and he would leap over it." He did the same with the microphone. *(Michael Ochs Archives)*

Lewd lyrics and a suggestive style did not scare off television producers, who lined up to book the rock 'n' roll sensation. Jerry Lee sang "Whole Lotta Shakin' Going On" twice on *The Steve Allen Show* in the summer of 1957, pounding the piano and kicking the stool across the stage, only to have Allen toss it back and, for good measure, throw some other furniture onto the stage. It was a far cry from Elvis and the braying basset hound.

Lewis followed his success by recording another male brag song, "Mean Woman Blues." Its double entendres were not difficult to decipher: "I like a little coffee / I like a little tea / Jelly, jelly is the thing for me." A bit too much like "Whole Lotta Shakin' Going On" the song did not catch fire, but "Great Balls of Fire" certainly did. Otis Blackwell, who had written "Don't Be Cruel" and "All Shook Up" for Elvis, created the song with Lewis in mind, after seeing Jerry Lee perform on *The Steve Allen Show*. As Lewis, Clement, and Phillips worked on "Great Balls of Fire," Jerry Lee began to hear the voice of his mother, lecturing and hectoring him. "How can the Devil save souls?" he shouted in the studio, to no one in particular. "It says make merry with the joy of God only." On and on he went, insisting "I've got the Devil in me" against Phillips's argument that he could do good as a "rock 'n' roll exponent." After several hours, he seemed to calm down, and then, suddenly, he turned from the sacred to the secular and sexual. "I do like to eat it," he said, and asked if the sound was on. "You ready to cut 'Great Balls of Fire?' What am I gonna eat? I would like to eat a little pussy if I had some." Lewis leaped into the song, recording what everyone knew would be a hit. Perhaps they should split royalties with the Holy Ghost, quipped Jack Clement when the session was finished. No one laughed. "I'm about to gag," Lewis announced.

"Great Balls of Fire" was even more sexually explicit than "Whole Lotta Shakin' Going On." A pounding piano and a deafening drum suggested that the song was less about foreplay than about the act itself. "Great Balls of Fire" opened after four chords with Lewis screaming, "You shake my nerves and you rattle my brain / Too much love drives a man insane / You broke my will / But, what a thrill / Goodness, gracious, great balls of fire!" His vocal interjections—"Oooh / Feels good" and "You're kind / So fine"—put listeners right in the bedroom. Critics were furious, predictably, but largely ineffectual. Perched at number 1 in country and western and R&B, and number 2 in pop, "Great Balls of Fire" benefited from extensive radio play. Once again television came calling. Lewis returned to *The Steve Allen Show* in November 1957, this time in living color. He performed the song as well on *Patti Page's Big Record TV Show* and CBS's variety series *The Howard Miller Show*. On Thanksgiving Day, Lewis spat in the eye of rock 'n' roll's detractors with an appearance on the no longer always squeaky-clean *American Bandstand*. "Great Balls of Fire" was the best-selling record in the history of Sun Studios. There were almost as many zeroes on his checks, Jerry Lee told Elmo Lewis Sr., as there had been F's on his third grade report card.[50]

Lewis's sensational success suggests that the repeal of reticence was well under way in the 1950s, with a big boost from rock 'n' roll. FDA approval of the birth control pill in May 1960, for better and worse, it is often said, ushered in an era of sexual liberation. Thanks to oral contraception, historian David Boroff observed in the early '60s, "the loss of chastity is no longer the fall from innocence; it is the fall upward, so to speak, to maturity and self-fulfillment." Admittedly significant, the sexual revolution was neither as new nor as sweeping in its impact as Boroff implied. The dawning of a new decade did not operate as an Iron Curtain or a Berlin Wall, separating the repressed from the uninhibited, the virgins from the free-lovers, the prudes from the pleasure-seekers. Baby boomers carried into the 1960s the complex and contradictory sexual messages of the formative '50s, during which "there was a whole lotta shakin' going on."[51]

"YAKETY YAK DON'T TALK BACK"

4

Rock 'n' Roll and Generational Conflict

Many Americans believed that rock 'n' roll was an irritant that provoked conflict between parents and teenagers and increased antisocial behavior. Acknowledging that there was no simple, causal equation between enjoying Elvis and arranging a rumble, they remained convinced that rock 'n' roll reinforced the most worrisome aspects of youth culture: antagonism to adult authority and expectations; conformity to peer-group norms; and an ephemeral, erratic emotional intensity. With journalist John Sharnik, many adults in the 1950s found Presley's "air of inarticulate suspicion" just as subversive as his onstage gymnastics: "It's like that hostile look you get when you've told your 13-year-old daughter that she can't wear lipstick, or stay up to watch the late movie."[1]

According to cultural critic Dwight Macdonald, with rock 'n' roll "teenism reached its climax, or its nadir" as a form of defiance of adult control. Popular music, however, was by no means alone as a symbol and a sign of generational conflict. Throughout the mass media and the marketplace, it seemed, teenagers separated themselves from the rest of the population. Their behavior was as "baffling to the lay adult," wrote Macdonald, "as if they were in the grip of a severe neurosis." How should parents respond? Were teenagers really all that rebellious? If so, what made them so? Were the standards of taste and

conduct of young people actually natural and functional aspects of
the transition to adulthood? Or might the tribal subculture of '50s
adolescents become a permanent way of life? As they pondered these
questions, Americans of all ages evaluated the relationship between
the state of the family, the threat of juvenile delinquency, the
purchasing power of boys and girls, and the immense popularity of
rock 'n' roll. On both sides of the generational divide, they tended to
reject authoritarian models for the family and choose accommodation
rather than open warfare, with adults seeking not to obliterate but to
modify teenage culture to approximate their own norms. Perhaps most
important, by the end of the 1950s intragenerational identification had
been reinforced and, to some extent, legitimized.[2]

Before the twentieth century, teenagers did not exist. When Tom
Sawyer and Booth Tarkington's Penrod reached the age of thirteen,
Dwight Macdonald observed, they remained children, "who accepted
the control of grownups as something they could no more escape than
the weather." By 1900, however, as the average age for the onset of
puberty declined while the age at marriage increased, youngsters struggled for greater autonomy during a prolonged period of dependence
on their parents. In the enormously influential *Adolescence: Its
Psychology, and Its Relation to Physiology, Anthropology, Sociology,
Sex, Crime, Religion, and Education* (1904), G. Stanley Hall provided
the first sustained, systematic analysis of these stress-filled years. Taught
by his own parents to refer to his genitals as "the dirty place," Hall
believed that the sexual impulses of adolescents should be acknowledged as "natural." But since he believed that civilized people should
exercise sexual restraint, Hall advised adults to provide an environment in which young people grow into maturity by learning to channel
their erotic energy into religious, athletic, and aesthetic activities.[3]

By the end of World War II, the term "teen-ager" was firmly established in the language. In the '50s, the *Dictionary of American Slang*
subsequently pointed out, the United States was the only country
"considering this age group as a separate entity whose influence, fads
and fashions are worthy of discussion apart from the adult world." The
transition from childhood to adulthood now routinely spanned most
or all of the teen years. In 1940, seventy-three of every one hundred
children between the ages of fourteen and seventeen were enrolled in
high school; at the end of the '50s, it was eighty-seven. A site of peer-

group socialization, the high school was one of several institutions in an increasingly self-contained teenage universe.[4]

As teenage subcultures solidified, parents seemed less willing and able to enforce norms of appropriate behavior. During World War II, some argued, many adolescents became reckless and violent. According to the FBI, crime for all age groups increased 1.5 percent during the first six months of 1943 but a whopping 40 percent for youngsters under 18. Shown in movie houses across the country, *Youth in Crisis*, part of the *March of Time* series, pointed out that when boys earned "a man's wages" they got into trouble, while girls sinned against common decency, advancing the specious rationalization that "it is an act of patriotism to deny nothing to servicemen."[5]

These concerns did not disappear with the return of peace. A policeman in *Blackboard Jungle* traced juvenile delinquency in the '50s to failures of supervision of boys and girls during their formative years: "They were six years old in the last war. Father in the Army. Mother in a defense plant. No home life. No church life." Even as they predicted an increase in delinquency throughout the decade, experts insisted that the problem was not limited to the hoodlums who ran afoul of the law. In abdicating their responsibility to teenagers, adults darkened what already seemed like a long, dim tunnel between childhood and maturity for millions of youngsters. That abdication had taken new and troubling forms. Alongside the classic broken home, journalist Harrison Salisbury found a growing middle-class component of the "shook up generation," the "psychologically broken home," characterized by emotionally distant fathers and suffocating mothers. "Split level delinquency in quiet suburban communities," Salisbury wrote, was just as dangerous as "the festering conflicts of the housing projects and old slums." In testimony before the U.S. Senate, A. C. Flora, an official of the National Education Association, noted that many parents were "willing to give our boys and girls their week's allowances and an automobile and turn them loose." Robert Segal, executive director of the Jewish Community Council of Metropolitan Boston, agreed, identifying the increase in working mothers, the prevalence of divorce, more unplanned leisure for young people, "the fluidity of modern life and the impact of comics, movies, radio and TV programs suggesting hostile behavior" as explanations of antisocial behavior among teenagers. John O. Reineman, director of probation for the Philadelphia Municipal Court, added that an uncertain future, including the possibility of a nuclear war, with "its predicted horror and widely publicized destructiveness," produced in teenagers an irresponsible "last fling" attitude. In this "rather sick civilization," concluded Karl Holton, chief probation officer of Los Angeles County, young people had less and less respect for "God or law or man or anybody else."[6]

Explanations, however, were easier to come by than workable solutions. Some Americans advocated a return to a more hierarchical, authoritarian family. "Are you afraid of your teenager?" asked Sumner Ahlbum in *Cosmopolitan* magazine. "Why don't we crawl out of the storm cellars where we've been cowering before the teen barrage of 'everybody else is doing it' and start fighting back ... ?" It would not be easy, traditionalists said, because discipline and corporal punishment were in retreat throughout American society. When Dad remembered getting his hands slapped with a ruler by a teacher, Mary Rose, a probation officer in the juvenile and family court in Denver, Colorado, lamented, "his son will pipe up and say, 'Well, they can't do that to you any more or they will get arrested if they do.'"[7]

Traditionalists demanded that moms subordinate themselves to the needs of their children, defer to their husbands, and, above all, stay at home. Noting that 5.2 out of the 5.3 million working mothers in 1952 had children under eighteen, Joseph Schieder, director of the Youth Division of the National Catholic Welfare Conference in Washington, D.C., condemned women for working when it was not an economic necessity. The selfish desire of American females to "keep up with the Joneses, to have a car, to wear a mink coat," he claimed, led them all too often to barter the interests of youngsters "for a fleeting bit of happiness." Walter Reckless, an inappropriately named professor of criminology at Ohio State University, asserted that women who did not hold jobs were also destabilizing domestic life because they, too, pursued personal gratification: many mothers "do the afternoon stint at the bingo game and come home and give the family a can of beans, you see, something of that sort." Was bingo playing common among American women? "I am just using it as a symbolic statement," Reckless admitted, but then added, "If it is not there, it is in the downtown department store or something else."[8]

To prevent mothers from emasculating their sons, traditionalists pressed fathers to reassert themselves as disciplinarians and role models. "You have a horror of seeing your son a pantywaist," a writer in *Better Homes and Gardens* warned, "but he won't get red blood and self-reliance if you leave the whole job of making a he-man to his mother." If they did not become homosexuals, sons of feckless fathers might become sullen and disobedient. Indulged or ignored, Jim Stark (James Dean) in *Rebel Without a Cause* (1955) was disgusted with his apron-clad dad. "She eats him alive and he takes it," Jim told his friend. "What a zoo. He always wants to be my pal. If he had the guts to knock Mom cold maybe she'd be happy." Traditionalists suggested that a belt to the behind might have kept Jim happy, too.[9]

But the traditionalists were in the minority by the 1950s. Parents did a disservice to their children when they permitted them to "pursue every whim and fancy without regard for others," A. C. Flora admitted, but "we have rightly discarded the attitudes symbolized by the woodshed whipping as the basis for securing conformity through fear." Councilwoman Rosalind Weiner Wyman of Los Angeles supported setting aside areas for teenagers to race cars on Saturdays and Sundays under supervision because "the minute you say 'No' just blankly and flatly they are going to do it some other way." Most parents, who had deferred gratification themselves during the Depression and World War II, did not want to deny their children cars, clothes, or commercial entertainment in a more affluent age. But they did want to influence their behavior. To do so, suggested sociologist James Coleman, parents should take the desire for autonomy and the peer-dominated adolescent society as given and then use them "to help young people internalize sound and sturdy values."[10]

Most teenagers, experts insisted, were not rebelling so much as testing their power; they expected and even wanted adults to regulate their behavior. Much of what was called juvenile delinquency, moreover, was the normal exuberance of youth. Had joyriding not been lumped together with auto theft by the FBI, they pointed out, the statistics on juvenile delinquency would not be all that alarming. Torn between a desire for independence and a craving for security, sociologists H. H. Remmers and D. H. Radler reminded parents, teenagers "often make reasonable demands in unreasonable ways and so tend to seem more childish than they really are." Although 80 percent of teenagers believed their mothers and fathers treated them as if they were younger than they actually were, Remmers and Radler reported, only 10 to 20 percent reported serious conflicts with parents. While 31 percent felt their parents talked too much about what they ought to do and never discussed with them what actually happened on dates, 70 percent deemed their moms and dads "just about strict enough"; 33 percent wanted more parental advice than they were getting. Therefore Remmers and Radler concluded that teenagers did not dislike parents so much as their own status as children: "Teenagers desperately want to break away from parental control, yet, at the same time, they feel a strong need for parental guidance."[11]

Adherents of this view often had little respect for the values of teenagers. Believing that the desire for autonomy and independence was superficial, they differed from the traditionalists less on ends than over means. Because fixed and rigorously enforced codes no longer commanded the assent of young people, these adults sought new ways to secure compliance with conventional norms. Strategies could be subtle or, as in the case of Enid Haupt, editor-in-chief of *Seventeen* magazine, transparent appeals to conformity. Haupt began with flattery: "Restless discontent with existing rules and with authority, is certainly the sign of a young, creative, thinking mind. . . . Rebel you will, rebel you must." But rebellion, she continued, should be constructive. When, for example, parents prohibited dating during the week, destructive rebels deceived them by secretly arranging a meeting at the home of a friend. Such an approach was dishonest and, in any event, unlikely to succeed. A constructive rebel polled friends to see if their mothers allowed a midweek date. If the tally was only two or three out of ten, "forget the whole thing," she suggested. But if five or more received permission to date during the week, the teenagers should "explain that your friends are important to you and that you would like to keep up with them." To sweeten the offer, teenagers might promise that if their grades went down, they would drop the arrangement without complaint and, as the coup de grace, propose that the date be dinner at home with another couple present. As if it were not already obvious, Haupt concluded with a recognition that constructive rebellion approximated capitulation: "In other words, whether your problem is at home or at school, try to offer the authorities a solution to the problem that will be acceptable to them."[12]

A few observers in the 1950s offered more searching examinations of the feelings and actions of adolescents. The enormous popularity among teenagers of J. D. Salinger's novel *The Catcher in the Rye* (1951) suggested that many of them were struggling, as was Holden Caulfield, to develop a distinctive and substantive identity amidst materialism, conformity, and hypocrisy. At home and at school, indeed everywhere there were adults, Holden found the "phonies coming in the goddam windows." For Salinger, adolescent idealism and defiance were not only natural but good, much-needed correctives to the preoccupation with appearances and the falsifying self-consciousness of adults. Unfortunately, Salinger implied, adolescents grew up: whenever Holden thought about his future, he came up empty, a rebel without a plan. Amidst the conventional aspirations of postwar America, Holden's aimlessness made him all the more authentic and attractive to youthful readers.

In *The Vanishing Adolescent* (1959), Edgar Z. Friedenberg provided a nonfiction defense of teenage rebelliousness, more comprehensive but no less passionate than Salinger's. During adolescence, he observed, young people learn who they are and what they feel. They shun solitude, adhering to the conventions of their own social group, often participating in "rituals which they do not really understand themselves." In defending what they believe to be their rights and prerogatives, young people tend "to be pugnacious and quarrelsome" and sometimes "naive and reckless." Thus the teenage years were a disturbed and disturbing period. Friedenberg hoped that through a dialectical process adolescent conflict with adults would produce healthy individuals and a less conformist, more critical, tolerant, and just society. He acknowledged, with regret, the reality that reassured Enid Haupt: as boys and girls learned "the complex, subtle and precious" differences between themselves and their environment in the 1950s, they did so "on the culture's terms." Even if adults allowed their children more autonomy, Friedenberg concluded, in his own effort to reassure, conflict need not be war; "it need not even involve hostile action." For most young people, most of the time, "things do not go terribly wrong. They go moderately wrong," and boys and girls become more or less responsible adults.[13]

Although nostalgia for the authoritarian family remained in evidence, the rhetoric of accommodation between the generations dominated the decade. Sometimes vague, the differences between parent and child were more personal than ideological, centering around dating, curfews, and sexual behavior. At the same time, a consensus emerged that young people did constitute a distinct class. Teenagers thought it separate and unequal; many adults deemed it actually or potentially powerful and dangerous. Told that rebellious-ness was a phase in human development, parents continued to fear that their child might demonstrate that he, too, was a "teenage were-wolf." And, given the adolescent predilection for "predatory assembly," she might join a pack of werewolves. As patterns of behavior formerly confined to African Americans and poor whites spread to middle- and upper-class kids, Harrison Salisbury asserted, public concern about delinquency grew. Citing rock 'n' roll as his prime example, Salisbury worried that the slums were becoming "tradition setters for antisocial conduct at all levels." Comparing rock 'n' roll to the "dancing mania of the Middle Ages," Macdonald charged that publicizing the music and other "irrational acts" like hot-rodding "stimulates more such acts." The stakes were high, and they grew higher on October 4, 1957, when the Soviet Union launched the first rocket-powered satellite into orbit. Had the Communists taken the lead in science and technology? Americans might take some solace in the popularity of rock 'n' roll among young Russians, who listened to the music over the radio and on bootleg recordings. But unless the teenagers of the United States switched their priorities from bandstands to Bunsen burners, the future might not be as rosy for individuals, families, and the nation.[14]

Even without rock 'n' roll, generational conflict would have had a prominent place in private and public discourse, but the furor over the music added visibility and a sense of urgency to the issue. Commen-tators in the national media warned parents that the "bad elements" in the neighborhood and at school gravitated toward rock 'n' roll. Years later, as he described '50s kids waiting in line at the Paramount Theater in Brooklyn, media critic Jeff Greenfield acknowledged that they differed markedly from middle-class parents' ideal teenager. The fans, Greenfield recalled, had "the hard faces of the children of the working poor." The boys "read auto specs at night, not college cata-logues. They wear St. Christopher medals, and white T-shirts with their cigarette packs held in the left sleeve, which is rolled up to the muscles." The girls "have curlers in their hair and scarves tied around their heads. They chew gum. They wear jeans and sweaters, and their crucifixes bounce on their breasts, some of which are remarkable examples of stress under pressure."[15]

As we have seen, parents linked rock 'n' roll with sexual license. They suspected that the music also distracted young people from their academic work. Dwight Macdonald cited a survey in support of this view. According to the poll, Elvis Presley fans got an average grade of C in high school. Even worse, only one of every ten Presley fans even tried to get the best possible grade. Students who preferred Pat Boone or Perry Como did much better, with an average grade of B. One of every three of them strove to get the highest grade within his or her grasp. The good kids—the ones who donated blood to the Red Cross, wore neat, stylish clothes, took care not to spill soup on the pretty Formica tops of the cafeteria tables, took honors classes, and hung around with the leaders of their high school—preferred pop, or even classical music.[16]

What was it about rock 'n' roll that made it an incubator for alienation and rebelliousness? It was not lyrics. There was no equivalent in rock 'n' roll lyrics to Jim Stark knocking his father over a couch as his mother screamed from the staircase in *Rebel Without a Cause*. To be sure, a few songs contained lighthearted, mocking dismissals of parents' expectations for their children. In several novelty songs written for the Coasters, Jerry Leiber and Mike Stoller defined the generation gap from the point of view of teenagers. With upbeat dance music and a humorous narrative, "Yakety Yak" climbed to number 1 on the pop charts in 1957. The song presents a hectoring, lecturing mother who enjoys invoking her authority as a parent and the power of the purse: "Take out the papers and the trash, / Or you don't get no spending cash; / If you don't scrub that kitchen floor, / You ain't gonna rock 'n' roll no more. / Yakety yak, don't talk back. . . ." "Yakety Yak" did satirize mothers who forced their sons to do menial "woman's work" in exchange for the otherwise "forbidden pleasures" of listening to rock 'n' roll or hanging out with friends. It implied, though it did not say, that children did (and maybe should) talk back. But the lyric is not a manifesto of disobedience, defiance, or rebelliousness. It's satire—and it's gentle.

So was "Charlie Brown," which reached number 2 for Leiber, Stoller, and the Coasters two years later. Here, in fact, whining adolescents as much as the authority of parents are the targets. Charlie's refrain, "Why's everybody always picking on me?" was repeated by warriors on both sides of the generational divide. It expressed the feelings of put-upon teenagers who thought their parents talked entirely too much about what their children ought to do, and it provided a text for parents who doubted that their kids had anything significant to complain about.

What was it, then, about rock 'n' roll? In no small measure, it was the insistent beat, which relaxed and released the body, for dancing and, well, for sex. Director Richard Brooks capitalized on that beat when he used "Rock Around the Clock" as the sound track in *Blackboard Jungle*. Onstage, rock 'n' roll performers were in tune with the beat. They were more aware of their bodies and more hedonistic and defiant than any singers had ever been. Most important of all, whether its lyrics were potent or puerile, rock 'n' roll was music for teenagers, about teenagers, performed by teenagers. By 1956, *Ebony* reported, there were over two hundred teen rock 'n' roll groups. Their names—the Teen-Queens, the Six Teens, Frankie Lymon and the Teenagers, the Youngsters, the School Boys—and the titles of their songs—"A Teenager's Romance," "Teenage Crush," "Young Love," "So Young"—served to welcome adolescents to a world all their own. Every rock 'n' roll concert was an occasion for affirming and celebrating teenage collective identity and solidarity. So often subject to the will and whim of adults, teenagers felt empowered by rock 'n' roll to listen, dance, and scream in their own space. Rock 'n' roll gave unprecedented power to teenage performers. "Rejuvenating juveniles," *Ebony* crowed, were "dethroning and retiring veteran artists faster than you can say 'oou oou I love you.'" Rock 'n' roll stars solved the problem of meddlesome parents, Grace and Fred Hechinger claimed, "by making their parents their dependents." Elvis was publicly, and genuinely, devoted to his mother, but he left the family home as soon as he could, and he bought the eye-popping possessions Gladys and Vernon Presley enjoyed. In rock 'n' roll, parents were peripheral and powerless, or they weren't there at all.[17]

Whatever the reasons, rock 'n' roll ignited arguments in many families about independence and deference, sex and abstinence, work and leisure. Many parents envied their teenagers as much as they feared losing control over them. Never before, they reminded themselves and their children, were cars, clothes, and a college education so readily available. Never before had parents provided so much and asked so little in return. And never before, some fumed, were children so ungrateful. For them, rock 'n' roll was hardly harmless fun. It was a metaphor for freedom without responsibility, for the loss of parental authority, and for everything that was inexplicable and incomprehensible about the younger generation. *Yakety yak, don't talk back*, many of their sons and daughters responded—or wanted to.

In some households, it was Mom and Dad who held their fire. "You restrain yourself from putting on the Irate Parent act," wrote the editors of *Changing Times* magazine. "Instead, you go away smoldering, wondering how you can possibly make the kids understand what you find so unacceptable about the music they enjoy." Ethan Russell described such a household and the tensions within it. As he sang Elvis's songs in front of the mirror in his home in San Francisco, Ethan imitated Presley's smile, "raising the corner of one side of my mouth. I tried to move like him, rotating one leg from the hip. And I tried to comb my hair like him. I used Vitalis, Butch Wax, Brylcreem, pulling the comb through my hair and seeing little white globules of grease ooze between the teeth." While Ethan found spending afternoons with his parents listening to Tony Bennett records excruciatingly painful, he knew that they hated the music he found thrilling. One day, Ethan's father, "vexed beyond endurance" at his son's bathroom rituals, and at the rock 'n' roll music blaring from the record player and the car radio whenever the boy was within reach of the dials, took Ethan and his brother to the local barbershop and ordered the barber to give the boys crew cuts. Mr. Russell's corrective action changed nothing, of course. Ethan's Elvis imitations returned well before his hair grew long enough to comb.[18]

We do not know what restrictions, if any, Terry Tudor's parents placed on him, but the Arizona teenager was sufficiently exorcised about an older generation that "just doesn't want the younger generation to have any fun" to write the magazine *Senior Scholastic* about it. "They had theirs," he asked, "so why can't we have ours?" Terry "put his emotions into it" as he danced to rock 'n' roll songs, just like "every other teenager who isn't 'square.' . . . Man, we like Fats Domino, Elvis Presley, and many other rock and rollers." Adults had no reason to blame juvenile delinquency on rock 'n' roll, Terry concluded: "I would like to say this: keep it up, ban the music we like, and the world will be worse off in five years than we are now. Thanks for nothing."[19]

In an "Open Letter to Parents," published in *Seventeen* magazine, an anonymous teenage girl was more conciliatory but no less convinced than Terry Tudor that parents and teens were "talking two different languages." She admitted she was "one big contradiction." She wanted to be on her own, "at least partly," and, "in a way," to keep her from making mistakes, she wanted her parents to tell her what to do. She shared her parents' views about "necking, drinking and going to places you consider off limits." On other matters, however, she refused to give ground, because, more than anything, she wanted "to be sure I have a weekend date and am part of the crowd." That was why she sulked when her mother suggested a classic dress instead of the Italian striped T-shirt with a hood all the other girls were wearing. And she sizzled when her parents attacked her boyfriend. Jimmy was not punctual, neat, well-mannered, ambitious, or a good student, she admitted, but she liked the way he "walks—sort of lopes—and the way he jumps into the middle of a sentence when he calls me up, as though we belong together." She admired Jimmy's bravery in arguing with his imposing math teacher. Her mom and dad laughed at the idea of anyone her age being in love, but despite moments of doubt, she was "really in love with Jimmy."

Interestingly, rock 'n' roll was at the top of her list of "things that I can't possibly decide your way." It was not, as her father characterized it, "musically atrocious" or "monotony carried to the point of torture. Torture? It's wonderful. Monotonous? That steady beat says to me: you're young—be glad—you're young—be glad." With thanks to her parents for giving her opportunities they did not have as teenagers, she suggested that "maybe if you'll stop thinking I'm more than just average, I just might be." She asked for their trust. Given her attachment to her peers, to Jimmy, and to rock 'n' roll, her parents may not have been all that ready to give it.[20]

The "Jimmys" of America and their more truculent and troublesome soul brothers seemed to be part of the rock 'n' roll package. Frantic reports of rock 'n' roll riots fed perceptions that the music was at best a nuisance, and at worst a spur to defiance and violence. "Headlines such as 'Immoral, Dangerous, Criminal,'" according to *The Cash Box*, were "boldly plastered across the page to attract the readers' attention. And all too frequently, they do." The resulting backlash, entertainment industry officials concluded, might "kill the goose that laid the golden guldens." Therefore, in conjunction with their efforts in the middle of the decade to tone down rock 'n' roll's sexuality, they launched a comprehensive campaign to dissociate rock 'n' roll from juvenile delinquency and enlist it in the drive for intergenerational under-standing and harmony.[21]

In doing so, the industry endorsed the view that the outlandish behavior of teenagers was a phase in the transition to adulthood. The teenagers of the 1950s were neither different from nor more dangerous than their counterparts who grew up earlier in the twentieth century. "Remember raccoon coats and flasks," *Cash Box* opined, "waterhose fights in the towns after a football game, panty raids, tearing up the insides of trains on the way to some event. How do you explain these wild escapades when they can't be blamed on rock 'n' roll?" That teenagers "react strongly, sometimes wildly, many times unknowingly, but, except in special cases which rock 'n' roll has nothing to do with, seldom viciously," was a "simple fact." Nor had there ever been a time, the editors added, "when the previous generation could fully accept the modes of conduct, the tastes and concepts of living of the younger generation." Rock 'n' roll channeled the emotions and excitement of the nation's youth into listening and dancing. The kids bounced up and down in their seats, clapped their hands, and sometimes shouted vociferously. There were far worse ways for them to dis-charge their energy.[22]

As they parried the "fright-shock" exaggerations of rock 'n' roll's detractors, the beneficiaries of the "goose that laid the golden guldens" argued by addition rather than subtraction. Since there were few incendiary lyrics to censor in the second half of the decade, the industry aimed more at context than text. While Elvis, Jerry Lee Lewis, and Little Richard remained relatively silent about generational conflict, "soft" rock 'n' rollers spoke for the music, associating it with traditional secular and religious values, including, at times, the author-itarian family. The enhanced prominence of clean-cut balladeers singing songs about chaste young lovers may have contributed to what historians of popular music call the "treacle" period in rock 'n' roll, marked by a decline in "originality, vitality, and volume." At the same time, the public relations campaign opened new markets to rock 'n' roll, on television and in the movies. Designed to enhance the image of rock 'n' roll with adults, the campaign did not dissuade them, however, that the music was *terra incognita*, accessible only to teenagers.[23]

Since "I'm Not a Juvenile Delinquent," by Frankie Lymon and the Teenagers, probably produced few converts to rock 'n' roll, the campaign moved beyond the recording studio and the concert hall. As he convalesced after a heart attack, President Eisenhower received several rock 'n' roll hits. "This is the music of Young America," wrote Ken Malden of radio station WBMS in Boston. "If this, their music, can make their president 'look alive and dig the jive,' they will consider it 'par for the course.'" The note of thanks from Eisenhower's secretary was silent on whether the president "dug the jive" or had even listened to the records. More significant was the public relations blitz for spiritually based messages of intergenerational harmony. To prove that the traditional three R's, "plus two new ones, rock 'n' roll, can add up to something worthwhile for everybody," Douglas "Jocko" Henderson, a DJ at WOV in New York City, suggested five commandments for teenagers on his 10:00 P.M. to midnight program: "1) Attend all your classes regularly. 2) Do your homework without fail every day. 3) Help your folks with chores around the house. 4) Your parents are good company—go places with them, as well as your friends. 5) Be home every night before this program begins."[24]

When DJs at KDKA in Pittsburgh and WBZ in Boston read a new list of "The Teen Commandments," an "inspirational life of rules of self-conduct," an avalanche of letters poured in from priests, preachers, principals, lawyers, bankers, and doctors, as well as thousands of young people, *Cash Box* exulted. So ABC-Paramount released a recording of "The Teen Commandments," by Paul Anka, George Hamilton IV, and Johnny Nash. It intended admonitions such as

> 1) Stop and think before you drink.
> 2) Don't let your parents down; they brought you up.

and

> 6) Choose a date who would make a good mate.
> 9) Avoid following the crowd. Be an engine—not a caboose.[25]

Of course, Dick Clark and Pat Boone played prominent parts in the program of parental pacification. Clark used *Seventeen* magazine, his own television shows, and his book, *Your Happiest Years*, to remove the stigma from rock 'n' roll by helping bridge the gap between the generations. Complaints about young people, Clark emphasized, echoed across the centuries. In his office in Philadelphia, he had a copy of a scroll discovered in an Egyptian's tomb, written about 2000 B.C., lamenting that youth were driving the country to rack and ruin. "No, it doesn't say rock and ruin," Clark joked to five teenage reporters for *Seventeen*. Denying that contemporary popular music was "a reflection on anyone's moral standards," he suggested that parents "worry far more than they should about rock 'n' roll."

In his analysis of generational conflict, Clark played at first to his teenage audience. He characterized young people as more knowledgeable about the state of the world, more conscious of psychology, and older emotionally than any preceding generation. Emotional maturity was one reason, he guessed, for the increase in early marriages. "Yearning to have another chance to go back, to do it all again," some adults were jealous or hypercritical of their teenagers. Others were too busy to pay attention, laughing off adolescent problems as unimportant and likely to solve themselves.

"But don't get me wrong," Clark hastened to say. "I don't agree with people who blame all the faults of teen-agers on their parents. . . . Most of the time, parents are worth listening to. I know mine were." Indeed, once he got past the preliminaries, Clark strongly and consistently advised adolescents to respect and obey their parents. He acknowledged that some parents were "overstrict and overprotective," opening their children's mail or forcing them into a course of study at school for which they had no aptitude or interest. In a few extreme cases, teenagers might "have to go elsewhere for aid." However, Clark did not deem mothers and fathers who "set up a sensible list of do's and don'ts for you and expect you to follow them" too strict. He approved of the action of one father who enforced a three-minute limit on his child's telephone conversations by starting an egg timer.

Clark's most important message was that "parents have a strange way of being right, most of the time." When children make concessions, parents become far more willing to make concessions themselves. Although "not all problems can be talked out of existence," differences that appeared to be unbridgeable could be solved "in a few minutes of simple conversation when all the facts are set out and inspected." Too often, Clark implied, teenagers were adamant and unreasonable, inclined to draw the line on trivial matters. He cited the example of a son who "squared off" with his father over the length of his hair. Six months later, long hair was out. Parents were patient, he stressed, "because they've seen it all happen before." But their patience was wearing thin. Authorities "far more learned than I," Clark wrote, had documented a breakdown in family communication, so teenagers had better think at least twice before challenging their parents.[26]

In *'Twixt Twelve and Twenty*, Pat Boone allied himself even more firmly than Clark with adult authority. Although he had obeyed his parents "out of love as much as by commandment," Boone believed that corporal punishment helped him control his body so that his "mind was ready to follow what was being said." In endorsing household chores as a good way to teach children responsibility, Boone went out of his way to disagree with the Leiber and Stoller song: "If you're on the 'yakety yak, don't talk back,' walk yourself to the laundramat, bring in the dog, and put out the cat stage, you just haven't accepted reality." Parents made rules for conduct inside and outside the home because they cared about their children. "For the record," Boone joked, "your parents had to be teenagers [themselves] at some time." If parents were too strict, the singer suggested, teenagers should redouble their efforts at empathy. There was no alternative. Unlike Clark, Boone did not discuss communication, negotiation, or compromise. He simply claimed that "no strict parent was ever won over to seeing your side of things by defiance, disobedience, or a comparative description of what all the other parents do." In arguing for the futility of resistance to those with power and authority, Boone used a metaphor that shed light on his view of the relationship between parents and teens. The harder a large dog wearing a choke collar "struggles and pulls," the singer wrote, "the tighter the collar gets."

Left to their own devices, teenagers often were impressionable, fickle, and restless. The injunction "act your age," taken by adolescents as an insult, was actually, Boone believed, "very good advice." Youngsters should not drive cars, date without a chaperone, wear spike-heeled shoes or a dinner jacket, or get a job until their parents thought they were ready. "I know we say, when we're on the receiving end, 'I'll let my children have Whizzers [motor bikes], and horses, and cars, and paint their fingernails red, and stay out 'til two,' but when the time comes and we understand, we change our minds. Believe me!" For boys and girls between twelve and twenty, Pat Boone's message was simple and straightforward: obey, and be consoled by faith that good things come to those who wait.[27]

In 1957, Boone starred in two teen-targeted and adult-approved films, *Bernardine* and *April Love*, part of a late '50s phenomenon that Thomas Doherty calls "the clean teenpics." A musical set in a high school, *Bernardine* was unrelievedly wholesome. A reviewer summarized the plot: "The adolescents in this film come from well-to-do families and their major problems concern whether they will pass their high school exams and who their dates will be for Saturday night.... Most teenagers attracted to this film will recognize and identify with such symbols as sneakers and sweaters, cokes [a product endorser for Coca-Cola, Boone blatantly plugged the soft drink throughout the film] and hamburgers, jukeboxes, high school clubs, problems of dating, and the desire to own a car." Bowing to Boone's refusal to kiss a woman onscreen, the script cast him as adviser to a friend who was ardently and ineptly courting a pretty telephone operator. For this reason, Boone sang the hit song "Love Letters in the Sand" all alone in the boys' clubhouse.

Bernardine glanced at the dark side of teen culture with the humiliation of Kinswood, a straight-A student, by his classmates, only to include him, without explanation, in the "in group" at the end of the film. The only explicit acknowledgment of generational conflict comes when Boone's buddy joins the army and his mother realizes that her son is a stranger: "There's only one thing I'm thinking and that's the foolish notion that I've always cherished that I understood my boy. And all the time he's been living a life so entirely separate from mine that I've never had an inkling of it." Having delivered its lecture to parents, *Bernardine* moves on, never looking back at the causes or consequences of the separation.

In *April Love*, Boone plays a troubled young man, impervious to the discipline of his widowed working mother. Arrested for joyriding in a stolen car, he is put on probation and sent to work on a farm for the summer. The film featured a drag race and some swing-based rock 'n' roll but was a conventional Hollywood musical, starting with the heavily promoted title song, a ballad with intergenerational appeal. Alongside its romantic plot (Boone and Liz, played by Shirley Jones, refer to a kiss that took place offscreen), *April Love* demonstrated how loving, no-nonsense authority could keep young people on the straight and narrow. On the farm, plain-talking Uncle Jed (Arthur O'Connell) becomes the father Boone needed and never had. When the two meet, Uncle Jed delivers the movie's traditional moral: "Heard a lot of talk you gotta treat kids different nowadays. I don't know what they mean by that. We raised our son the way we was raised—to fear God, to respect his elders, and to mind his manners. And 'til a better way comes along, and I ain't heard of one yet—that's the way it's gonna be with you as long as you're here." Boone grumbled about Uncle Jed's guidance, but he did not rebel against his patriarchal authority. Another young man had been snatched from the jaws of juvenile delinquency.[28]

As it featured rock 'n' roll stars like Boone and Presley in dramas and musicals, Hollywood also offered "rock 'n' roll teenpics," which packed as much music as possible in about ninety minutes. In their inane and trite plots, Doherty has argued, these films trafficked in generational conflict but concluded with generational reconciliation and an acknowledgment on both sides that teenagers constituted no threat to contemporary American values. They were designed to refute the association between rock 'n' roll and teenage violence for which the motion picture industry bore substantial responsibility. Following the success of *Blackboard Jungle*, a spate of juvenile crime melodramas used rock 'n' roll as background music or in their publicity to attract young viewers into the theater. An advertising kit for *Teenage Crime Wave* set out the strategy:

ROCK-AND-ROLL IN THE STREETS!
If your situation permits use a sound truck or car featuring current rock-and-roll tunes. Highlight blowups of teenage crime headlines and picture credits for maximum effect.

GO AFTER DISC JOCKEYS!
Interest disc jockeys with rock-and-roll following in the problem of teenage crime. Seek out favorable comment on your picture from them on the air![29]

In sharp contrast to the JD films, the rock 'n' roll teenpics emphasized that the music of teenagers was a "harmless outlet," and the
youngsters themselves no less than lovable. In *Don't Knock the Rock*
(1956), some "Carrie Nations with their hatchets" keep a rock 'n' roll
show out of the small town of Melandale. To win over the town elders,
Alan Freed and the town's teens present a historical pageant of art
and culture in America. Reminded that as youngsters they went over-
board for the Charleston and the Lindy Hop, the adults relent as Freed
delivers the movie's sermon: "Parents need not worry about today's
generation. They'll grow up to be the same fine sort."

A popular and profitable film, *Rock, Pretty Baby* (1956) shifts the
focus of generational conflict to the family. Jimmy Daley (John Saxon)
wants to play rock 'n' roll, while his father (Ed Platt) insists that he
become a doctor. So Jimmy becomes a rebel with a cause, pawning his
medical books to buy an electric guitar. But he goes too far, destroying
his parents' home by hosting a party there. Jimmy's mom (Fay Wray)
saves the day, telling Dr. Daley that the boy is "so hurt and confused
he doesn't know what he is doing." The chastened dad gets five traffic
citations as he races to see Jimmy's band perform on a televised
amateur hour. "Sometimes it takes a father longer to grow up than his
son," he tells Jimmy. Along with the almost effortless reconciliation,
Rock, Pretty Baby demonstrates how rock 'n' roll short-circuits sex.
As college-age frat boys begin to neck with high school coeds, Jimmy's
band strikes up a rock 'n' roll tune and the girls rush to the dance floor.

Shake, Rattle, and Rock! (1956) told the story of DJ Gary Nelson
(Mike Connors), who stages a benefit to raise money for a "Teen
Town" clubhouse that will help juvenile delinquents reform. When
young hoodlums start a brawl there, the do-gooding DJ finds himself
accused of inciting a "rock 'n' roll orgy." The ensuing trial pits Nelson,
defending "5,000 kids held together by common interest," against
SPRARCAY (Society for the Prevention of Rock and Roll Corruption
of American Youth), a thinly disguised reference to Asa Carter's White
Citizens Council. SPRARCAY members show film clips of Africans
dancing to a drum beat, identifying them as the disgusting and
depraved originators of rock 'n' roll. Nelson answers with his own
clips, of Americans dancing to the Black Bottom, Charleston, and
Turkey Trot. They grew up to be responsible adults, he claims. "We
never participated in those decadent antics," SPRARCAY members

reply. In the *deus ex machina* conclusion, someone spots a SPRARCAY member in Nelson's film clip. With SPRARCAY discredited as a bunch of hypocrites, the remaining adults are ready to "give the kids a chance to work their own way out of their teens." The dance floor and the jukebox, they now agree, are more wholesome attractions than alleys and pool rooms.[30]

It is difficult to know how many adults saw these films or how teenagers responded to them. Young viewers, Doherty suggests, may well have been attracted to *Don't Knock the Rock* because it featured Little Richard, and to *Shake, Rattle, and Rock!* because Fats Domino and Joe Turner performed in it. They may have used the plot inter-ludes between the rock 'n' roll songs to chat or smooch, identifying more with one girl's confession in *Rock, Pretty Baby!* ("All I think about is necking and petting") than with the aborted "make-out" at the frat house. And they may have seen the platitudes of the rock 'n' roll teenpics as a validation by adults of teenage culture rather than a solution to generational conflict. Advertised as "the wonderful story of today's rock 'n' roll generation the way they wanted it to be told!" *Rock, Pretty Baby* invited them to do so.[31]

With its family-friendly packaging, rock 'n' roll was ready for prime time. As we have seen, some rock 'n' roll performers were becoming familiar faces on television variety programs in 1957, but in that year they got an unexpected boost from a most unlikely source. Since the 1940s, first on radio and then on television, Ozzie and Harriet Nelson and their two sons, David and Ricky, had appeared to play themselves on *The Adventures of Ozzie and Harriet*, embodying the '50s self-image of prosperity and harmony in their two-story, nine-room, colonial-style white house with green shutters. On their situation comedy each week, the Nelsons' suburban life was wonderful. Harriet attributed it all to good old-fashioned family values: "If modern kids are sassy, lack responsibility, treat home strictly as a stopover between dates, and have no respect for earning money, it may be because the old-time ties that bound have been broken. With the Nelsons they have become a firm anchor to happiness." Jack Gould, the television critic for the *New York Times*, agreed, praising *The Adventures of Ozzie and Harriet* as "fine family fun" and "as realistic as the neighbors down the street."

Offscreen, however, the Nelson family was not so tranquil. Far from easygoing, Ozzie was a workaholic who made virtually every decision

Ozzie and Harriet Nelson with sons and TV co-stars Ricky (center) and David. Ricky's onscreen rock solos were designed to show that the music was no threat to sitcom family values. *(Ralph Crane/Timepix)*

on his program. He was also a demanding, domineering parent. Born in 1940, Ricky was an adorable, wisecracking kid on TV but actually a shy, secretive, and sometimes sullen teenager. After he was black-balled from the Elskers, a club at Hollywood High School for "the in-crowd," Ricky began to hang out with a tough gang called the Rooks. He dressed in motorcycle boots and a leather jacket, raced his blue Chevy Bel Air down Laurel Canyon, tattooed his initials on his hand in India ink, and smoked some marijuana. Cruising Hollywood Boulevard with the Rooks, Ricky got into fights and once was arrested for stealing construction lanterns. At the same time, he fell in love with rock 'n' roll. Jim Miller has suggested that rock 'n' roll "functioned for Ricky Nelson much as it functioned for the rest of his generation. Embedded in an ostensibly defiant pattern of gestures, the music and its idols offered a focus for fantasies of youthful revolt and sexual mastery—a ritual representation of potentially unruly impulses." As he sang and learned chords on the guitar, Ricky emulated rockabilly's sound and tone. Carl Perkins's "Blue Suede Shoes" changed his life, he later remembered.

Ozzie and Ricky bickered and battled constantly, over the length of the boy's hair, his poor performance in school, and his disreputable friends, but they did not fight over rock 'n' roll. Ozzie was a shrewd businessman, with an instinct for the main chance. A former band-leader, he understood the extraordinary popularity of the music with young audiences. In January 1957, for example, Ozzie watched Tommy Sands play an Elvis Presley–like character in *The Singing Idol* on *Kraft Television Theater*. "Teen-Age Crush," the song Sands introduced on the made-for-TV movie, zoomed to number 3 on *Billboard*'s charts. In the right setting, Ozzie concluded, rock 'n' roll could be more inno-cent than insolent. He treated rock 'n' roll on his show as the special property of teenagers. In one episode, twenty-something David arrives at a costume party dressed as Yul Brynner's character in the Broadway hit *The King and I*, while Ricky impersonates Elvis. In another, David (who actually preferred the Modern Jazz Quartet and Frank Sinatra) listens to classical music in the living room while rhythm and blues blares in Ricky's bedroom.

When Ozzie found out that Ricky had performed for a girlfriend in a record-your-own-voice booth, he arranged for his son to make his professional debut as a singer. Ricky recorded three songs, "You're My One and Only Love," "A Teenager's Romance," and the Fats Domino hit "I'm Walkin,'" the only tune Ricky knew how to play on the guitar. "It was scary," Ricky recalled. "I had gone straight from singing in the bathroom to the recording studio." Satisfied with the sessions, Ozzie decided to have Ricky perform on *Ozzie and Harriet*. On April 10, 1957, Americans were introduced to Ricky Nelson, the rock 'n' roll singer. In an episode set on an ocean liner crossing the Atlantic, Ricky sits in as a drummer with the ship's orchestra. Ozzie gets the band-leader's permission for his son to sing a rhythm and blues tune, and Ricky, clad in a black tuxedo, lip-synchs "I'm Walkin'." Almost imme-diately, tens of thousands of letters poured in to the television show. Three hundred Ricky Nelson fan clubs were formed. Released three weeks later, "I'm Walkin'" made it into the Top Twenty while the flip side, "A Teenager's Romance," cracked the Top Ten. Several more pop singles followed, as did an album, released in November, which proved to be a chart-topper as well. Each song, of course, provided an occasion for a show-closing performance on *Ozzie and Harriet*, with pretty girls smiling and swaying to the music, and an opportunity, as well, to assure adults that the music was safe, polished, and, above all, appropriate for teenagers to listen to. While Ricky sang "Your True Love," crusty, gravel-voiced, veteran character actor Edgar Buchanan told Ozzie, "By George, I like that rock and roll beat." Ozzie himself sang "Baby, I'm Sorry" right after Ricky performed the song on the show. Rock 'n' roll helped attract teenagers to *Ozzie and Harriet*—and sell Ricky's records—without alienating any of the older, traditional fans of the show. If rock 'n' roll was good enough for the Nelsons, and for Edgar Buchanan, then it couldn't do much harm to America's kids.

Ricky Nelson was a talented rock 'n' roll artist who became one of the best-selling male vocalists of the era. A superb band, led by virtuoso country guitarist James Burton, helped, but Ricky deserved to be the star attraction. Making good use of a limited vocal range, he sang with a quiet, sincere, and strong romantic passion, staking out the large expanse of cultural terrain between the chaste Pat Boone and the explosive Elvis. Most significantly, as Jim Miller has recognized, Ricky became a rock 'n' roll model of decency and restraint. With his pretty face and hair styled in a pompadour, he sang ballads with his eyes closed, and rockabilly while standing stock still: "He was all voice and no body—an impression reinforced by his deliberate omission of songs that conveyed even the slightest hint of lust."[32]

Even in its less objectionable form, rock 'n' roll remained the music of teenagers. With rock 'n' roll, observed journalist Bob Rolontz, "the teenager really comes into his own as an arbiter of musical taste." Because young people's preferences paid off "with an unmistakable jingle in the cash register," the music industry had begun cultivating them "as a vast potential sales market." In catering to teenagers, rock 'n' roll was at the leading edge of "market segmentation," a phenomenon with pivotal cultural as well as economic ramifications. For young people, sociologist David Riesman argued, music was "one of the principal areas for peer-group training in the appropriate expression of consumer preferences; by learning to talk about music, one also learned to talk about other things." Even more than most of its musical predecessors, rock 'n' roll had its own "slanguage" and fashion accessories. It helped build a consensus that teenagers, as

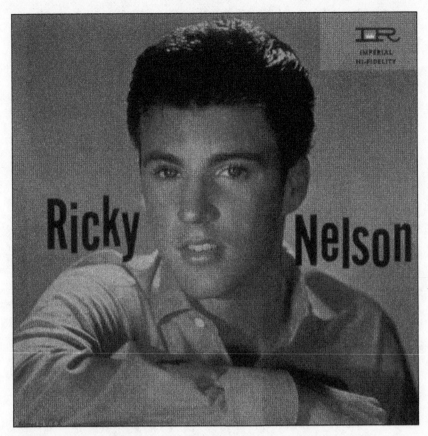

Ricky Nelson sang ballads with his eyes closed and rockabilly while
standing still, delivering romantic songs that were anything but raunchy.
(Michael Ochs Archives)

Dwight Macdonald put it, "constitute the latest—perhaps the last—
merchandising frontier. Clothes and food and drink and typewriters
are designed for them, magazines are edited for them, special kinds of
non-music are created for them." In their consumer preferences,
teenagers had become a sharply differentiated part of the population,
a special interest group, Macdonald called them, like the farm bloc or
organized labor. Along with the discretion to spend came power.
"Being patrons themselves," Edgar Z. Friedenberg observed, teenagers
"cannot always be patronized."[33]

Demography and prosperity fed the power of teenagers in the 1950s.
In 1958, seventeen million teenagers lived in the United States. Unlike

their Depression-conscious parents, "baby boomers" had never experienced scarcity. What adults considered a luxury, '50s youth deemed a necessity: with neither hesitation nor guilt, they spent about $10 billion of their own money, in addition to what their parents purchased for them. About two-thirds of "their own money" came from allowances paid out each week by parents, the rest from earnings. More than a third of teenage boys in the late '50s had after-school jobs, twice the percentage in 1944. In earlier generations, working children turned their paychecks over to their parents. In the more affluent postwar period, Mom and Dad made no such claim on their earnings. The weekly disposable income of teenagers varied with age. Boys had on average $4.16 at age thirteen, $8.26 at sixteen, and $16.65 at eighteen; girls' incomes were two or three dollars less.[34]

According to Eugene Gilbert, founder of Gilbert & Company, a consulting firm specializing in teenage buying habits, teenage income was unique. With the exception of lunch and school supplies, it was "free money," to be spent at the whim of the possessor. Equally important, fewer and fewer parents sought to control or even influence their children's spending. In the '50s, Gilbert emphasized, "both parents tend to be uncertain in matters of taste, confused about values, and all too ready to abdicate decisions—whether about cereals, car colors, furniture or clothing—to sons and daughters who have definite preferences, shared with large numbers of their contemporaries. In similar fashion, immigrant parents used to lean on their children as arbiters of taste and interpreters of the American way." Gilbert exaggerated, but only a bit. The influence of teenagers over products used by the whole family—a house, a refrigerator, a coffee table—remained negligible, though young people were sometimes consulted in the purchase of a car or a television set. With goods and services used by the teenagers, however, young people did call the shots. Fifty-seven percent of teenagers bought records and athletic equipment with their own money, 40 percent their own shirts, 36 percent their own shoes. Even when Mom and Dad paid, the children made the choice. Eighty percent of boys and ninety percent of girls in the United States believed that they had decided where their parents would take them to shop. Most of the time, they had "all or most of the say" over purchases of radios, records, fountain pens, watches, toothpaste,

deodorants, shampoos, jewelry, shoes, coats, and suits. More than a
third of teenagers thought their preference decisive in the family's
choice of a vacation destination.[35]

Although both teenagers and parents in the 1950s embraced an ethic
of material acquisition, consumption tended to increase the gap
between the generations. Teenagers pressed their families to use
prepackaged, "heat 'em and eat 'em" TV dinners, Macdonald complained, "and now the family dinner table, once the high altar of
domestic life, stands deserted while Mom, Dad, Junior, and Sis
consume their provender in the dark, off disposable compartmented
trays." They watched television as they wolfed down dinner, and they
raced up to their rooms or bolted out of the house. Parents were
coconspirators, of course, in the centrifugal family. Less willing or able
to control their children, middle-class parents found it easier to buy
them off. If parents had any idea of "organized revolt" against the
power of their children, *Life* magazine sighed, "it is already too late.
Teen-age spending is so important that such action would send quivers
through the entire national economy." Actually, parents were more
interested in relief than revolt. An advertisement by a telephone
company just after the decade ended played to their sentiments: "Your
teenage princess will appreciate the privacy of her own Princess exten-
sion—and you'll appreciate the resulting peace and quiet around the
other telephones in the house!"[36]

Peers, not parents, had preeminent influence over teenagers.
Adolescents were more likely to ask one another than their parents
about dating, what to wear, what movie to see, what record to buy.
For this reason, Eugene Gilbert employed teens to ask survey ques-
tions of their fellow teens. Gilbert also advised his clients—Esso gas,
Borden's milk, *Seventeen* magazine, Mars candy, Van Heusen shirts,
Hires soft drinks—to market their products first to the leaders in high
schools: "What they approve counts for more than what Mom and
Dad approve at home." Hires responded with a promotion campaign
that paid popular high school girls to ask for Hires Root Beer on dates.
R. J. Reynolds Tobacco Company sponsored Alan Freed's CBS radio
show, "The (Camel) Rock 'n' Roll Dance Party." Gilbert's interviewers
asked teens, "Do you feel that you could have any influence on your
friends' purchase of a particular brand of gasoline?"[37]

In the identification and exploitation of a separate teenage market, rock 'n' roll led the way. As early as 1953, the editors of *The Cash Box* recognized that "for every teenager you have in the nation, you have a potential record buyer. For that's the age at which the record buying public is born." The enthusiasm of a teenager, moreover, was infectious: "He forms fan clubs. He writes letters. He distributes literature and pictures.... He becomes a publicity man, a personal salesman." Three years later, *The Cash Box* celebrated "an entirely new development," the designing of records for an exclusive teenage audience that "stems almost directly from the rise of rock 'n' roll." Before the 1950s, there were kiddie records, aimed at the very, very young, and songs "aimed at everyone above kiddie age." Now, "the switch has gone all out for teenagers' demands."[38]

As rock 'n' roll defied its critics and gained in popularity, the new differentiation based on age became more pervasive and more permanent throughout the entertainment industry. Radio programmers, jukebox operators, television executives, and Hollywood studios jumped on the bandwagon. In 1955, the first "teen type" magazines, *Dig* and *Teen*, appeared on newsstands. Unlike their predecessors, including *Seventeen* and *Senior Scholastic*, these publications treated the teenager as a peer. More interested in making the years between twelve and twenty as enjoyable as possible than in the transition to adulthood, these magazines featured articles about romance and rock 'n' roll.[39]

Manufacturers of other products targeted teens as well, often using rock 'n' roll to win their attention and allegiance. A few held back. Designers of premiums and boxtops, the *New York Times* explained, who had capitalized on every craze from Davy Crockett to spacemen, were slow with offers related to rock 'n' roll because parents disapproved of the music. Manufacturers who sold products directly to teenagers, however, did not hesitate. Coca-Cola used rock 'n' roll music and pink and black, Elvis's favorite colors, in its advertisements. So did the Ralston Purina Company, maker of cereals and pet foods. Ralston used a singing ad on the television shows it sponsored: "Who-ho-ho-ho, Rock that rock, and Roll that Roll, Get that Ralston in the bowl." General Electric played rock 'n' roll records to attract teenagers to a demonstration of its cooking equipment. As they waited their turn to try out the appliances, the teens danced to the music. Everyone, it seemed, was getting into the act, from the Lion Brothers Company in Baltimore, which turned out forty-seven thousand emblems each month for teenage rock 'n' roll clubs, to the Arthur Murray School of Dancing, which reported an influx of teenage pupils that swelled registrations by more than 10 percent.[40]

Since rock 'n' roll called attention to teenager fashion, the cosmetics and clothing industries offered an array of products identified with rock 'n' roll stars. According to Eugene Gilbert, they were breaking new ground. Although merchandisers had exploited the children's field, with Howdy Doody, Hopalong Cassidy, and Ding Dong School products, Gilbert found that before rock 'n' roll "no major symbol" had been accepted by the teenagers. When Frank Sinatra's appeal to bobby-soxers was at its peak, the "merchandising plans built around him . . . were minor and amateurish." Elvis Presley, however, was "getting a colossal buildup," with merchandisers "attempting to make the Presley name the watchword to look for on every sort of product catering to the teen and pre-teen taste." By the end of 1957, seventy-eight Elvis Presley items had grossed $55 million. Presley helped plug the products, making personal appearances in department stores. In addition to a fluorescent portrait of Elvis, fans could purchase shoes, skirts, blouses, T-shirts, sweaters, charm bracelets, handkerchiefs, purses, pencils inscribed "Sincerely Yours," soft drinks, Bermuda shorts, blue jeans, toreador pants, pajamas, and pillows. They could make contact with a pen pal who idolized Elvis. And they could choose one of three shades of lipstick, marketed in connection with the Presley merchandising campaign: "Heartbreak Pink," "Hound Dog Orange," and "Tutti Frutti Red."[41]

Although the editors of *Billboard* warned against "the ostrich act and wishful thinking," many adults remained in denial, unsettled by the purchasing power of teenagers and its impact on American culture. In a much-quoted speech to the first disc jockey convention in Kansas City in 1958, Mitch Miller, director of artists and repertoire for Columbia Records, whose credits included "I Saw Mommy Kissing Santa Claus" and "Mule Train," blasted the music industry for pandering to "the eight- to fourteen-year-old mentality."[42] The industry was complicit, Miller charged, not only in losing contact with adults by concentrating almost exclusively on rock 'n' roll records but in fostering the impression that teenagers created the music they consumed. "The kids don't want recognized stars doing their music," he fumed. "They don't want real professionals. They want faceless people [their own age] doing it in order to retain the feeling that it's their own."

Miller insisted that consigning kids "to the land of fifth rate entertainment" was bad business. In making the argument, he discharged his anxiety and animus toward teenagers. The music had a "paralyzing monotony," he asserted. Rock 'n' roll performers had to be "whisked off" the stage after three minutes "before the natives grew restless." They denied themselves "the dignity of last names" out of an awareness of the "temporary nature of their success." Rock 'n' roll, Miller insisted, had no entertainment value for anyone over fourteen. At one and the same time, it seemed, Miller recognized, resented, and repudiated the teenage market. "It's true we need the youngsters," he told the assembled DJs, only to add that the "pre-shave crowd" holds "zero percent" of the buying power of the country.

Mitch Miller's screed was an exercise in cognitive dissonance. As demographic, economic, and cultural realities pressed themselves upon him, he clung all the more fiercely to his long-held views, arguing more by epithet and non sequitur than logic: Rock 'n' roll was "musical baby food," whose popularity would soon wane; the music's hold on listeners was evidence of "the worship of mediocrity, brought about by a passion for conformity"; teenagers appeared to present a lucrative market for records and other products, but since adulthood lasted a lot longer than adolescence, businessmen and -women should take "the long view." What strategy did this entail? To prepare the nation's youth to appreciate really good music, Miller implied, the current market for rock 'n' roll records and radio fare should be downplayed or ignored.

A much respected figure, with a long string of hits on his résumé, Miller received a polite and sympathetic hearing; his views were circulated in industry publications and the national media. Few, however, were ready to follow his advice to ignore the teens and go after "a broader, healthier audience." Pat Cowley of WKLO, Louisville, Kentucky, was a longtime Mitch Miller fan, "and I will continue to be," but was certain that "you can't go against the public, no matter how much you feel it's right!" Chuck Blore of KFWB in Los Angeles agreed. "If rock 'n' roll happens to be 50 to 75 percent of what people want, then 50 to 75 percent of our music is rock 'n' roll. When the listeners' taste changes, our music policy will reflect that change." Cowley, Blore, and their colleagues in the entertainment business had good reasons to stick with the teenage market: the baby boom guaranteed that it would grow well into the next decade, and perhaps beyond it.[43]

There was (and is) no such thing as The American Teenager, of course. Thirteen-year-olds in junior high school shared little with nineteen-year-olds in college or with a full-time job. Differences attributed to race, religion, and region, ethnicity, gender, and class bred heterogeneity in the age group as well. Some fifteen-year-olds enjoyed *Seventeen* magazine, while others were mad about *Mad*. Some liked Chuck Berry, others Pat Boone, and still others Bach, Brahms, or Brubeck. Although the concept was artificial, Dwight Macdonald pointed out that in the 1950s "statisticians treated teenagers as a separate, homogeneous class, "and . . . current usage leans that way, too." At the end of the decade, as the theory of market segmentation took hold among applied economists, a consensus on teenage culture formed as well: it might be "an absurd contradiction of irreconcilable terms," but teenage culture was almost universally recognized as "a fortress unto itself" with its own way of life.[44]

But the jury was still out on the cultural and social impact of the postwar generation. Most observers noted that teenagers had coalesced only to conform. "Employers will love this generation," Clark Kerr, head of the University of California, predicted in 1959. "They are going to be easy to handle. There aren't going to be any riots." Citing a Gallup survey indicating that 90 percent of young people in the United States were satisfied with their lives, Grace and Fred Hechinger quoted one teen as typical of her generation: "I want to be average. I have everything I want; I have security, clothes, love, a pet, a boyfriend. I wanted a typewriter; I got a typewriter." Teenage rebellion, the Hechingers stressed, was concerned with "appearances rather than substance, with intensity rather than depth." The "Frustrated Young Boys are satisfied with beach parties and temper tantrums."[45]

A few commentators sensed that the inchoate and sometimes incoherent alienation and antiauthoritarianism of teenagers might find other outlets in the 1960s. David Riesman had "the feeling" in 1959 that "the children hold the strategic initiative." Adults "will probably have to be 'nice to the kids' despite their fear and hostility," Edgar Z. Friedenberg warned, and "they will most certainly try to maintain by seduction and manipulation the dominance they previously achieved by coercion and punishment." Power had shifted, however, in American families and American society. The "loss of authority is real," Friedenberg asserted. "The adult empire is tottering. All empires are."[46]

Even the Hechingers speculated that young people might "establish new beachheads of reform." Writing after the lunch counter sit-ins and Freedom Rides in behalf of civil rights, nuclear test ban rallies, and the establishment by President Kennedy of the Peace Corps, the Hechingers saw some signs of a "readiness to 'explode out of' the private world of youth—even at the risk of discomfort." Young people who were passionate about political and social issues, they wrote, were far less likely to become the prisoners of "personal drives and undisciplined appetites—even in a society that has succumbed to these selfish preoccupations."[47]

Most young people were quiescent in the 1960s, just as Clark Kerr predicted. A significant number, however, did take up the Hechingers' challenge, combining the personal and the political as they did so. These activists were acutely aware of their membership in an "adolescent society." Its roots were in the '50s, when the relationship between youth and the modern economy changed, and mass culture, with rock 'n' roll often in the lead, invited teenagers to identify themselves as a distinct and distinctive generation.

"ROLL OVER BEETHOVEN, TELL TCHAIKOVSKY THE NEWS"

Rock 'n' Roll and the Pop Culture Wars

5

"Y ou know my temperature's rising, / the juke box is blowing a fuse," Chuck Berry proclaimed. "My heart's beating rhythm / and my soul keeps singing the blues. / Roll over Beethoven, / tell Tchaikovsky the news." The news, of course, was that rock 'n' roll was a "national pastime," a powerhouse in American popular culture. "Maybe politically and socially you were a little shaky," *Cash Box* crowed in 1957, "but man the whole music business rises, takes off its hat and salutes you." Advances in technology following World War II, including the introduction of the LP, the 45, and high fidelity, and the production of inexpensive phonographs, prepared the industry to serve a mass market. Thanks to rock 'n' roll, the customers appeared right on cue. Teenagers in the '50s purchased more records than did adults— and they bought lots of them. In the latter half of the decade, record sales nearly tripled, from $213 million in 1954 to $613 million in 1959.[1]

Rock 'n' roll also helped resuscitate radio. Unable to compete with television as a medium of family entertainment, radio replaced live musicians, comedians, and actors in soap operas with a much cheaper source of programming, rock 'n' roll records. After school and late at night, radio "narrowcasted" to teenagers, who used car radios and portable transistor radios to take the music wherever they went. Rock 'n' roll DJs became powerful figures on radio, commanding high salaries and the loyalty of listeners as arbiters of musical taste.[2]

Like radio, the motion picture industry used rock 'n' roll to fend off the challenge of television. In the 1930s and '40s, Hollywood had heroes with adolescent appeal—the Dead End Kids, Hopalong Cassidy, and Flash Gordon—but they appeared in B movies, churned out by second-rate studios llike Monogram, Republic, and Universal. Before 1956, Tom Doherty argues, executives at the major studios did not exploit, or even fully recognize, the potential of the teenage market. *Rock Around the Clock* (1956) made them sit up and take notice. While their couch potato parents stared at the small screen in suburbia, adolescents raced to theaters and drive-ins to see and hear Bill Haley, the Platters, and Alan Freed. The first box office smash targeted exclusively to teens, the film had a worldwide gross of $2.4 million, about eight times the cost of production. By the end of the year, six more rock 'n' roll pictures were in the can. Hollywood producers continued to search for blockbusters with intergenerational appeal, but rock 'n' roll had a profound and permanent impact on the industry. For producers, exhibitors, and distributors who connected with teenagers, wrote one observer in 1958, "the rewards will be fabulous in years to come."[3]

Not everyone in the entertainment industry benefited from the revolution wrought by rock 'n' roll. Members of the American Federation of Musicians, for example, were devastated by the shift from live music to platter spinning on radio. The AFM prohibited musicians from appearing on radio or television or allowing disc jockeys to use tapes or transcriptions of them without compensation. Canned music, insisted James Petrillo, president of the AFM, was inferior, "mechanical" music, beneficial only to the disc jockey and the radio station.[4]

With rock 'n' roll, the market share of record company majors dropped dramatically. Between 1946 and 1952, the majors produced all but 5 of the 162 million-selling records. By the end of 1957, the "indies" dominated the pop singles charts; two years later, they had twice as many rock 'n' roll hits as their much bigger competitors. The majors retained their virtual monopoly on albums, which were far more expensive to produce, but executives recognized that rock 'n' roll posed a threat to the bottom line. Despite a few exceptions—Elvis at RCA, Gene Vincent at Capitol, Bill Haley and Buddy Holly at

Decca, and the Big Bopper at Mercury—they decided that rock 'n' roll was a fad they could outlast, beat back, or replace. The majors tried "everything but the music," said Ahmet Ertegun, president of Atlantic Records. They tried to tempt teenagers with calypso, polka, and novelty songs. They revamped the marketing of singles and albums to reach younger listeners; they reduced delivery time to ten days after cutting; and they promoted their records more aggressively to disc jockeys. Still, the independents' success with pop singles continued into the 1960s, when the majors bought many of them.[5]

The influence of artists and repertoire men (there were no A&R women) in the large record companies helps explain the antipathy to rock 'n' roll. Senior executives in the industry, A&R men identified potential hits and matched them to the personality and style of artists under contract. Trained in middle-of-the-road music, they thought rock 'n' roll inane. "You couldn't expect a man who loved 'April in Paris,'" Ertegun explained, "to like lyrics like 'I wanna boogie your woogie' and 'Louie, Louie.'" Equally important, rock 'n' rollers had made A&R men virtually superfluous. The editors of *Cash Box* explained: "Whereas formerly to get a good sound recording, you had to gather a group of skilled musicians, a top arranger, and an experienced singer, today that is no longer necessary. A publisher can go into a tiny studio with the author usually singing his own song accompanied either by himself or by a small group, and come out with a side which . . . has the appeal to sell—and sell in large quantity." Since rock 'n' roll hits came from "areas which mature, adult people have very little contact with," A&R men were unlikely to discover hit songs or star performers. Little wonder, then, that Mitch Miller, the paradigmatic A&R man, led the charge against rock 'n' roll.[6]

With plenty of reasons to resent rock 'n' roll, AFM members and executives in the major record companies supported the declaration of war on the music by ASCAP (American Society of Composers, Authors, and Publishers), a powerful organization representing interests on Broadway, on Tin Pan Alley, and in Hollywood. Formed in 1914, ASCAP fought for the enforcement of copyright laws and the collection of royalties for its members. In the 1920s and '30s, the organization battled frequently with radio stations over fees for the recorded music that was emerging as a staple of programming. In the late '30s, ASCAP demanded a 100 percent increase in the royalty rate, from 5 percent to 10 percent of overall radio billings. When the two sides deadlocked at the end of 1940, ASCAP music was taken off the air. In anticipation of a strike, the broadcasters formed their own licensing organization, Broadcast Music Incorporated. Whereas ASCAP had been dominated by New York artists, the makers of Tin Pan Alley music, BMI took on virtually all performers, publishers, and writers, including R&B and country and western musicians. In contrast to ASCAP's complicated formula to distribute earnings, which allocated a higher percentage to more established artists and songs, BMI paid an equal sum per play. BMI also treated live and recorded performances equally and did not discriminate between performances on network radio and those on independent stations. By using national sampling to track performances, BMI enhanced the influence of listeners in the vast areas between Brooklyn and Beverly Hills. The editors of *Variety* observed that with BMI supplying music, the radio industry "finally faced the one thing it always feared, and found that ASCAP music is not indispensable." After ten months and the threat of an antitrust suit by the Justice Department, ASCAP settled the strike, on terms less favorable than it had initially proposed. BMI flourished during the 1940s and '50s, in no small measure because it represented virtually every artist associated with rock 'n' roll.[7]

By the middle of the 1950s, BMI licensed 80 percent of all music on the radio, but ASCAP refused to roll over. By charging that its rival had conspired with radio station owners and independent record company executives to foist rock 'n' roll on young listeners, ASCAP attempted to seize the aesthetic and cultural high ground. This was a fight against "low quality" music, race music, sexual license, and juvenile delinquency, BMI opponents proclaimed, as well as a struggle for control of key components of the entertainment industry. As they tapped into the animus against rock 'n' roll, ASCAPers asked unsettling questions about the relationship among the economy, entertainment, and culture in the United States. Were corporations giving Americans the entertainment they wanted? Or did they manufacture desire for an inferior, inexpensive, and subversive popular culture while maintaining the illusion of choice? Should government protect passive consumers and increase the options available to them? ASCAP helped push these questions into the public arena. The pop culture wars had a significant cultural impact. They left rock 'n' roll reeling. They also chipped away at confidence in the sovereignty of the consumer, leaving a lingering suspicion of manipulation in the mass media marketplace.[8]

In 1953, thirty-three ASCAP members, including music luminaries Alan Jay Lerner, Ira Gershwin, and Virgil Thomson, filed a $150 million lawsuit against BMI and the major radio networks. By owning BMI stock, the plaintiffs argued, the broadcasters could influence radio personnel, especially disc jockeys, to play BMI-licensed songs. As ASCAP pressed its case in court, its leaders lobbied the U.S. House of Representatives and Senate to investigate BMI for antitrust violations and to pass legislation forcing broadcasters to divest their holdings in BMI. In court and in Congress, they pointed to the popularity of rock 'n' roll as evidence of a clear and present danger to the American public.[9]

In the summer of 1957, Senator George Smathers of Florida introduced a bill "to provide that a license for a radio or television broadcasting station shall not be granted to, or held by, any person or corporation engaged directly or indirectly in the business of publishing music or of manufacturing or selling musical recordings." Drafted by ASCAP, the legislation initially drew support from both sides of the aisle: Senator John F. Kennedy, a Democrat, inserted anti-BMI editorials into the *Congressional Record;* and Senator Barry Goldwater, a Republican, proclaimed that "the airwaves of this country have been flooded with bad music since BMI was formed." A who's who in the music industry lined up to testify as the hearings on the bill began in March 1958.[10]

The first witness, Broadway librettist/lyricist Oscar Hammerstein II, insisted that the public's taste in popular music had been "artificially stimulated" by BMI in a conspiracy with radio station owners. Listeners loved the music of Cole Porter, Jerome Kern, Victor Herbert, and George Gershwin, Hammerstein averred. Their songs deserved a place in "the permanent catalogue of the nation's music." By contrast, rock 'n' roll, bebop, and "corny guitar songs" had to be played incessantly on the radio to become hits, and they "die as soon as the plug stops."[11]

Arlan Coolidge, chairman of the Department of Music at Brown University, told the subcommittee that despite increased sales of classical music and the availability of symphonic, operatic, and choral music on educational television, "the growth of a healthy music culture in the United States has been retarded." On a recent automobile trip, Coolidge had been "shocked by the perpetual blanket of banality" spewing out of his car radio: "Every advertiser knows that constant repetition of an idea gradually sinks into public consciousness." Since virtually all the music teenagers heard came from the radio and jukeboxes, their tastes were impoverished. Young people imagined that they knew what they liked and liked what they knew, but, in fact, they knew only "what was ground out by the disc jockeys. . . . They have heard the rock and roll and the cheaper music and that to them is music."

Coolidge recognized that forcing boys and girls to accept higher standards might be neither possible nor desirable, but "there must not be tacit approval of a condition which favors the cheap and restricts the worthy." Teenagers "did not come into the world with bad taste"; they would appreciate good music, if it was carefully selected and presented to them. Consequently, he urged "all action, legislative or voluntary, which would break monopolistic or near monopolistic control of the music which goes out over the radio or TV or from the coin machines."[12]

Of the supporters of the Smathers bill who appeared before the Senate subcommittee, the star witness was Vance Packard. A journalist and social critic, Packard became famous in 1957 as the author of the bestseller *The Hidden Persuaders*, a warning to consumers that advertisers had designed appeals to their subconscious motivations. Packard began his testimony where *The Hidden Persuaders* had left off: "My particular beat or field of special interest is the manipulation of people, wherever it rears its head, and it is getting to be a pretty big beat, because the professional persuaders in our society, especially the Madison Avenue brand, are becoming too powerful and too ingenious for comfort." Packard believed that some of the fundamental freedoms of Americans, "key tenets of our American creed cherished by our Founding Fathers," including the dignity of the individual, freedom from conformity, and freedom of choice, were "being nibbled away" by rapacious corporate interests. Through subliminal messages "Americans are being standardized, homogenized, hypnotized, and sterilized."

These concerns, Packard claimed, led him to an investigation of popular culture in general, and music in particular: "My interest in the manipulation of musical taste arose before I ever heard of any dispute between the songwriters and the broadcasters. I have no interest in that dispute; I wouldn't even know how a tune is composed. In fact, I can't even carry a tune." Packard then invoked the racial, sexual, and generational disputes swirling around rock 'n' roll in the 1950s in a blistering bombardment of BMI.

The broadcasters used their "privileged position of power" in radio to generate a demand for the music in which they had a financial stake. The cheapest types of music available to them, Packard reiterated, were rock 'n' roll, hillbilly music, and Latin American music. That virtually all of this music was BMI controlled was no coincidence. The broadcasters flooded the airways "with whining guitarists, musical riots put to a switchblade beat, obscene lyrics about hugging, squeezing, and rocking all night long." Rock 'n' roll was "inspired by what has been called race music modified to stir the animal instinct in teenagers. Its chief characteristics now are a heavy, unrelenting beat and a raw, savage tone. The lyrics tend to be either nonsensical or lewd, or both. Rock and roll might best be summed up as monotony tinged with hysteria." Intent on manufacturing a market for low-cost music, the conspirators "would be willing, I am convinced, to drive us all back to the dark ages of music, if necessary, in order to achieve their goal, and frankly, judging from the present state of the music I hear my children listening to on their radios, the broadcasters wouldn't have to drive us very much further."

Having failed "to lure respectable songwriters" to BMI, the leaders of the organization decided to "fish the rock 'n' roll lake for all it was worth." They discovered that rock 'n' roll songs were "simple in the extreme to compose." "Peggy Sue," Packard pointed out, consists of nineteen short lines, in which the girl's name is repeated eighteen times. Even more telling was the composition and performance history of "Hound Dog." The song had been "scribbled out in pencil on ordinary paper" and handed to a singer moments before the recording session began. The musicians, who had also been given no time to rehearse, improvised a rhythmic background. Rock 'n' roll surged, Packard concluded, only after RCA Victor and BMI "bought up for $40,000 the contract of a pallid, sullen young man named Elvis Presley." They drummed the music into the minds of millions of impressionable teenagers using "the parlor psychological treatment of reiteration and reiteration." Soon after their greatest coup, exposure on prime-time TV for "Elvis and his restless pelvis, . . . rock and roll became a mass mania . . . from which we still haven't recovered." BMI and its allies had lined their pockets by creating "a new musical trend in America." Through "intensive plugging," they made rock 'n' roll appear to be the music young Americans loved to listen to.[13]

After fourteen supporters of the Smathers bill completed their testimony, BMI and its allies presented a spirited rebuttal. *Variety* reported that the polished BMI performance "was designed as a counterbalance against the ASCAP testimony—lawyer against lawyer, publisher against publisher, composer against composer, singer against singer." Among its twenty-four witnesses, BMI included operators of small radio stations, spokesmen for the motion picture industry, and constituents of every member of the Senate Commerce Committee. Ironically, the defenders of rock 'n' roll, not the traditionalists at ASCAP, wrapped themselves in the ideology of free market capitalism, consumer choice, and opposition to censorship. The witnesses dismissed the claim that rock 'n' roll had been foisted on the public as the whine of men and women unable to meet the popular demand of the contemporary market.[14]

Several witnesses took advantage of openings Vance Packard unwittingly had given them. Packard's denigration of hillbilly music alarmed politicians who knew how much southerners loved it. After all, as early as 1954 Democrat Adlai Stevenson had given a talk at a ceremony honoring Jimmie Rodgers, and a young Republican representative named Howard Baker had offered a resolution in the Tennessee legislature calling for a weeklong celebration of country and western music. Not surprisingly, then, Governor Frank Clement of Tennessee sent the subcommittee a telegram denouncing Packard's comments as "a gratuitous insult to thousands of our fellow Tennesseans." When BMI represented writers and publishers of country music, Clement pointed out, they helped make Nashville "one of the major music capitals of the world." Senator Albert Gore, an amateur fiddler himself, added that country music expressed the hopes and aspirations of the "pioneer stock" of mountain people of Tennessee: "I would not like to see all country music branded intellectually cheap." Gore threatened a floor fight if the bill cleared the subcommittee. As Gore fulminated, an ASCAP witness remarked, "If you attack country music, you attack southern womanhood, I see."[15]

Mae Boren Axton continued the attack on Packard. The writer of "Heartbreak Hotel," Axton lived in Florida, George Smathers's home state. A well-dressed mother of two, a schoolteacher, active in her church and community, married to a teacher, coach, and athletic director, Mrs. Axton asked subcommittee members to "judge for yourselves whether people like me, who wrote compositions called rock 'n' roll music, are really the villains we have been painted." She doubted that Packard was "qualified to understand why teenagers like rock 'n' roll music" and was horrified at accusations that she or any other person associated with BMI or rock 'n' roll "had deliberately and callously either caused or contributed to juvenile delinquency." If such allegations were true, she said, "I certainly would be a modern Dr. Jekyll and Mr. Hyde."[16]

Sydney Kaye, chairman of the board of BMI, insisted that additional government regulation of the music industry was unnecessary and harmful. The evidence of a conspiracy in restraint of trade cited by ASCAP, he told the senators, was "so irrelevant, so trivial, so easily susceptible of explanation" that it lacked "not only individual but cumulative probative force." BMI would plead guilty only to "the guilt of competition." Indeed, Kaye charged, it was ASCAP that had a long record of monopolistic practice. In contrast to ASCAP's tight restrictions on accepting new members, BMI adopted "an open door policy." Had not cowboy singer Gene Autry learned that it was easier to get an invitation to the White House than an ASCAP membership card? Before BMI was formed, about 1,100 writers and 137 publishers shared revenues from performing rights. In 1956, over 6,000 writers and almost 3,500 publishers did so.

Virtually all broadcasting stations, Kaye pointed out, had agreements with both ASCAP and BMI. For a fee, the radio stations could play, as frequently as they wished, any music licensed by these organizations. Broadcasters did not make or save money by choosing the music of one to the exclusion of the other. Kaye flatly denied that BMI and the broadcasters manipulated the music market. That BMI was responsible for more than twice as many pop hits as ASCAP was easy to explain: the latter refused to respond to changes in the musical marketplace or to represent artists with a contemporary sound. In what by 1958 was a familiar refrain, Kaye observed that every generation criticized the taste of young listeners, whether they enjoyed the waltz, jazz, ragtime, or the tango. "You can't catch up with public taste," he concluded. Since every radio station sought to please its audience, broadcasters would not discriminate even if they wanted to: "Music for programs is selected by tens of thousands of persons" through polls, purchases, and call-ins to DJs. In the fullness of time, good music endures and fads fade: "All we do is take what comes— we don't try to act as censors."[17]

From the outset, it was clear that most senators subscribed to the free market position staked out by BMI. Perhaps sensing that ASCAP had failed to stir up public pressure for regulation, Smathers lived up to his reputation as a lazy legislator, appearing only twice in the hearing room. The members of the subcommittee could eat their cake and have it, too, by expressing personal distaste for rock 'n' roll while endorsing the status quo in the name of unencumbered consumer choice.[18]

Owning a network and promoting a product, Senator A. S. (Mike) Monroney of Oklahoma told an ASCAP witness, "are as normal as ham and eggs in our great American system of ballyhoo." Along with Professor Coolidge, Monroney lamented the decision of NBC television to take the *Voice of Firestone*, a fine music program, off the air. But the decision to cancel, the senator observed, came because its ratings were not high enough to merit a spot on the network. It had nothing to do with the use of "BMI music versus ASCAP." Nor was it made, as Coolidge suggested, because jukebox and radio station owners were plugging rock 'n' roll. As long as advertisers made ratings their Sermon on the Mount, Monroney believed, "the radio and television diet of America is decided, not on what will lift up America but what will sell more soap or more deodorants."[19]

As he presided over the hearings, Senator John Pastore of Rhode Island kept ASCAP from appropriating rock 'n' roll for its own ends. At times he acted like an attorney for the defense. He elicited from Vance Packard an admission that his research had been commissioned and paid for by the Songwriters Protective Association, an ASCAP affiliate. Pastore agreed that through music "you can reach the fine innate nature of an individual," but in exchanges with virtually every ASCAP witness, he asserted that the Congress should not—and probably could not—improve the quality of music by regulating the entertainment industry. "I don't like rock 'n' roll too much," Pastore told Oscar Hammerstein II, "but there are a lot of people who do. And I don't think it is within the province of Congress to tell people whether they should listen to *South Pacific*, or listen to some rock 'n' roll." Congress should intervene only to keep obscene music from the airwaves—and legislation on this subject was already on the books.

Rock 'n' roll, Pastore implied, did not present a danger so clear and present that it justified constraints on consumer choice. "Now, I don't mean to be impertinent," the senator said to Professor Coolidge, "but if the stamping of the feet is the result of the music that a child is listening to and induces that child to buy more bubble gum, what does the Congress do about it? . . . What do we do about it?" Congress cannot dictate to a record company executive, a radio station manager, or a jukebox operator "as to the kind of music he is going to play, no more than I can tell that man what kind of coffee he is going to sell."

Pastore did not buy the argument that BMI and the broadcasters had created in teenagers a taste for rock 'n' roll. He asked Coolidge to "look at it objectively," posing a series of questions that betrayed his own point of view: "Do you think that a disc jockey played rock 'n' roll because he wants that child to hear rock 'n' roll or because he thinks that child wants to hear rock 'n' roll? . . . Why does this child want to hear rock 'n' roll instead of Beethoven? What does a disc jockey have to do with it?" The senator believed that the ASCAP witnesses underestimated the intelligence of the American people: "I mean it is not that pliable." Neither teenage nor adult listeners suspended their own judgment just "because eight disc jockeys get together to push a song." Even if Congress passed the Smathers bill, Pastore pointed out, "you would have rock 'n' roll blared as long as any disc jockey was willing to play it and we couldn't stop him."[20]

Pastore refused ASCAP's request for three days to refute the BMI testimony rather than the one that had been scheduled. When John Schulman, general counsel of the Songwriters Protective Association, read a twenty-four-page statement of rebuttal, the senator interrupted him frequently, once to take issue with disparaging remarks about Leiber and Stoller's "Yakety Yak." Pastore's daughter Louise enjoyed the record, he said, and so did many, many young people. When Judge Samuel Rosenman rebutted the rebutters on behalf of BMI, Pastore listened attentively. "Never in my experience," Rosenman declared, "have I seen such sweeping charges made against so many people with such flimsy evidence."

As he closed the hearings, Pastore revealed the results of his own "freedom of music on the air" test. He had called several local radio stations requesting a performance of the ASCAP song "Louise" to celebrate his daughter's birthday. Although the senator had not identified himself, every disc jockey complied. So much for a conspiracy to exclude ASCAP. Pastore believed that the regulations ASCAP proposed would harm thousands of singers, musicians, and songwriters and the owners of small independent stations, throwing "every Tom, Dick and Harry into the soup," and they would have little or no impact on the quality of music available to listeners.[21]

The Smathers bill was dead, but the battle between BMI and ASCAP raged on. With the "payola" revelations of 1959–1960, opponents of BMI, disc jockeys, and rock 'n' roll gained the upper hand. Indeed it seemed at the time that the scandal had delivered a lethal blow to rock 'n' roll.

The term "payola" was coined by *Variety* in 1938 to refer to gifts, favors, or cash surreptitiously dispensed by record companies to get orchestra leaders and disc jockeys to play their songs. By the 1950s, influential disc jockeys were receiving hundreds of records to listen to every month. Payola was a good way to get their attention. For the indies, which had modest marketing budgets, it was often the only way to promote rhythm and blues and rock 'n' roll records. "Payola to disc jockeys is at an all-time peak," *Billboard* reported early in the decade. Some DJs preferred a flat-rate deal of $50 to $100 per record, while others negotiated a percentage of sales. When one distributor refused to pay because a disc jockey had deals with five other companies, his label's records suddenly disappeared from the airwaves. A company trouble-shooter settled the "strike" by pressing several greenbacks into the hands of the DJ.[22]

Payola was an open secret. Industry insiders disagreed only about its scope and significance. Disc jockeys, of course, denied that they themselves received payola and claimed that only underpaid spinners employed in the backwaters of radio paid for play. Payola could wreck the career of a disc jockey, they maintained, because popularity depended on giving the public what it wanted. The "DJ who lets his interest lapse," wrote the music-radio editor of *Billboard*, "is in danger of having the field pass him by. He will be outpaced by more alert DJs who are quicker to sense the public's music taste and who are hip to the developing and overlapping music patterns." For this reason, Alan Freed insisted he would not "take a dime to plug a record. I'd be a fool to; I'd be giving up control of my program."[23]

Some DJs were not so sanguine. Art Ford of WNEW in New York supported the establishment of a policing board composed of disc jockeys and distributors to "weed out the black sheep." Bill Randle, an influential spinner at WERE in Cleveland, believed that payola was a multimillion-dollar business. He had no proof that the hundred top disc jockeys were acting in concert, or were in the pocket of the record companies, but "it has to be accepted that somehow . . . they seem to react the same toward tunes, artists etc." Reluctant to condemn his colleagues, Randle also claimed that payola was neither more pervasive nor more dangerous than similar practices in other areas. It was "ridiculous," he concluded, to think that even a well-placed bribe could buy a hit or make a singer a star.[24]

It could help a lot, though. It was "axiomatic in the music business," Paul Ackerman wrote in *The Nation*, that a "bad" (i.e., commercially unappealing) song could not be made a hit, no matter how much it was plugged, but a "good" song needed extensive airplay to "achieve its hit potential." Manufacturers, distributors of records, and disc jockeys all too often accepted payola as a necessary if not sufficient condition in anointing a song worthy of the attention of listeners.[25]

In the early '50s, music industry publications warned record companies and radio stations that if they did not clean house they would face a crisis of public confidence and possible government regulation. Closely allied with Tin Pan Alley, *Variety* deemed payola a "Frankenstein," rampant in rhythm and blues and country music. A normal operating expense for the "indies," payola had forced the majors to make deals with disc jockeys "to unload their merchandise." *Billboard* in 1951 saw little prospect of a cure. Even *Cash Box*, with its close ties to R&B and country and western music, acknowledged that "some disc jockeys . . . can be had for anything from a can of beans to a Cadillac." Insisting that most platter spinners were honest, *Cash Box* called for a moratorium on vague stories about payola but vigorous prosecution of anyone who betrayed the public trust.[26]

A few radio stations took steps to restrict payola. In 1952, WFMS distributed a booklet to its employees calling payola a "monster" and promising to dismiss any announcer who engaged in the practice. DJs were enjoined from mentioning the labels of records or from expressing their own opinions about them: "The audience is not interested whether it is a Capitol, Decca, Columbia, or Victor release. It is interested in the selection and the artist."[27]

To limit payola and reduce the power of disc jockeys, many stations adopted the Top Forty format. Introduced by Todd Storz at KOWH in Omaha and then WTIX in New Orleans, Top Forty limited DJs to songs on the *Billboard* charts, with only a few slots available to new releases or personal preferences. The format relied much less on the discretion and, for that matter, the personality of the disc jockey. Top Forty quickly became popular because many listeners liked to hear their favorite songs played over and over again. A Top Forty program style, with a playlist limited to mainstream pop singles, interrupted by station identification, news broadcasts, and commercials, spread throughout the nation during the decade.[28]

Efforts to eliminate payola, however, remained halfhearted and ineffective. The major record companies as well as the independents came to accept it as a cost of doing business, and not a terribly substantial one at that. Implicated in the practice themselves, they had no incentive to blow the whistle. Moreover, many in the music industry viewed payola as a victimless crime, having little or no impact on consumer choice. They noticed that the public continued to buy millions of records, despite a spate of articles about pay for play in *Newsweek*, *Time*, and other mainstream magazines.

So, in the mid-'50s, the brouhaha over payola faded a bit. At the Smathers hearings, ASCAP attorney Seymour Lazar pronounced payola part of BMI's corrupt plot to promote its music, but the charge did not give him the traction he desired. Under questioning by Senator Pastore, he admitted that the major labels did not favor BMI music and that, at most, there was a "potential danger" to ASCAP. When record promoter Bob Stern offered to refute Lazar's testimony about the pervasiveness of payola, Pastore felt no need to reply to him, let alone invite him to appear.[29]

All that changed with the quiz show scandals of 1958–1959. Television producers Jack Barry and Dan Enright, investigators revealed, had conspired with the sponsor, Revlon, to "fix" the game shows *The $64,000 Question* and *Twenty-One*. They had supplied contestants who were audience favorites with the correct answers, coaching them to pause, cogitate, grimace, stammer, and wipe their brows before supplying them. To portray Herbert Stempel as a struggling ex-GI, Barry and Enright outfitted the graduate student from New York City in a marine-style haircut, a loose-fitting double-breasted suit, a shirt with a frayed collar, and a cheap watch, with a tick loud enough to mark the tense moments in the isolation booth. When Stempel proved to be too nerdy and nervous to connect with viewers, the producers forced him to lose to the young man "you'd love to have your daughter marry," handsome, suave Charles Van Doren, an English instructor at Columbia University, descended from a long line of distinguished American intellectuals. Angry that he was cast aside, outraged that he had had to give the wrong answer when he knew the right one (that *Marty* won the Academy Award for the Best Picture of 1955), Stempel took his story to the authorities, and the scam unraveled. Van Doren confessed that he had been "involved, deeply involved, in a deception." When Barry and Enright told investigators that "deception is not necessarily bad . . . it's practiced in everyday life," some observers declared that American innocence had ended. Others condemned the cynical immorality imbedded in corporate capitalism. The quiz show hoax, President Eisenhower proclaimed, was a "terrible thing" to do to the American people. "Have We Gone Soft?" John Steinbeck asked in a letter reprinted in *The New Republic*: "If I wanted to destroy a nation I would give it too much and I would have it on its knees, miserable, greedy, and sick." Convinced that "on all levels, American society is rigged," Steinbeck wondered whether it could survive.[30]

The quiz show scandals provided the opening (and the audience) opponents of BMI and rock 'n' roll had been looking for. That Barry and Enright owned several radio stations helped make the connection between payola and the rigging of game shows even easier to make. Equally sensational were allegations that at a convention at the Americana Hotel in Miami Beach, Florida, in May 1959 record companies spent $117,664 to entertain disc jockeys. Prostitutes were flown in from Chicago to service the jocks. Informed of the mayhem in Miami, the Special Subcommittee on Legislative Oversight of the House of Representatives, chaired by Oren Harris of Arkansas, launched "the first exhaustive probe of the entire music industry in the history of America." Meanwhile, the Internal Revenue Service intensified its investigations of the tax returns of dozens of influential DJs. ASCAP, *Variety* reported, took credit for "shifting the spotlight from the TV quiz rigging to the disc jockey payola." Politicians panting for publicity probably needed little prodding, but ASCAP lobbyists did play a role in focusing their attention on DJs, small record companies, and rock 'n' roll. Left relatively untouched were A&R men and the major labels, whom ASCAP needed to help restore "high quality" music.[31]

A few observers understood what was going on. "Cynics in broadcasting wonder whether the disc jockeys are not relatively small fry when it comes to payoffs," wrote Jack Gould in the *New York Times*. They had been singled out, he explained, by "the writers of Broadway and Hollywood hit tunes—who have been dismayed to witness the dominance of rock 'n' roll on the nation's airwaves." The editors of *Billboard* agreed: "Many frustrated music men—out of step with current song and recording trends—see in the present goings on a chance to return to a position of eminence."[32]

Many radio station owners, however, decided to sacrifice their DJs to ensure that their licenses would be renewed. Others took advantage of the scandal to settle scores, clean house, or reduce expenses. One of the first disc jockeys to go was Tom Clay of WJBK in Detroit. As his popularity with teenagers soared, Clay, whose annual salary was $8,000, was approached by record distributors. "I never told a person he had to pay me to get records played," Clay claimed. "They asked me to take money. Were they wrong, or good businessmen?" In eighteen months he pocketed $5,000 or $6,000. Apparently, the manager at WJBK learned in August 1959 that the DJ had accepted payola, warned him, but took no action. But when the House of Representatives announced its investigation, Clay was fired.[33]

The bloodletting continued, as the subcommittee staff announced that payola was "all over the place." Joe Niagara of WBIG in Philadelphia resigned abruptly after a meeting with the management of the station. WXYZ in Detroit canned Mickey Shorr, who had allegedly accepted a $2,000 loan from a local rock group, the Royal Tones. Stan Richards, Bill Marlowe, and Joe Smith, three of the most popular DJs at WILD in Boston, were let go. So were four jocks at WCMS in Norfolk, Virginia, after they played the record "Pahalacaka" over and over, some 320 times in one day, to prove that listeners would not embrace a bad record no matter how much airtime it received.[34]

As the scandal fed on itself, state prosecutors got into the act. On the books in several states, but rarely used, commercial bribery statutes appeared to make payola a violation of the law. The most vigorous activity occurred in New York, the home of ASCAP, where district attorney Frank S. Hogan subpoenaed the financial records of eleven companies and several disc jockeys. Among his targets was King Records, an "indie" based in Cincinnati. Promising full cooperation, the president of King, Sydney Nathan, admitted that he paid more than a dozen DJs, some of them in New York, as much as $100 a month to play the company's records. The payments, which had ceased "many months ago," had been made openly, by check, because King did not regard payola as a violation of the law. "It is a dirty rotten mess," Nathan told prosecutors, "and it has been getting worse and worse in the last five years. It is getting so you can't get your records played unless you pay."

In 1960, Hogan indicted five disc jockeys, two radio station record librarians, and one program director on misdemeanor violations of the commercial bribery statute. The defendants, the district attorney claimed, had accepted payola for a decade but because of the statute of limitations could be charged only with receipt of bribes from twenty-three record manufacturers and distributors totaling $116,850 over the last two years. The "chief offenders" among the record companies were all "indies": Alpha Distributing, Superior Record Sales, Roulette Records, and Cosnat Distributing. Significantly, Hogan took no action against any of the companies, arguing that it was common practice to prosecute only one party to an alleged bribery and to give immunity to the others to get them to testify. He won several high-profile convictions; equally important, most of the DJs were fired as they awaited trial.[35]

The Federal Communications Commission and the Federal Trade Commission moved against payola as well. FCC commissioner Robert E. Lee declared the practice "a sneaky commercial" that violated the requirement that paid sponsors be identified. The FCC directed all 5,236 radio and television outlets to submit sworn statements indicating whether any employees had taken cash or gifts in exchange for on-the-air plugs during the last year. Licensees were also required to set forth actions taken to prevent payola from occurring in the future. Station owners found chilling the implication left by the FCC that they might be responsible for the actions of disc jockeys, even if they were not aware of them.[36]

In a twenty-page brief to the FCC, ASCAP president Stanley Adams asserted that the practice of payola "goes much deeper than a few 'isolated' cases." At least 146 of the 277 Top Fifty hits of 1959, Adams charged, benefited from play for pay. To combat the practice, ASCAP advocated prohibiting radio stations from accepting any remuneration in exchange for playing a musical composition. ASCAP also revived its suggestion, aimed at BMI, that the FCC order broadcasters to relinquish financial interests in "performance rights" organizations. In March 1960, the FCC ruled that many stations had failed to comply with Section 317 of the Communications Act of 1934, which required stations to mention on the air any material that had been furnished to them for free. Acknowledging that noncompliance may have resulted from ambiguities in the statute, the commission put stations on notice that they could no longer evade punishment by pleading reliance on "accepted industry practices."

The National Association of Broadcasters denounced the FCC ruling. Broadcasters now had a Hobson's choice: clog the airwaves with self-incriminating announcements or purchase all of their records. Acknowledging that payola was bad, the NAB nonetheless insisted that the receipt of free records by a broadcasting station did not destroy "that station's objectivity in making its determination as to which music should be aired." One industry executive called the regulation "ridiculous. It is like demanding that the *Saturday Review* or the *New York Times Literary Supplement* pay for the books they're going to review." If stations had to buy all of their records, the impact would fall disproportionately on independent broadcasters and record companies. Only a few radio stations could afford to spend $10,000 to $20,000 to stock new releases. Many small stations would take fewer chances, sticking with the heavily promoted records of the major labels. The regulations victimized the listening public, the NAB concluded, since the variety of music available to them would be reduced.[37]

The Federal Trade Commission assigned forty staff members to the payola investigation. By August 1960, the FTC had charged 106 record manufacturers and distributors with deceptive acts or practices designed to "suppress competition and to divert trade unfairly from their competitors." FTC chairman Earl Kintner estimated that an "exceedingly high percentage" of the nation's 256 distributors and 481 record labels used payola as a "standard commercial procedure." The most pervasive practice involved payments to disc jockeys to play records repeatedly. Most of the defendants readily acknowledged making payola payments but denied that they had broken the law. "Sure we paid disc jockeys," a spokesman for one distributor told reporters. "We met competition. Every company was involved in one way or another. We merely fought the battle to sell records, and that was to pay some of the bigger disc jockeys." No one had been defrauded, another distributor maintained: not only was the number of plays per day no guarantee of public acceptance, but "as there is no objective standard to determine the superiority of one record over another, there is no deception."

In the end, virtually all of the defendants signed consent decrees, claiming no crime had been committed but promising, in effect, that they would not do it again. By 1961, Kintner believed that payola had been "pretty well stamped out." John T. Walker, assistant to the director of litigation at the FTC, agreed. Walker congratulated the "big manufacturers" for their efforts to eradicate payola, and if others "were slipping around, I think we'd hear about it from competitors." The FTC had no jurisdiction over disc jockeys, but its investigators believed that at least 255 DJs or other radio station employees in fifty-six cities in twenty-six states had taken payola. FTC files on all disc jockeys were turned over to the FCC, the IRS, and the House subcommittee.[38]

The full force of all of these institutions of the federal government fell on Alan Freed. As the editors of *Cash Box* noted, he "suffered the most and was perhaps singled out for alleged wrongs that had become a business way-of-life for many others." Present at the creation, Freed remained a poster boy for rock 'n' roll, a cheerleader for many controversial performers, including Chuck Berry and Jerry Lee Lewis. Arrogant and argumentative, even when he hadn't had too much to drink, Freed was easy to portray as a wild, greedy, and dangerous man. After all, his critics pointed out, he had been indicted for inciting a riot in the Boston Arena in 1958, when he told an already restive teenage audience that the police "don't want you to have a good time." Freed's past and present as the "founding father" of rock 'n' roll explains the vigor and vindictiveness so evident in his pursuit and prosecution. The payola probe was payback time, an opportunity to eviscerate rock 'n' roll, its institutional infrastructure, and its principal proponents. Freed became payola's first fatality, an object lesson for the music industry.[39]

There is no doubt that Freed played for pay. On the very day Charles Van Doren confessed on national television, Freed made a "new arrangement" with four distributors of the records he would play on his radio and television programs. From the new releases his clients sent, Freed would select a "Pick of the Week," a "Sleeper of the Week," and a "Spotlight Song of the Week." To cover his tracks, he asked that future payments be made in cash. But Freed had already left a paper trail. When the payola scandal broke, the management of ABC sent all disc jockeys a questionnaire about payments received for playing records and financial holdings in "any music publishing, recording, or merchandising concern." Freed had told his superiors at the network when he signed his contract in 1958 that he had interests in the music business. A year later, they sought plausible deniability. Asked repeatedly, "Are you going to sign? Everybody's signing it," the disc jockey refused. But if Dick Clark signed the affidavit, Freed promised, he would follow suit.

To break the stalemate, Freed sent a letter to ABC, branding the payola affidavit "improper and uncalled for." Although from "time to time" Freed had invested in various music ventures, all of them "a matter of public record and common knowledge," he had zealously protected the quality and integrity of his radio program. Freed's intransigence helped seal his fate at the network. Whether he signed or not, an official at ABC told Freed's lawyer, "he is fired." On November 22, 1959, Ben Hoberman, manager of WABC radio, dismissed the DJ. Declaring that the decision had nothing to do with payola, he declined to elaborate, citing only the "contractual rights" of the station.

The next day Freed learned that WNEW-TV would also let him go. "We want to do it nicely," Bennett Korn, the station's general manager, told the DJ. The decision "by mutual consent" to terminate Freed's contract was unrelated to payola, Korn informed reporters: "At no time did we suspect he did anything wrong." The parting of the ways had been "long in coming," a consequence of differences over payment of guests on Freed's *Big Beat Heat* program and WNEW's desire "to

control our own show." On November 27, Freed interrupted Little
Anthony and the Imperials' rendition of "Shimmy Shimmy Ko Ko
Bop" to announce his "resignation" from *Big Beat Heat*. Sobbing, he
maintained he had done nothing wrong, but then added: "Payola may
stink, but it's here and I didn't start it. . . . I know a lot of ASCAP
publishers who will be glad I'm off the air." At a press conference that
night, the embattled DJ admitted that he had taken gifts in exchange
for playing records and had been paid by record companies and
distributors for "consultation work." He called these activities "the
backbone of American business."

The target of the New York district attorney, the FBI, the IRS, the
New York State attorney general, and the House Special Subcommittee on Legislative Oversight, the unemployed DJ was so tense "he
couldn't sit down," his ex-wife remembered. "For the first time in his
life he felt total panic. . . . He didn't know which way to turn." Freed
alternated between despair and an alcohol-enhanced bravado. In an
ill-advised interview with columnist Earl Wilson of the *New York Post*,
he made more damaging admissions. Would he accept a Cadillac
offered by a record company? Wilson asked. It would "depend on the
color," Freed replied. He would not take the car as a quid pro quo for
playing a record but would be "an idiot" if he refused a gift after having
done someone "a hell of a turn, inadvertently helping a company by
playing a record for it." Freed also implied that he was about to blow
the whistle on several prominent people, including Dick Clark: "he's
on 300 stations. I'm on one. . . . If I'm going to be a scapegoat, he's
going to be one, too."

Everyone who knew him well recognized that Freed was a broken
man. Still a marquee name, Freed managed to get some work in the
next two years, at KDAY radio in Los Angeles and WQAM in Miami.
But at each job he was fired soon after he was hired. "Often a moody
and injudicious man off radio," journalist Bob Rolontz observed, Freed
"became more so as his fortunes plunged downward." In 1964, a
federal grand jury indicted Freed for evading income taxes between
1957 and 1959. The charges involved failure to report as income the
payola "he received for pushing records."

Bankrupt, despondent, and frequently drunk, Freed relocated to
Palm Springs, California. He spent his last days alone, telephoning
colleagues in the music business to ask for money to cover his rent

and grocery bills. On January 20, 1965, Alan Freed died of uremic poisoning, a condition caused by failure of the kidneys.[40]

While Alan Freed was payola's first fatality, Dick Clark perfected the politics of personal preservation. With close ties to the ABC television network (he was the producer as well as the host of *American Bandstand*) and several major record companies, Clark was too valuable a commodity to lose. If Freed was unpredictable, Clark was pliable. If Freed was associated with African-American performers and an edgier rock 'n' roll, Clark was willing to sell his teenage audiences a more mainstream musical fare. An entrepreneur building a music industry empire, Clark installed himself as a silent partner in music publishing and record distribution companies, with stock worth hundreds of thousands of dollars, while DJs indulged in penny-ante practices of payola. Part of the music establishment, Dick Clark was protected by the music establishment.

When the payola scandal broke, Leonard Goldenson, chief executive officer of ABC, summoned Clark to his office. Clark flatly denied that he had taken any payola but told Goldenson, defiantly at first, that he had interests in music publishing, manufacturing, and distribution: "I make a little bit of money, where am I going to invest it? I don't know anything about the hot dog business. . . . Why shouldn't I invest in the music business?" Unmoved, Goldenson gave his TV star a "pistol to your head" ultimatum: sell his music-related holdings or resign from ABC. Clark chose divestment.

As soon as Clark made his decision, Goldenson helped shield him from the authorities. Unlike any other employee of ABC, including Alan Freed, Clark prepared his own payola affidavit. The document defined payola narrowly, as an explicit agreement between a disc jockey and another person to play a particular record. Informed that Tony Mammarella, Clark's right-hand man at *American Bandstand*, had taken money from seven companies for "advice" about "overcoming deficiencies in their distribution," Clark and Goldenson added a paragraph to the affidavit to distance themselves from him: "Early yesterday morning one of my programming associates revealed to me certain information which he had concealed from me. I had no previous knowledge or suspicion of these facts. His resignation has been accepted."

On November 18, 1959, a few days before Freed was fired, ABC issued a statement exonerating Clark and expressing complete confidence in him. After examining "all available evidence," the management of the network believed that "he has neither solicited nor accepted any personal considerations, money or otherwise, to have any performer appear, or to play records, on any of his programs." The statement added that Clark had voluntarily divested himself of all music-related holdings to conform with the new policy at the network. After reading the statement to reporters, Clark expressed appreciation "that the people I work for stand behind me." As he spoke, musicians struck up "Bandstand Boogie," Clark's theme song, and teenagers in the audience applauded.

ABC had not, in fact, investigated Clark's guilt or innocence or his holdings in the music business. The network had taken its star at his word. A month after ABC's exoneration, the *New York Post* reported that Clark retained interests "in almost every phase of the music industry." Asked whether Clark had fully divested, ABC vice president Michael Foster replied: "I'm damned if I know. . . . I doubt if anyone [at the network] knows." Despite this uncertainty—and an FTC accusation of payola infractions against Jamie Records, in which Clark had a substantial interest—ABC gave him a raise in January 1960. The network brass noticed that *American Bandstand*'s ratings were strong, the support of its sponsors steadfast. And they knew that the television shows he hosted brought in more than $5 million in advertising revenue, almost 5 percent of the network's total billings.

A few months later, Clark caught another break. In Philadelphia, district attorney Victor Blanc issued thirty-nine summonses to DJs and record company personnel for alleged payola infractions. Among the targets were Chips Distributing and Jamie Records, two firms in which Clark had invested. Since, by accident or design, Clark was not a corporate officer in either of these companies, he escaped Blanc's scrutiny. In his probe of local radio stations, moreover, Blanc exempted WFIL—Clark's station—because the FCC and the FTC had given it a clean bill of health. Stating publicly that Clark was "not involved" in his investigation, Blanc asked him to chair a group helping DJs to avoid entanglements with payola.

In June, ABC released a brief press biography of Clark, celebrating his rapid rise "to the top of the entertainment industry," his six weekly shows for the network, his fan mail, and his forty million viewers. No mention was made of payola. In September, Walter Annenberg's *TV Guide* (Annenberg's Triangle Publications owned the rights to

American Bandstand) ran a cover story about the DJ, "Guilty Only of Success." Claiming that he was "all talked out" about payola, Clark told *TV Guide*, "I was exonerated. I like to leave it at that."[41]

Clark was not indicted, nor was he convicted of a payola-related crime. In his poised and polished testimony before the House Special Subcommittee on Legislative Oversight in the spring of 1960, Clark "wiggled off each baited hook flung out" by his interrogators. But no subcommittee member exonerated him of complicity in the deceptive practices of the entertainment industry. Instead, along with much of the press, several congressmen suggested that he was up to his eyeballs in "Clarkola." With rock 'n' roll as their prime example, they concluded as well that a few corporate moguls "rigged" the music market in the United States.[42]

In his testimony before the subcommittee, punctuated frequently with "I cannot recall" and "it is difficult to say," Anthony Mammarella refused to implicate his former boss in any wrongdoing. Other witnesses, however, did not hesitate to do so. Angry that ABC had made him a "sacrificial lamb," Alan Freed told the subcommittee that when it came to payola he was a "piker" compared with Clark. By defining payola so narrowly in his affidavit, Freed pointed out, Clark permitted himself to deny that he played for pay. As commonly practiced, payola consisted of winks and nods, and payments in anticipation of or shortly after a plug. Under the definition of the document Clark drafted, Freed, too, was "as clean as the driven snow."[43]

Even more damaging to Clark was the testimony of Harry Finfer, vice president of two Philadelphia-based companies, Jamie Records and Universal Record Distributing, who had promoted songs to *American Bandstand* for years. Finfer told the subcommittee he had paid Mammarella for listening to records, and giving advice about them and had sent $500 as a gift in honor of his newborn child. In June 1957, because of Clark's "expert knowledge of records," Finfer and his partners at Jamie allowed the TV DJ to become a 25 percent owner of the company by purchasing 125 shares of stock for $125. Clark had helped Jamie get off the ground by playing Duane Eddy's "Moving and Grooving" and inviting the guitarist to appear on his show. He then guided Eddy "in various releases he put out with him." Starting in July 1959 (but retroactive to May 1958), Clark received a $200-a-week salary from the company as well "for giving Jamie the benefit of his

Dick Clark told the House Special Subcommittee on Legislative Oversight that he might have favored records in which he had a financial interest "without realizing it." *(Bettman/Corbis)*

advice and experience with respect to the sale of records." When ABC ordered Clark to divest himself of his holdings in music-related companies in November 1959, three major shareholders of Jamie purchased his stock for $15,000.[44]

As careful as Finfer to avoid acknowledging a quid pro quo to pay for play, several other witnesses indicated that they had assigned song copyrights to Clark or a company with which he was associated. Clark, it turned out, held 162 copyrights, 145 of which he had received gratis. George Goldner, majority stockholder in Real Gone Music and N Music, was responsible for four of them. When he assigned the copyrights of "Could This Be Magic," "So Much," "Every Night I Pray," and "Beside My Love" to Clark's companies, Sea-Lark and January, Goldner did so "hoping that he would play my records. . . . It was a calculated risk on my part." Goldner insisted that he had no understanding with Clark, with whom he did not even have a conversation.

"You did feel certain that the magic would be worked" and the records played? asked Representative John Moss of California. "I had hoped for that, yes sir," Goldner replied.[45]

George Paxton and Marvin Cane, the principal owners of Coronation Music, told the subcommittee a similar story. Following a conversation with Clark's assistant Vera Hodes, Cane assigned to the January Company half of the royalties to "Sixteen Candles." Since there was no "stipulation" that Clark would plug the record, the partners were "more hopeful than confident" that the then-uncharted tune would get airtime on *American Bandstand*. They were not disappointed. Clark played "Sixteen Candles" twenty-seven times in the three months after copyright had been assigned to January. By the beginning of 1960, the song had sold 468,235 copies.[46]

Songwriter and music publisher Bernard Lowe expressed his gratitude for Clark's help in promoting his song "Butterfly" by offering the DJ 25 percent of the publishing rights. Clark refused, according to Lowe, but agreed to accept a check for $7,000 made out to his mother-in-law, Margaret Mallery. When she cashed the check, Mrs. Mallery wrote on the back of it, "Reimburse loan." Subsequently, Lowe admitted, he had assigned 50 percent of the performance rights to "Back to School" to Clark. "Was he a good kind of partner to have in this business?" asked Congressman John Bennett of Michigan. Was he "worth more in playing the records than other disc jockeys?" "I would say so," Lowe replied, only to reverse himself. "For financial gain, I don't think it meant anything." Lowe asked Clark to join his company "just because we were very friendly."[47]

To parry the proposition that he pushed the platters from which he profited, Clark hired Computech, a data processing firm based in New York City. Bernard Goldstein, vice president of Computech, presented to the subcommittee the results of his survey of the records played on *American Bandstand* between August 5, 1957, and November 30, 1959. Using a complicated formula to establish a relationship between the popularity of a record and the number of times it had "a right to be played," Goldstein concluded that on average titles in which Clark had a direct or indirect financial interest were not played more often than their standing on the charts suggested they should be played.[48]

Clark later acknowledged that with the Computech study he hoped to create "the biggest red herring I could find—something that would shift the attention away from my scalp." But he did not have much success in muddying the waters. The subcommittee staff had little difficulty poking holes in Goldstein's "300 pounds of information." Among the study's flawed premises was the assumption that a record ranked number 1 on the charts ought to be played only twice as many times as one at number 50. To increase the percentage of *Bandstand* plays of records in which Clark had no financial interest, moreover, Goldstein counted every play of "Bandstand Boogie," the show's theme song. The subcommittee swore in three statisticians who asserted that the Computech study offered no substantive evidence on the point at issue. One of them, Joseph Tryon, professor of economics and statistics at Georgetown University, claimed that Clark "clearly and systematically favored the records in which he had some interest. He favored them first by playing them more often, he favored them by playing them longer, he favored them by playing them earlier relative to when they became popular. And it also appears that he favored those in which he had the strongest interest—he favored those records most."[49]

A study of records that were not hits in which Clark had an interest completed long after the payola hearings adjourned suggested that the TV DJ did feather his own nest. According to John A. Jackson, *Bandstand* played 53 percent of the records issued by three of Clark's firms, "an inordinately high percentage of plays for any record company." Cane, Finfer, Goldner, Lowe, Paxton, and just about everyone else in the industry knew that as host and producer of *American Bandstand* Clark was in a unique position to give a record "exposure"—and help himself and his friends as the bands played on.[50]

In his testimony to the subcommittee, Clark searched for space between the Scylla of self-incrimination and the Charybdis of non-cooperation. He was more concerned about limiting his own liability than defending the music business. Clark insisted that he had never taken payola, which he once again defined as an explicit agreement "to play a record or have an artist perform on a radio or television program in return for a payment in cash or any other consideration." He acknowledged that it "seemed incredible" that he would not have known that Tony Mammarella, whom he "loved and respected" and with whom he shared a tiny office, was receiving payments from record companies. But he denied "categorically" any knowledge of improper, unethical, or illegal practices by Mammarella during their association on *American Bandstand*. Moreover, the only gifts of more than nominal value that Clark had ever received from a business acquaintance were a fur stole, a necklace, and a ring from Lou Bedell of Era and Dore Records. The Clarks were reluctant to accept the presents but did not know how to refuse them. The gifts, Clark emphasized, were not part of any agreement or understanding that he had or would give special treatment to Bedell's records or performers.

Clark provided the committee data pertaining to the thirty-three music-related business with which he had been connected. He maintained that before his discussions with the management of ABC "the conflict between my position as a performer and my record interests never clearly presented itself to me." Clark had "no doubt" that some of the copyrights were assigned to his firms "at least in part" because he was a network television performer, but he had "neither asked for, nor promised anything" to acquire them. He might have favored records in which he had a financial interest "without realizing it," he conceded, but he had never consciously done so.

The DJ cum entrepreneur claimed that for some time he did not know that his firms were using payola as a promotional expense. He disliked accounting and did not read financial statements carefully, he told the subcommittee. "The only thing I ever failed in my life is mathematics." When he did realize, "somewhere along the line," that his companies paid for play, he did not deem it "terribly important." Clark would no more think of telling an officer of a music company "how to run his business than the man in the moon, because it was his responsibility, and this was not a particularly unusual practice in this business." Was he guilty of payola because he did not intervene to stop his companies from making payments? "If you own any stock in RCA Victor, Mercury or Decca, or United," Clark shot back, "you are as guilty of payola as I am."

Clark believed that "the crime I have committed, if any, is that I have made a great deal of money in a short time on little investment." In the record business, he maintained, substantial profits were by no means unusual. Nor were they illegal or immoral. Perhaps he had made mistakes along the way. Perhaps the music business needed new ethical standards. Indeed, since he had divested, he could now "program my shows, pick my records and select performers free of any fear that somebody might think that I am playing the angles." Given the practices that prevailed throughout the 1950s, however, Clark had not done anything for which he should be ashamed.[51]

Interested in revelations about conspiracies to foist mediocre music on an unsuspecting public, members pummeled Clark. The only exception was chairman Oren Harris, who had a good reason to be reticent. During a probe of the FCC in 1956–1957, Harris's colleagues on the subcommittee learned that the chairman had purchased (for $500 and a promissory note for $4,500, which he never paid) a 25 percent interest in a television station in Arkansas. Soon after the deal, the FCC, which had denied the station a power increase, reversed itself. The embarrassed congressman sold his interests but retained his chairmanship. Reluctant to probe too deeply into Clark's conflicts of interest, Harris tended to ask innocuous questions (Why did members of Clark's audience "squeal so loud?") and praised the network DJ as a "fine young man" who had benefited from a system he did not invent. Now that Clark had voluntarily divested, Harris hoped he would "make your mark in life as you have an opportunity to do."[52]

Clark's other interrogators were not nearly so deferential. "Apparently you know how to count," Steven Derounian of New York declared derisively, "and I think more students in the country are going to want to fail math if they can be as successful as you are." Incredulous at Clark's protestations of innocence and ignorance, Derounian described the document the network DJ had prepared for ABC as "a Christian Dior affidavit," tailored to his need. "You say you did not get any payola, but you got an awful lot of royala." Congressman Bennett suggested that ABC and Clark had "cooked up" the affidavit "to assure the public this whole matter has been scrutinized and was now taken care of." Bennett got Clark to admit that he had left *American Bandstand* viewers "with the impression that you had no interest in any record that you were playing."[53]

Congressman Moss observed acidly that his evaluation of Clark was "perhaps a little less modest than your own evaluation of yourself." The only network TV disc jockey in the United States, Moss added, Clark had been "sufficiently prudent not to overlook any opportunity" to use his position to make money. He had even taken $7,150 from American Airlines for a plug at the end of the program, even though the carrier did not provide transportation for guests, as he announced. Clark did not respond to the popular demand for music; he attempted "to create a demand in an area of music." And he had been "very successful in creating that desire." Everyone knew why songwriters, record manufacturers, and distributors came to Clark—and why they did not request a quid pro quo: "They did not have to, because it was understood—this is the osmosis I referred to the other day—it was understood." Nor did Moss believe "that the ugly thought never once entered your mind."[54]

Battered and belittled, Clark never lost his composure. With the backing of ABC, he resumed his career and over the next four decades built an entertainment empire worth more than $200 million. Payola prosecutions, regulations, and congressional investigations, however, took a toll on rock 'n' roll. Few fans, to be sure, accepted Congressman Moss's definition of the music as "raucous discord" or Derounian's description of performers as "unwashed kids." And few in the industry really believed that payola was responsible for the popularity of rock 'n' roll. Kevin Sweeney, president of the Radio Advertising Bureau," called payola "the most over-played news story of 1959." Nonetheless, radio stations and record companies responded to the media attention and political pressure by switching to more "melodic" music. Some of them returned unopened platters sent to them by independent record companies, playing it safe with songs vetted by the majors. Since "the finger of suspicion is more likely to be pointed now at a disc jockey who is spinning a 'far out' brand of rocking music," *Variety* reported, many broadcasters used the Top Forty format or prohibited DJs from choosing the records they played. WEOK in Poughkeepsie, New York, banned the use of the term "disc jockey" altogether, referring to its spinners as "musicasters." Boston's WILD dropped rock 'n' roll. So did WMAQ in Chicago, WNTA in Newark, New Jersey, Dallas's Texas' KVIL, and Denver KICN. Rock 'n' roll "squats in the dark, accused," wrote John Tynan in *Down Beat*.[55]

Were fans also "in full flight from the rock, the roll, the big beat and the teen tunes"? Journalist Charles Suber reported that attendance was down at live concerts. Sales of rock 'n' roll records had not yet declined, but "it takes a while for five years of brainwashing to wear off." After a struggle that had lasted for most of the decade, rock 'n' roll, it appeared, was about to roll over.[56]

"THE DAY THE MUSIC DIED"

6

Rock 'n' Roll's Lull and Revival

Between 1958 and 1963, rock 'n' roll faltered. Several factors contributed to the lull. The ASCAP-led assault was the most important. The payola probes left rock 'n' roll gasping for airtime, as many radio stations switched to mellow, melody music. Large record companies promoted polka, calypso, folk music, ballads, novelty songs, and a softer, lushly orchestrated fare. Some independents went pop or merged with a major. In these years, moreover, the ranks of more hard-line rock 'n' roll performers were depleted. Fans listed the losses that presaged the end of an era: "Elvis in the Army, Buddy Holly dead, Little Richard in the ministry, Jerry Lee Lewis in disgrace, and Chuck Berry in jail."

Some of these singers exited voluntarily or by accident. Others were pushed offstage. All of them, directly or indirectly, were casualties, if not of a conspiracy, than of the assault against rock 'n' roll, to which the payola scandal added momentum. At the end of the "Ike Age" many Americans, inside and outside of the entertainment industry, remained unsettled by and hostile to rock 'n' roll, which retained its association with the blurring and redrawing of racial, sexual, and generational boundaries. The war to reclaim the cultural space in the United States for mainstream values raged on.

Opponents of rock 'n' roll recognized that the horse they were beating was not dead. Rock 'n' roll had become less vital, edgy, and

161

creative, but its decline was producer induced, not consumer driven. Even as manufacturers promoted mainstream music they called rock 'n' roll, there remained a market for the real thing. A few new rocka- billy and rhythm and blues artists reached that market. And the records of established rock 'n' roll stars continued to sell even when the stars themselves were overseas, behind bars, in the grave, or other- wise out of commission. Across the United States—and Europe—rock 'n' roll still had the capacity to agitate, motivate, and arouse. The Beatles, the Rolling Stones, and dozens of other British musicians— whose explosion into the American market would be known as the British Invasion—cut their musical teeth on Berry, Holly, Presley, Lewis, and Little Richard. In fact, historian Alice Echols argues, the British Invaders "conquered America with her very own music—early rock 'n' roll, hard-driving R&B, and the blues." Many of their early recordings were note-for-note versions of rock 'n' roll classics. They would, of course, turn out to be much more than cover artists, but as the revival began, the Brits and their American fans understood that the 1960s began in the '50s, when rock was young.[1]

Things seemed bleak before the Invasion, however, because one by one the voices of the great American rock 'n' roll performers had been stilled. Little Richard Penniman was the first to go. Little Richard was a volatile and unstable man, ambivalent about his sexuality and inclined to give some credence to charges that rock 'n' roll encour- aged licentious behavior. After a visit in 1957 from Wilbur Gulley, a missionary of the Church of God of the Ten Commandments, who knocked on doors in the "star belt" neighborhoods of Los Angeles, Little Richard reconnected with the religious teachings of his youth. With Gulley's guidance, he came to believe that "if you want to live with the Lord, you can't rock 'n' roll, too. God doesn't like it." Exhausted by a relentless travel schedule and petrified that he was about to be charged with income tax evasion, Little Richard decided while on tour in Australia to retire from show business. Some members of his entourage remembered that when the engine of his plane caught fire, the singer promised the Lord that he would abandon the devil's music if his life was spared. Others believed that he took the launching of the Sputnik satellite by the godless Communists as a sign from heaven that he should rejoin the Christian flock. All agreed, however, that he tossed jewelry worth thousands of dollars into the ocean as a down payment on his pledge to live a more spiritual life. Departing Australia ten days before his bookings were scheduled to end, Little Richard returned to the United States to enroll in Oakwood College, a Seventh-day Adventist school in Huntsville, Alabama: "I wanted to work for Jehovah and find that peace of mind."

At Oakwood, he embarked on a new life. He served as an usher at revival meetings. He restricted his diet to vegetables cooked in vegetable oil, "as the church instructs." And he took a wife, Ernestine Campbell, a recent high school graduate, who was working for the navy. Within months, however, his resolve weakened. He skipped classes, frequently taking to the road in one of his garishly colored Cadillacs. Six hours late on his wedding day, Little Richard was not much of a husband, preferring the company of young men to spending time with Ernestine. After he was arrested following a fracas in a men's bathroom in a Trailways bus station in Long Beach, California, she divorced him.

Although Little Richard remained attracted to a higher calling, he was ready to return to show business. He recorded dozens of sacred songs sans pompadour, makeup, and slam-bam sound in 1960, but the lure and lucre of rock 'n' roll were too great. He participated, surreptitiously, in several rock 'n' roll recording sessions with a group called the Upsetters. In 1962, he began his comeback, with bookings in England on a bill with singers Sam Cooke and Gene Vincent. To lay to rest rumors that he would sing gospel music, promoters placed ads in the newspapers announcing, "Little Richard has been booked purely as a rock 'n' roll artist, and his repertoire WILL consist of old favorites like 'Rip It Up' and 'Long Tall Sally.'" One of his most enthusiastic fans was Paul McCartney. Among the very first songs McCartney remembered singing were "Tutti Frutti" and "Long Tall Sally." And when the Beatles performed in Liverpool in the early '60s, they asked Little Richard to join them. Little Richard returned to the United States and resumed an erratic and campy career as a rock 'n' roll shouter. Although he never regained the popularity he had had in the '50s, he had never really been out of fashion.[2]

Although Jerry Lee Lewis was also attracted to and repulsed by the sacred and the profane, he was not about to retire voluntarily from rock 'n' roll, as Little Richard had. But by marrying his thirteen-year-old cousin, Myra Gale, the daughter of the bass player in his band,

Lewis gave his opponents the weapon they needed to wreck his career and discredit as dangerous the music impressionable girls Myra's age loved to listen to.

With "High School Confidential" climbing up the charts (even before the release of the movie for which it served as a theme song) and "Breathless" likely to follow, Lewis was a hot property in 1958, the stud in the stable of Sun Records. As the singer embarked on a thirty-seven-day tour of England, Sam Phillips begged him not to tell reporters about Myra. "She's my wife," Jerry Lee replied. "There ain't nothin' wrong about that." True to his word, he told journalists in England that he was married to the girl standing demurely beside him, clad in black slacks and a black and white blouse. Myra was fifteen, he lied. She "might look young and be young, but is growed." Lewis compounded his troubles by providing some details of his previous two marriages. "Age doesn't matter back home," Myra chimed in. "You can marry at ten if you can find a husband."

Reporters for the *Memphis Press-Scimitar* quickly discovered that Myra was thirteen and the couple had exchanged vows five months before Lewis was divorced by his second wife. All hell broke loose. English papers pleaded with teenagers to boycott Jerry Lee's concerts and "show that even rock and roll hasn't entirely robbed them of their sanity." Editorial writers demanded that Lewis be deported from the United Kingdom as an undesirable alien. When he performed at the Granada Theater in Tooting, hecklers shouted, "Cradle-robber," switching to "Sissy" when the singer ran his silver comb through his hair. After the hooting at Tooting, the remainder of Lewis's concert tour was canceled. "Baby-Snatcher Quits," the *London Daily Herald* gloated. Asked how the scandal might play in the United States, the singer was defiant: "Back in America, I got two lovely homes, three Cadillacs and a farm." Squeezing Myra's hand, he added, "What else could anyone want?"

Back home, Lewis was denounced and derided. *Newsweek* provided the details of the singer's expulsion from England, followed by a story about Pat Boone's graduation magna cum laude from Columbia University. In the *New York Herald Tribune*, columnist Hy Gardner cackled that the Lewises were about to have an addition to the family: "He bought her a doll." Sam Phillips scrambled to contain the damage. Jerry Lee married Myra again to ensure that the union was legal.

Phillips and Lewis paid for an open letter in *Billboard* in which the singer acknowledged that "some legal misunderstandings . . . inadvertently made me look as though I invented the word indecency." Lewis insisted that his once stormy life had straightened out, but amidst the musical McCarthyism of the late '50s he could no longer be optimistic about the future. "I hope that if I am washed up as an entertainer it won't be because of this bad publicity," he concluded, "because I can cry and wish all I want, but I can't control the press or the sensationalism that these people will go to get a scandal started to sell papers. If you don't believe me, please ask any of the other people that have been victims of the same."

The letter didn't help, and Phillips's attempt to make a quick buck off of his all too hot and rapidly cooling property made matters worse. A week after Lewis came back to the United States, Sun cut and released "The Return of Jerry Lee," a bizarre novelty record consisting of questions posed by the announcer "Edward R. Edward" (actually Memphis disc jockey George Klein) and answers culled from Lewis's hit singles. "Where did you meet your young bride?" Klein asked. "Boppin' at the high school hop!" "What did Queen Elizabeth say about you?" "Goodness gracious! Great balls of fire!"

"The Return of Jerry Lee," on a record and in real life, was a disaster. In 1958, there was nothing frivolous about a sex scandal. Blacklisted by most radio stations, Lewis could no longer connect with an audience. Sales of "High School Confidential" stalled. Neither side of the singer's new single, "Break Up" or "I'll Make It All Up to You," made it into the Top Fifty. In 1959, the prophetically titled "I'll Sail My Ship Alone" crept onto the pop charts, at number 93, but sank back when DJs ignored it. Personal appearances were equally disappointing. After one night at Café de Paris, a nightclub in New York City, Lewis returned to Memphis. Empty seats and scoffing patrons were more than he could stand. In an act that he later called "very cowardly," Dick Clark declined to book Lewis on *American Bandstand*. Once heir apparent to the title "King of Rock 'n' Roll," Lewis was persona non grata in his profession.

Lewis continued to record for Sun and perform live in concert venues, mostly in the South, but for years there wasn't much shakin' going on. Record producers lost their nerve. They overdressed, overdubbed, and smoothed out Lewis songs, prompting biographer Jimmy

Guterman to wonder whether "this was rock and roll? With background choruses out of the blandest pop and pop-country forms?" Lewis's promotion manager, Guterman asserts, wanted to turn him into Pat Boone. He didn't—and probably couldn't—but it would take years in the wilderness before "the Killer" regained confidence in his own voice and style and a new generation discovered him.[3]

Chuck Berry was a sexual threat and a target of opponents of the civil rights movements as well as foes of rock 'n' roll. With eight songs on the Top 100 pop charts and four R&B best-sellers, Berry was at the apex of his career in 1958. The next year, while touring Mexico and the American Southwest, Berry met Janice Escalante, a fourteen-year-old Mexican-Indian girl, and brought her back to St. Louis to work as a hat checker in his nightclub. When she was not at Club Bandstand, Escalante allegedly worked as a prostitute. Picked up as she plied her trade, she explained how she had come to St. Louis—and the police launched an investigation of Chuck Berry. When Joan Martin, another of Berry's alleged victims, declined to cooperate with authorities, they restricted themselves to the Escalante case, indicting the singer for violating the Mann Act, a federal law making it a crime to transport a minor across state lines for immoral purposes. Had he not been a rock 'n' roll headliner, and an African American who had opened a nightclub in a predominantly white section of town, Berry almost certainly would not have been prosecuted.

It took two trials to convict him. The first resulted in a guilty verdict but was overturned by an appeals court which found that trial judge Gilbert Moore "intended to disparage the defendant by repeated questions about race." Referring to Berry as "that Negro," Moore intervened frequently to assist the prosecutor. When a witness described the establishment in which Berry and Escalante had stayed in Colorado as "just a regular small hotel," the judge exclaimed, "He asked you what kind of hotel! Was it a white or colored hotel?" "In Denver we don't observe any differences between our citizens," the witness responded, igniting another outburst from Moore: "I didn't ask you what kind of people you observe, just answer my question." After a lengthy second trial, which ended in 1962, Berry was sentenced to three years in prison and a $5,000 fine. The press sensationalized the case, making rock 'n' roll a defendant, responsible for illicit sex and the racial unrest in St. Louis. One headline declared, "Rock 'n' Roll Singer Lured Me to St. Louis,

Says 14-Year-Old." Several articles inserted lyrics from Berry's "Sweet Little Sixteen" alongside accounts of testimony at the trial.

Berry continued to record and perform between trial dates but faced continued harassment. In August 1959, he was imprisoned briefly in Meridian, Mississippi, for trying to date a white girl who asked for his autograph. In February 1962, Berry surrendered to authorities, serving his sentence first at Leavenworth, then in a prison in Springfield, Missouri. His legal problems had a devastating impact on his career, of course. Berry's original compositions, including "Bye Bye Johnny," a commentary on Elvis's decision to abandon live concerts to concentrate on a career in the movies, got little radio play and disappeared. So did his experiments with the blues, including an excellent recording of Maceo Merriweather's "Worried Life Blues." Yet Berry's classics continued to sell well. In September 1959, Chess Records released the singer's third LP, "Chuck Berry Is on Top," which included "Maybellene," "Johnny B. Goode," "Little Rock and Roller," and "Roll Over Beethoven." The album was so successful that Chess tried again in 1962, using many of the same songs, in a release entitled "Twist with Chuck Berry."

During these years, English musicians were listening to Berry as well. When they performed in a club in Hamburg, Germany, in the summer of 1960, the then little known Beatles sang Berry's "Too Much Monkey Business" every night. When they became international stars, the Beatles included "Roll Over Beethoven" in most of their concerts. And Berry's tune "Back in the USA" was the inspiration for McCartney's "Back in the USSR." "Don't give me any sophisticated crap," John Lennon liked to say, "give me Chuck Berry." With boosts like these, Berry was able to resume his career when he was released from prison in October 1963.[4]

On the surface, Elvis Presley's removal from rock 'n' roll was unrelated to assaults on the music. As Chuck Berry's "Bye Bye Johnny" claimed, Elvis embraced pop music, including gushy ballads and gooey background choruses, to increase his appeal to adults and his bank balance. And in classifying him 1-A, the Selective Service Board in Memphis treated Presley as it did every other able-bodied male who was eligible for the draft.

The singer's strategy, however, was dictated by the intense criticism of rock 'n' roll. Elvis's astute manager, Tom Parker, was determined

In Hamburg, Germany, early in their career, the Beatles played the
music, and copied the look, of '50s American rock 'n' rollers. *(Astrid
Kirchherr/K&K)*

to build for him a career that would last a lifetime. "In keeping with
that goal," music historian Peter Guralnick has argued, "it was necessary to distance his boy from the hurly-burly." Because Parker was
convinced that "the very controversy that had originally fueled Elvis's
fame was now serving to limit it," he decided in 1957 to "remove Elvis
from the fray." Without ever making explicit what he was doing, even
to his client, Parker drastically reduced Elvis's personal appearances
and whisked him off to Hollywood, where, Guralnick writes, the
image on the silver screen "always flickered, the candle burned but
never flamed—and fame, carefully nurtured, need never go away."[5]

   In 1957, the Memphis draft board informed Elvis to prepare himself
for induction. One member exulted that he had an opportunity to put
the rock 'n' roll star in his place. "After all," he snarled, "when you
take him out of the entertainment business, what have you got left? A
truck driver."[6] Elvis expected Parker to fix things. When the manager
failed to act, he was "devastated, just down, depressed," a friend
recalled. Parker urged Presley to ask for a sixty-day deferment so that

Paramount Studios could complete the film *King Creole*, but he told reporters the singer would not "consider making another request, because I know how he feels personally about it." Would Presley's popularity slip away while he was serving his country? Elvis thought this "the sixty-four dollar question," telling reporters he wished he knew the answer. But Parker was serenely confident. Movie releases, a backlog of RCA singles and albums, and publicity about the world's most popular private getting a GI haircut or completing basic training would keep him in the public eye.

While other rock 'n' rollers were vilified, Presley the private was portrayed as a patriot. In interviews he played his part well. Expressing gratitude for "what this country has given me," Elvis told a *Memphis*

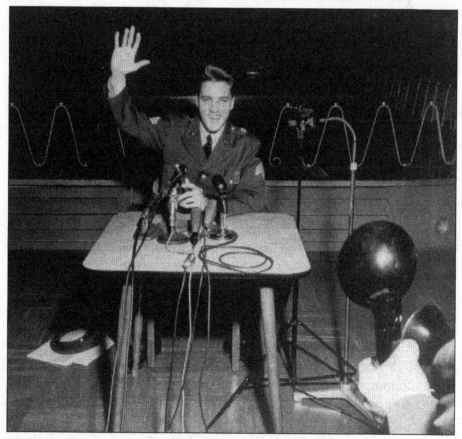

While other rock 'n' rollers were vilified or ruined by scandal, Elvis escaped the hurly-burly as a patriotic private in the army. *(National Archives)*

Press-Scimitar reporter that he was "ready to return a little. It's the only adult way to look at it." After having worked in a factory, in a defense plant, and as a truck driver, he told columnist Vernon Scott, he was not worried about manual labor in the army: "I'll do whatever they tell me, and I won't be asking no special favors." Elvis acknowledged that his military service would be hard on his parents, especially his mother, who was "no different from millions of other mothers who hated to see their sons go." When he showed up at the induction station on March 24, 1958, to be examined, weighed, and deemed fit to serve, with *Life* magazine cameras clicking away, Elvis stuck to the script. "If I seem nervous, it's because I am," he said. But he looked forward to a "great experience. The army can do anything it wants with me. Millions of other guys have been drafted, and I don't want to be different from anyone else." As he devoured his army-issued box lunch, and Tom Parker marched around the building handing out balloons that advertised *King Creole* to the large crowd that had gathered, a telegram from Governor Frank Clement arrived. Clement congratulated his constituent for showing that "you are an American citizen first, a Tennessee volunteer, and a young man willing to serve his country when called upon to do so."[7]

Unlike Jerry Lee Lewis, Greil Marcus has written, but like so many other Americans who came of age in the 1950s, Elvis Presley knew there were limits; he had a sure sense of where he wanted to go and "mainstream savvy in his soul." He chose to adopt Tom Parker's strategy as his own, though it meant suppressing his rebellious instincts. He understood as well that indulging his sexual appetites could ruin his career, as it had Lewis's. Although he believed that if Jerry Lee really loved Myra, "I guess it's all right," Elvis was not about to make the same mistake. While he was stationed in Germany, Elvis met and fell in love with fourteen-year-old Priscilla Beaulieu. He brought Priscilla to Graceland to live with him, but he did not marry her until 1967.[8]

When he was discharged from the army in 1960, Elvis reclaimed the throne in popular music, just as Parker had predicted. He began to prepare for a new film, *G.I. Blues*. And for $125,000, the largest fee ever paid for a guest performer, he agreed to appear on a television special hosted by Frank Sinatra. "Old Blue-Eyes" had once declared Elvis's music "deplorable, a rancid-smelling aphrodisiac," but times had changed, and so had both men. On the show, Presley and Sinatra sang each other's signature songs, "Love Me Tender" and "Witchcraft." The King of Rock 'n' Roll was back, as a balladeer. According to James Miller, Elvis never completely lost "the old edge—of anxiety, of nervous energy, of tittering raunchiness"—that marked his singles for Sun and were defining characteristics of '50s rock 'n' roll. With, but more often without, that edge, Elvis recorded 149 Top Forty singles and reached the album charts with ninety-two LPs before he died in 1977. A rebel and a conformist, he responded to the options as he understood them in the late 1950s. He struggled to keep his life and his music from becoming banal and dull, Marcus has written, while living in a society that "did enclose extremes." Elvis retreated from rock 'n' roll because he wanted to and because he had to.[9]

Some saw the hand of God striking out against rock 'n' roll in the plane crash near Clear Lake, Iowa, on February 3, 1959, that killed the Big Bopper, Ritchie Valens, and Buddy Holly. Although the Civilian Aeronautics Board blamed pilot error, the crash was not wholly unrelated to the assault on rock 'n' roll. If opportunities for these once and future stars had not narrowed in the late '50s, they might not have found themselves in the hinterland in winter, traveling from town to town in broken buses and rickety aircraft. Immortalized by Don McLean's anthem "American Pie" (1971) as "the day the music died," the accident took out three rock 'n' rollers who had already felt the impact of the industry-induced lull.

Jiles Perry Richardson, the Big Bopper, was the least prominent of the headliners who died that day. A disc jockey in KTRM in Beaumont, Texas, in the mid-'50s, Richardson gave himself his nickname, announcing on the air, "Bee-bop's big and I'm big, so why don't I become the Big Bopper?" In May 1957, during a KTRM "Disc-A-Thon," Richardson claimed a world's record for continuous broadcasting. During the six day marathon, he played 1,821 records and reportedly dropped thirty-five of his 240 pounds. A year later, the Bopper became a singer. Produced by Mercury-Starday Records, "Chantilly Lace" was an ode to cute and quiet, wiggly, giggly, and pony-tailed girls (like Richardson's wife, "Teetsie"), who wore see-through lace lingerie as they stood by their men. To almost everyone's surprise, "Chantilly Lace" became a smash hit. The third most played song of 1958, it reached number 6 on the *Billboard* pop charts. The sequel, "Big Bopper's Wedding," however, had struggled to make it into the Top

Forty. Richardson hoped that a tour of the United States and Australia with Buddy Holly would breathe new life into his career.[10]

Ritchie Valens hoped the Winter Party Dance Tour would prove that there was a market for his Latino/African/Anglo hybrid of rock 'n' roll in America's heartland. Born in a Los Angeles barrio in 1941, Richard Valenzuela grew up in an ethnically and racially mixed neighborhood, hanging out with Chicanos, African Americans, and a few white kids. A bit chunky, Ritchie was self-conscious and shy until he picked up his guitar and started singing. At Pacoima Junior High School, he invented a game song, "Mama Long," in which audience members made up lyrics, risqué when girls weren't around, as two black classmates harmonized. He enjoyed the songs of many rock 'n' rollers but was so taken with Little Richard that friends began to call him Little Ritchie.

While attending San Fernando High School, he began singing with a group called the Silhouettes. Among the songs he performed was his own composition "Donna," inspired by a crush he had on sophomore Donna Ludwig, an Anglo whose father ordered her not to go out with "that Mexican." Ritchie was discovered by independent record producer Bob Keane, just then establishing a new label, Del-Fi. His first single, a country-influenced rock 'n' roll tune, "Come On Let's Go," reached number 42 on the charts in 1958. That same year, "Donna" rocketed to number 2. On the flip side was the exuberant "La Bamba," whose lyrics were sung entirely in Spanish, interrupted frequently by a frenzied guitar. With "La Bamba" at number 22, Ritchie Valens was hailed as the "Chicano Elvis." Dick Clark and Alan Freed came calling. So did Hollywood, with a small role in *Go Johnny Go*, which was scheduled for release in August 1959.

Although he had a new name, Valens did not hide his Chicano roots or his fascination with African-American music. He planned to develop more fully the multicultural strains in rock 'n' roll. At the end of 1958, he recorded "Framed," the rhythm and blues classic about a man convicted for a crime he did not commit. Although Valens imitated a black accent in "Framed," he assumed that the song was relevant to Chicanos—and, for that matter, Anglos—as well. Before he went on the Winter Party Dance Tour, his first outside of California, he was preparing a rock 'n' roll version of the great Spanish standard "Malaguena," which drew on the style of African-American guitarist Bo Diddley.

It is impossible to determine where Valens would have taken his hybrid form of rock 'n' roll. We do know, however, that after he died none of the major record companies tried very hard to acquire the rights to his music. Del-Fi disappeared in 1964, and Keane did not rerelease Valens's songs until 1981. Bootleg versions of "Donna" and "La Bamba" circulated during these years, but the sound quality was poor because the producers had no access to the masters. Though he was never forgotten in the Chicano communities of the West and Southwest, Valens did not become a national icon until 1987, when the film *La Bamba* captivated a new generation of rock 'n' roll fans.[11]

Valens was thrilled to be part of the Winter Party Dance Tour because the headliner, Buddy Holly, was his idol. Born in Lubbock, Texas, in 1936, Holly labored for years in the rockabilly vineyards, held back in part by his plain face and Coke-bottle glasses. Dumped by Decca Records at the end of 1956, he formed a new group, the Crickets, and a partnership with producer Norman Petty. Their first release, "That'll Be the Day" (based on a phrase uttered by John Wayne in the film *The Searchers*), in 1957, leaped to number 1, and stayed on the Top Forty for sixteen weeks. Two more smash hits followed almost immediately: "Peggy Sue," with Holly singing solo, reached number 3; "Oh Boy!," performed with the Crickets, made it to number 10.

Like many '50s rock 'n' roll performers, Holly crossed racial barriers. As improbable as it seems, Holly was often thought to be an African American. On one occasion, he emerged onstage at the Apollo Theater in New York City, astonishing young Leslie Uggams, who was seated in the audience. "I knew his records," she recalled, and anticipated seeing "another brother out there doing his number. Then this white guy comes out and everybody says, 'Oh, that's Buddy Holly!' . . . I said, 'He's white, isn't he?' But he was terrific."

In 1959, Holly's career was in transition. For about a year, as the opposition to rock 'n' roll began to crest, his records had been less successful. The suggestive "Early in the Morning" got only as far as 32 on the lists, while "Rave On," which the Catholic Youth Organization denounced for promoting juvenile delinquency and "a pagan culture," barely made it into the Top Forty. Holly had also broken with the Crickets and Norman Petty. Recently married to Maria Elena Santiago, a native of Puerto Rico, once a receptionist at Peer-Southern

Music, Holly was learning the Spanish language and listening to Latino songs. He looked forward to conversations with Ritchie Valens about Chicano rock 'n' roll. And he planned to record gospel and the blues, including an album with Ray Charles and another in tribute to Mahalia Jackson. It was not to be. While Waylon Jennings, Dion DiMucci, and the rest of the Winter Party Dance Tour troupe took the bus to Moorhead for the next gig, the four-seater Beechcraft Bonanza with three rock 'n' rollers and pilot Roger Peterson went down in a snowstorm soon after takeoff.[12]

Holly's death breathed new life into his career. An album of his greatest hits, *The Buddy Holly Story*, reached number II on the charts and was on and off the Top 100 for the next seven years. "The 'death rattle' goes on perpetuating the performer and very often filling the record company coffers," Mike Gross wrote in *Variety*. "Material on Holly is kept in the active file to handle the flood of requests for photos and bioinformation that continually pours in."

In England the appetite for Holly's records was virtually insatiable. *The Buddy Holly Story* reached number 7 on the British charts, and another LP, *That'll Be the Day*, a reissue of recordings he made in Nashville in 1956, went to number 5. As late as 1963, two Holly singles and another album, *Reminiscing*, were in the U.K. Top Five. Virtually every British rock 'n' roller, starting with the Beatles, listened to and learned from Holly. The Beatles' first record, made in a small Liverpool studio, was "That'll Be the Day," and the first forty songs written by Lennon and McCartney were inspired by him. First called the Quarry Men, then Johnny and the Moondogs, the Beatles chose the name that stuck because they wanted "something . . . like Buddy Holly's Crickets." They dressed like Holly, with suits and skinny ties, McCartney recalled, and Buddy's example convinced John Lennon that an ordinary-looking guy with glasses could become a rocker. The first thing the Beatles told an editor of *Look* magazine when they arrived in the United States was that they wanted to meet Elvis Presley. The second was that Buddy Holly had had a significant impact on them.

He was a role model for other British Invaders as well. Keith Richards respected Holly because he "wrote his own songs, had a great band, and didn't need anyone else." According to Richards, the Rolling Stones' sound derived in part from Holly's song (borrowed from Bo Diddley) "Not Fade Away." Eric Clapton claimed that duplicating a Buddy Holly echo effect while playing in the stairwell at home changed his life: "It sounded like a record, and I thought, 'Yeah, this could be. . . . The world had better watch out.'" And Elton John started wearing glasses, his biographer claims, to copy Buddy Holly—not because he needed them.[13]

While rock 'n' roll flourished in England in the early '60s, with 350 bands in Liverpool alone, the music receded in the United States. Oldies and goodies continued to sell, but only a few new artists emerged. Roy Orbison was one of the most talented of them. Making full use of an extraordinary vocal range, including a high falsetto, Orbison had a string of rockabilly hits between 1960 and 1965, including "Only the Lonely" (1960), "Crying," (1961), "Blue Bayou" (1963), and "It's Over"(1964). The lyrics were sometimes shopworn, but he filled them with a haunting introspection and plaintive sadness, setting the mood with a distinctive stage persona, the solitary singer in dark clothing and sunglasses.[14]

In the freshness of his sound, Orbison was exceptional. And during the lull, rock 'n' roll limited itself in subject matter and theme to teenage romance, well before or after love was made manifest, and to celebrations of the young and the restless in the United States. Greil Marcus claims that this music appealed to Americans who wanted only to "applaud, to say Yes and mean it," to declare that the American Dream had arrived or was about to, and that the good life was filled with fun. This was the message of the surf music of the Beach Boys, Jan and Dean, and scores of other groups. "You can always write about social issues but who gives a damn," said Beach Boy Brian Wilson. "I like to write about something these kids feel is their whole world." And he did, in "Surfin' USA" (1963), "Surfer Girl" (1963), "Fun Fun Fun" (1964), "I Get Around" (1964), and "Don't Worry Baby" (1964). In the early '60s, rock 'n' roll (coincidentally and in a way he never intended) helped John F. Kennedy fulfill his campaign promise to get the nation "moving again."[15]

Some listeners wanted more than they were getting; they missed music that took risks and spoke to a fuller range of human experiences. Although loath to admit it, record manufacturers and radio station owners knew that demand for a more hard-driving rock 'n' roll had not diminished. They watched with dismay as record sales stag-

nated, after doubling between 1955 and 1959. In 1960, when the number
1 pop song was the easy-to-listen-to "A Summer Place," by Percy Faith,
sales decreased 5 percent. In 1963, while the number of teens in the
United States continued to surge, receipts were an anemic 1.6 percent
greater than those of the previous year. Music industry executives sat
between a rock ('n' roll) and a hard place. Burned once by the custo-
dians of a complacent consensus, they chose to keep the faith and
mark time—and attach the phrase rock 'n' roll to many of the mainstream records they produced—until something else captured the
kids' imagination.[16]

As they waited, they created a commercially viable ersatz rock 'n'
roll. Based in Philadelphia, the home of *American Bandstand*,
"schlock rock" offered teenage fans white, middle-class idols. Some of
them, such as Paul Anka, Bobby Darin, and Neil Sedaka, were
talented. On the whole, though, as music historian Reebee Garofalo
has pointed out, the phenomenon replaced distinctive regional sounds
with homogenized voices, raucous riffs with lush orchestration, sexual
themes with teenage yearning, rebellious white southern singers and
rhythm-and-bluesy black ones with boys-next-door (and a few girls)
whose looks were more important than their musical ability.[17]

Fabian Forte was the paradigmatic "schlock rock" hunk. Discovered when he was sixteen by Bob Marcucci, cofounder of Chancellor
Records, Fabian found his fans through the technical wizardry of
studio engineers: "If my voice sounds weak, they pipe it through an
echo chamber to soup it up. If it sounds drab, they speed up the tape
to make it sound happier. If I hit the wrong note, they snip it out and
replace it by one taken from another part of the tape. And if they think
the record needs more jazzing, they emphasize the accompaniment.
By the time they get done with the acrobatics, I can hardly recognize
my own voice." Fabian broke into the Top Ten in 1959 with "Turn Me
Loose." Before he was done, he produced eight Top Forty hits.[18]

"Schlock rock" was overwhelmingly white, but it produced one
black superstar, Chubby Checker, who ignited the dance craze known
as "the Twist." Originally released by Hank Ballard and the
Midnighters, "The Twist" had had a respectable sale in rhythm and
blues markets but did not cross over into pop. Cameo/Parkway
Records and *American Bandstand* turned "The Twist" into family
entertainment, soon after Dick Clark's wife suggested that singer

Ernest Evans take the name Chubby Checker, a not-so-subtle reference to Fats Domino. Although few got the joke, Checker twisted his way to the top of the pop charts in 1960, and again in 1962. As if to demonstrate that nothing succeeds like excess, dance after asexual dance followed, from "the Fly" to "the Fish," "the Limbo Rock" to "the Loco-Motion," "the Watusi" to "the Mashed Potato."[19]

Rhythm and blues–oriented and gospel-inspired rock 'n' roll, sung by African Americans, flourished during the lull. Much of it had crossover appeal. Indeed, since popular music abhors a vacuum, the lull may have helped make room for African-American performers. In the early '60s, the Platters, the Drifters, and the Coasters scored with white suburban audiences. So did Sam Cooke, who moved from gospel to pop, from the Soul Stirrers to the *Tonight Show*, hitting the charts with "You Send Me" in 1957, and then capitalizing on "The Twist" with "Twistin' the Night Away" in 1962. During these years, white songwriters and producers collaborated with black singers to develop a polished, "uptown" R&B style. The "girl groups" managed by independent producers Luther Dixon and Phil Spector led the way. The Ronettes, the Crystals, the Shirelles, and other "girl groups" secured a place for females in rock 'n' roll. They stuck to the sunny side of the street. With hit songs like "Be My Baby" (1963), "Da Doo Ron Ron" (1963), and "Dedicated to the One I Love" (1961), in fact, the "girl groups" perpetuated gender stereotypes and steered clear of racial references.[20]

Founded in 1960 by Berry Gordy, Motown produced a rhythm and blues sound with more staying power than "the girl groups," who were swept away by the British Invasion. When it became "Hitsville USA," Motown was the largest black-owned corporation in the United States, with African Americans filling virtually all creative positions, as artists, studio musicians, writers, and producers. For Gordy, black entrepreneurship was a means to an integrationist end. Motown proved that by dint of their own efforts blacks could achieve prosperity and acceptance into the mainstream of American life. He was willing to pay a price for it: "the Motown Sound," or as the label logo identified it, "the Sound of Young America," aimed to please rather than provoke.

Gordy was born in 1929, after his middle-class black family relocated from Georgia to Detroit. His father owned the Booker T. Washington Grocery Store, and was a firm believer in Washington's philosophy of self-help. Gordy dropped out of school in the eleventh

Berry Gordy made Motown, with its black artists and management, into "Hitsville, USA." During the '60s, 174 Motown singles reached the Top Ten. *(Motown Records Archives)*

grade to become a professional boxer, then opened a record store. After it failed, he worked on the assembly line at Ford Motors. In the 1950s, Gordy wrote several hit songs for rhythm and blues vocalist Jackie Wilson and managed the career of the Miracles. His family provided financial support for his first label, Tamla, and within a short time he had put in place the elements of the Motown empire: a studio, several labels, a publishing company, a management agency, and long-term contracts with a stable of immensely talented African-American R&B, gospel, and pop artists. From 1961 to 1966 alone, Motown performers included the Miracles, the Temptations, the Supremes, Martha and the Vandellas, the Four Tops, Marvin Gaye, and Stevie Wonder. These stars helped make the corporation the nation's leading seller of singles in 1965. During the '60s, Motown released 535 singles; 357 of them reached the pop or R&B charts, 174 of them the Top Ten. Six records reached number 1 on the pop charts alone, 29 on the R&B charts alone, and 21 were at the top of the heap on both pop and rhythm and blues listings.

The "Motown Sound" made brilliant use of studio technology to produce lively and danceable songs. Enormously popular among black as well as white consumers, Motown music was a watered-down version of gospel and the blues. Although it can legitimately claim inspiration from the church, Peter Guralnick has written, Motown music "rarely uncorks a full-blooded scream, generally establishes the tension without ever really letting go, and only occasionally will reveal a flash of raw emotion."[21] When it came to lyrics, as well, Gordy was mindful of the audience he was trying to reach and countenanced nothing political, let alone militant. Gordy's goal, to be more precise, was fulfillment by blacks of the American Dream; the means was a demonstration by example that a nation enriched itself when it opened careers to talent, regardless of race. The "sharp mohair suits and silk gowns" of Motown vocalists, Brian Ward argues, were "conspicuous images of success." In requiring performers to take lessons on etiquette, elocution, and deportment—how to walk, talk, sit properly and get up—Gordy had the same aim.

A creative but single-minded genius, Gordy did not want to jeopardize his business by linking Motown music with the sexual and racial controversies associated with rock 'n' roll. Consequently, Motown lyrics were as romantic and noncoital as those of the "girl groups." The titles of hits by the Miracles were typical of Motown's subject matter: "Shop Around" (1960), "You've Really Got a Hold on Me" (1962), "Oo Baby Baby" (1965), and "My Girl Has Gone" (1965). Before the mid-'60s, Motown lyrics also dealt neither with the oppression or poverty of blacks nor with the civil rights and voting rights movements. Motown did put out an album in late 1963 featuring Martin Luther King Jr.'s "I Have a Dream" speech—only to have King bring suit because it competed directly with the "official" March on Washington recording. Gordy's eyes were on the prize, but the prize was commercial and financial, at least at first, and certainly for now. In 1966, with some reluctance, Gordy permitted Stevie Wonder to cover "Blowin' in the Wind," as Motown's first "topical" record. By then, rock 'n' roll was no longer under wraps.[22]

Motown was the most commercially successful but by no means the only African-American sound on records and radio in the early '60s. As Guralnick has demonstrated, during these years soul music began to reach a mass audience. "Once it emerged from the underground," he asserts, "it accompanied the Civil Rights Movement almost step by step, its success directly reflecting the giant strides that integration was making." The product of a particular time and place, an optimistic and dangerous time, a time of struggle and success and frustration, sweet soul music transformed "the bitter fruit of segregation . . . into a statement of warmth and affirmation."[23]

Soul Music would not emerge as a mass culture phenomenon until the mid-'60s, but it was gathering steam during the lull. Ray Charles got hot in 1959 with "What'd I Say" (1959)—and then scored again and again with "Ruby," "Georgia on My Mind," "Hit the Road, Jack," and "I Can't Stop Loving You." The first of James Brown's many, many hits came in 1960, with "Think" and "You've Got the Power." That year, with the blessing of her father, the Reverend C. L. Franklin, eighteen-year-old Aretha Franklin moved to New York and signed a five-year deal with Columbia Records. And in 1960 as well, Stax Records was established in an unused movie theater in a shabby neighborhood in Memphis, Tennessee, by two whites, Jim Stewart and his sister, Estelle Axton. As "Soulsville USA" it would become the label of Booker T and the MGs, Sam and Dave, Isaac Hayes, and many other soul singers.[24]

Soul music was a harbinger. By 1964 the times were a-changing. That year, the 1950s, as embodied in the worldview of Pat Boone and Beaver Cleaver, ended. Of course, the critique of American culture and society in the '60s did not come out of nowhere. The seismic shifts were most noticeable along racial, sexual, and generational fault lines. The fissures of the '50s were widening into cracks, and a few chasms. And members of the post–World War II "shook up" generation, now 'twixt twelve and thirty, were in the vanguard of change. In the Port Huron Statement of the Students for a Democratic Society in 1960, Tom Hayden had introduced them to themselves: "We are the people of this generation, bred in at least moderate comfort, housed in universities, looking uncomfortably to the world we inherit."

The year 1964 was a pivotal one for race relations in the United States. In the summer, Congress passed and President Lyndon Johnson signed the most far-reaching civil rights bill in a century. The legislation outlawed racial discrimination in public accommodations and gave the federal government the power to enforce the law. It was increasingly clear, however, that legislation alone could not and would not provide equal opportunity for African Americans—and that many were tired of waiting. Riots that summer, in New York City, Rochester, three cities in New Jersey, and four others in the Northeast established race as a national rather than a sectional "problem." A new term, "backlash," entered political discourse. In an increasingly polarized environment, young people were credited with the idealism that brought them to the South as Freedom Riders—and blamed for fomenting racial discord. Journalist Theodore White was not the only commentator to conclude that militants preyed on "adolescent troops whose moral restraint had been entirely eaten away by dramatic producers and eloquent intellectuals on television, who somehow persuaded them that revenge for Mississippi and Alabama could be taken by looting and violence in the cities of the North."[25]

The Gulf of Tonkin Resolution of August 1964, the functional equivalent of a declaration of war against North Vietnam, made it likely that many American adolescents would soon become "troops" in more than a metaphorical sense. Although the war was actually a poor man's fight, with only a tiny percentage of college graduates serving in the military, the nation's campuses became hubs of antiwar agitation.

Energized by the civil rights and antiwar movements, college students began to look more critically at what activist Mario Savio called the "depersonalized, unresponsive bureaucracy" that infected virtually every institution in the United States. The Free Speech Movement at the University of California at Berkeley in the fall of 1964 demanded for students the right to solicit for political causes without restriction. It spread to universities throughout the country. Within months young people were the most visible members of two distinct but overlapping movements, the New Left and the counterculture.

Many of them drew inspiration from their generation's music. In February 1964, when the Beatles landed in New York City, rock 'n' roll came out of its holding pattern. Within three months, the "Fab Four" had twelve singles on the *Billboard* Top 100, occupying at one time the top five positions. At the end of the year, more than $50 million of Beatles merchandise, from dolls to dishcloths, had been sold. As we have seen, the Beatles brought something borrowed as well as something new to the music scene in the United States. On tour, in the

studio, and in interviews, they continued to pay homage to Chuck
Berry, Buddy Holly, Little Richard, and other rock 'n' roll heavy-
weights of the '50s. Included in their repertoire as well were more
recent classics, including the Shirelles' "Baby It's You" and Smokey
Robinson and the Miracles' "You've Really Got a Hold on Me."
Lennon and McCartney revealed that early on they had called their
group the Foreverly Brothers; George Harrison confessed that he had
once changed his name to Carl, to acknowledge his debt to rockabilly
performer Carl Perkins.[26]

Initially, the Beatles were reluctant to reignite the culture wars
that had been so damaging to rock 'n' roll. They strove to appeal
to teenagers without annoying adults. The lyrics of the group's early

Beatlemania at Shea Stadium, 1965. Compared to the Beatles' "100-proof
elixir," even Elvis was mere "dandelion tea," the *New York Daily News* had
commented on their first American appearance. *(Michael Ochs Archives)*

hits—"Love Me Do," "She Loves You," and "I Want to Hold Your Hand"—were no more sexually threatening than some of the music dismissed by critics as "treacle" a few years earlier. In choosing *The Ed Sullivan Show* for their first televised appearance in the United States, the Beatles hoped to win a seal of approval as middle-class family entertainment.[27]

But the power the Beatles had to influence young Americans was already apparent. As he sat in the audience at a concert in San Francisco, Ken Kesey observed that the group "could have taken this roomful of kids and snapped them." Bob Dylan noticed the same thing: "Everybody else thought they were for the teenyboppers, that they were gonna pass right away. But it was obvious to me that they had staying power. I knew they were pointing the direction of where music had to go."[28]

The Beatles could not and did not hide their irreverence toward authority, their impatience with efforts to shape and contain youth culture, and their affinity for political and social change. They were, indeed, "cute," but there was something subversive about them, something that worried the Reverend Billy Graham enough to make him break his rule against watching television on the Sabbath and become one of the seventy-three million Americans to see them perform on *The Ed Sullivan Show*. That same something prompted the *New York Daily News* to deem Elvis Presley's "gyrations and caterwauling . . . but lukewarm dandelion tea compared to the 100-proof elixir served up by the Beatles." The interview they gave in the airport lounge in February 1963 begins to explain why Reverend Graham deemed them "symptoms of the uncertainty of the times and the confusion about us." Asked to account for the group's success, Lennon explained:

"We have a press agent."

"What is your ambition?"

"To come to America."

"Do you hope to get haircuts?"

"We had one yesterday."

"Do you hope to take anything home with you?"

"The Rockefeller Center."

"Are you part of a social rebellion against the older generation?"

"It's a dirty lie."

"What about the movement in Detroit to stamp out the Beatles?"

"We have a campaign to stamp out Detroit."

"What do you think of Beethoven?"

"I love him," Ringo Starr interjected. "Especially his poems." At another press conference, the group was asked if they had a leading lady for their new film, *A Hard Day's Night*, scheduled for release in July. "We're trying for the Queen," said George Harrison. "She sells."[29]

The Beatles remained playfully irreverent, but over the course of the decade, in such songs as "Paperback Writer," "Nowhere Man," and "Eleanor Rigby," they began to use rock 'n' roll as a medium for a critique of modern industrial culture. When he struck out on his own, John Lennon became explicitly political, with "Revolution," "Give Peace a Chance," "Working Class Hero," and "Imagine." By then, rock was far more radical (and far more dependent on the lyrics) than it had ever been. Bob Dylan led the way in 1965, enlisting rock 'n' roll in politics, when he performed "Like a Rolling Stone," clad in a black leather jacket in front of an electric band. Meanwhile, dozens of British rock 'n' roll groups followed the Beatles to the United States, taking up residence on the pop charts. Many of them—and a new generation of American artists—tapped into the new zeitgeist with a sexually graphic, racially charged, psychedelic music. If the Beatles had been content to hold a girl's hand, the Rolling Stones demanded satisfaction that was rather more intimate. "Erotic politicians, that's what we are," said rocker Jim Morrison. "We're interested in anything about revolt, disorder, chaos, and activity that appears to have no meaning." He wasn't entirely serious, nor was he, for that matter, entirely accurate, either about rock 'n' roll or the predilections of its fans. Children of the 1950s, when "the teen breakout from jailhouse America began," they were also deeply concerned about order and meaning, and they carried into the new decade some complex, contradictory, and unsettled ideas about themselves and their society.[30]

EPILOGUE: "BORN IN THE USA"

The Persistent Power of Rock 'n' Roll

In the 1950s, rock 'n' roll was a meeting place, a breeding ground, and a staging area. The metaphorical equivalent of the interstate highway system built by President Eisenhower during the decade, the music carried messages across the country. It was, after all, the most pervasive and potent form of popular music in American history. In contrast to the theme of containment that dominated the nation's domestic and foreign policy, rock 'n' roll shook loose many teenagers—and shook up their parents. The baby boomers who were weaned on it embraced it—then and now—as a force for change, legitimizing their energy, impatience with the status quo, and dreams of freedom.

The influence of rock 'n' roll was not always pivotal. Although it accelerated the pace of integration in the entertainment industry and raised questions about racial boundaries in the United States, the civil rights movement would have unfolded much as it did without rock 'n' roll. The music played a crucial role, however, in fostering intra-generational identity. To a significant extent, a distinct teenage culture, with its own mores and institutions, did develop during the decade. A catchy and insistent rock 'n' roll led the way by encouraging boys and girls to resist the authority of parents, be more sexually adventurous, and learn from their peers about what to wear, watch, and listen to, when to study, and where to go on Saturday night. With the development of a separate market for teenagers, differentiation based on age became more pervasive and permanent in American culture and society. The values of young men and women were by no means fully formed, nor were they necessarily all that different from those of their parents. But in increasing numbers these young people were unwilling to be policed or patronized. As the '50s ended, the vast majority of baby boomers had not yet become teenagers: rock 'n' roll and the youth of America had history (and demography) on their side.

In the ensuing decades, rock 'n' roll demonstrated its persistent power—and its protean appeal. Rock 'n' roll was present at the creation of the 1960s, when "the shook-up generation" transformed an inchoate sense of disaffection and dissatisfaction into a political and cultural movement. Indeed, it is impossible to imagine the '60s in the United States without rock 'n' roll. The music and now the lyrics were sometimes the backdrop but often the inspiration as well for love-ins, sit-ins, demonstrations, the destruction of draft cards, tuning in, turning on, and taking off. Somehow, through the music and other stimulants to the soul, young people sought to bring together, "right now," a nation divided by race and class, and by regional and local values.

In August of 1969, Americans got a graphic demonstration of rock 'n' roll's capacity to define the experience of a generation of young men and women. More than three hundred thousand young people descended on Max Yasgur's dairy farm in the little Catskills town of Bethel, New York, for the "Woodstock Music and Art Fair," subtitled "An Aquarian Exposition." Discouraged by their parents from attending what turned out to be a chaotic, toiletless, muddy, drug-filled festival, they came anyway, in cars, on motorcycles, and on foot, ready to squat on the hillside facing the stage and sleep in bedrolls, in a tent, or under clouds. Rock artists were the big attraction, with Janis Joplin, Jimi Hendrix, and the Jefferson Airplane among the all-star lineup. For three days, *Newsweek* reported, the participants proclaimed the dawning of an Age of Aquarius in "history's largest happening," a tribal gathering that endorsed "communal living away from the cities, getting high, digging arts, clothes and crafts exhibits, and listening to the songs of revolution." According to Michael Lang, the twenty-four-year-old

rock-group manager who organized the festival, Woodstock demonstrated "that what this generation is all about is valid. This is not just
music, but a conglomeration of everything involved in the new
culture." Janis Joplin agreed that a new, idealistic—and powerful—
constituency was ready to transform American society and culture:
"There's lots and lots and lots of us, more than anybody ever thought
before. We used to think of ourselves as little clumps of weirdoes. But
now we're a whole new minority group." And Jimi Hendrix predicted
that "this was only the beginning." Through mass gatherings, a new

"History's largest happening," Woodstock, said one observer, demonstrates
"that what this generation is all about is valid." Pictured: Jefferson Airplane.
(Henry Diltz/Corbis)

generation would build community and begin to change things. "The whole world needs a big wash, a big scrub-down."[1]

Not everyone, of course, was as enthusiastic or optimistic about Woodstock. The festival underscored a persistent theme in rock 'n' roll, a theme that undercut the dream of unity: the United States was divided by age into "us" and "them." "If you were part of the culture," a young man said, "you had to be there"—and were obliged to share your digs, drinks, and drugs with total strangers. But if you weren't, no one expected you to understand. Such attitudes frightened many people over thirty. While the promoters stressed that there were no rapes, robberies, or assaults during the festival, critics bemoaned three deaths (one from a drug overdose), hundreds of bad LSD trips, the pervasiveness of marijuana, and a health emergency that compelled the organizers to bring in fifty doctors. "To many adults," a writer for *Time* opined, "the festival was a squalid freakout, a monstrous Dionysian revel, where a mob of crazies gathered to drop acid and groove to hours of amplified cacophony." They could not avoid the conclusion that "the children of the welfare state and the atom bomb do indeed march to the beat of a different drummer, as well as to the tune of an electric guitar." In an editorial that anguished over the "nightmare of mud and stagnation," the *New York Times* compared the pilgrimage to Bethel to lemmings following one another into the sea, Tulipmania, and the Children's Crusade. "What kind of culture is it that can produce so colossal a mess?" the editors asked.[2]

Woodstock turned out to be a less cosmic phenomenon than it appeared to be in 1969, when beat poet Allen Ginsberg called it "a major planetary event," The Jefferson Airplane proclaimed, "Look what's happening out in the streets/Got a revolution, got to revolution," and Yippie Abbie Hoffman predicted as imminent "the death of the American dinosaur." But there is no denying that "the generation attuned to rock, pot, and sex" wrought significant changes in the United States.[3] Or that the rock festival became, as *Time* put it, "the equivalent of a political forum for the young."[4]

The politics of ecstasy did not last, of course, and while rock 'n' roll remained potent through the remainder of the twentieth century, it fragmented in the age of multiculturalism and became less of a national force. Sometimes rock 'n' roll was political in the conventional sense of the term, with performers and members of the audience demanding a nuclear freeze, environmental reform, or aid to farmers. More often, it was, as it had been in the '50s, more cultural and personal than political or programmatic, a paean to freedom, autonomy, and authenticity, a suspicion of institutions and authority, and a call for communal gatherings filled with good vibrations.

There is no better illustration of the persistent power of rock 'n' roll—or of its complicated and contested impact—in the last quarter of the twentieth century than the career of Bruce Springsteen and the response of his fans to his music. Born in Freehold, New Jersey, in 1949, Springsteen was an unhappy loner until "his life was saved by rock 'n' roll." When he was nine, he watched Elvis on *The Ed Sullivan Show*, "and I had to get a guitar the next day." Since rock 'n' roll "was never, never about surrender," it helped him shrug off an angry and arbitrary father and the authoritarian nuns at school. Rock, he would remember much later, "provided me with a community, filled with people . . . who I didn't know, but who I knew were out there. We had this enormous thing in common, this 'thing' that initially felt like a secret . . . a home where my spirit could wander." As he watched the young Springsteen onstage, music critic John Landau described him as "dressed like a reject from Sha Na Na . . . [parading] in front of his all-star rhythm band like a cross between Chuck Berry, early Bob Dylan, and Marlon Brando." Springsteen never lost the '50s sensibility he exuded early in his career, but Landau was surely right in recognizing that he also represented "rock 'n' roll's future."[5]

By 1975, the '60s were clearly over. After Watergate, Vietnam, and the oil embargo, the United States was certainly not on the cusp of revolution. But while pet rocks, disco, and the sitcom *Happy Days* remained icons of popular culture, Springsteen's *Born to Run* became rock's first certified million-selling platinum album—and in the same week the singer appeared on the cover of *Time* and *Newsweek*. His songs visited familiar subjects: cars, romance, struggles with parents, authority, and life's expectations. But Springsteen brought to them poetry and passion, and a celebration of the heroism of a life lived each day with personal integrity. Journalist Eric Alterman was fifteen years old when the album was released: "*Born to Run* exploded in my home and my mind and changed my life. . . . [It] offered me an alternative context for my life, a narrative in which hopes and dreams that felt ridiculous were accorded dignity, and, no less important, solidarity."[6]

A rock 'n' roll sensation, whose concert performances were legendary, Springsteen followed *Born to Run* with *Darkness on the Edge of Town* in 1978, *The River*, which catapulted to first place on *Billboard*'s album chart in 1980 on the strength of the mega-hit single "Hungry Heart," and a solo acoustic album, *Nebraska* (1982). Sometimes light and sometimes dark, Springsteen's lyrics are intensely autobiographical, exploring the lives of men assaulted by a society that trivializes honest labor and values money and status above all things. But Springsteen always celebrates their pride and will to resist. Springsteen concerts, observers agree, resemble revival meetings, with congregants waiting, as critic John Rockwell did, for the singer to deliver the sermon that will "help inspire the country."[7]

Rock 'n' roll fans are often fanatically loyal to their favorite performers. When Springsteen appeared in Madison Square Garden, standing on a speaker with one arm raised high in the air, Stephen Fried detected in the subservient devotion of concertgoers to him an analogy to Nazi rallies in the 1930s. Not surprisingly, politicians eager to tap the youth market tried to associate themselves with popular rockers. During the 1976 presidential race, President Gerald Ford invited Peter Frampton to the White House. The Allman Brothers played so many concerts for Jimmy Carter that campaign workers asked jokingly whether Greg would be appointed head of the Food and Drug Administration.[8]

Springsteen lent his name to political causes as well, playing benefit concerts for Vietnam veterans and antinuclear groups. In 1980, the New Jersey assembly made "Born to Run" the state's "Unofficial Youth Rock Anthem." With the success in 1984 of *Born in the U.S.A.*, which contained seven top singles, stayed on *Billboard*'s charts for two years, and had domestic sales of eighteen million albums, political image makers salivated at the prospect of hijacking Springsteen's audience for their candidate. Springsteen thought the political message of the album's title song was transparent. He had written about a young man who gets into "a little hometown jam," chooses Vietnam over jail, and returns home to learn that the factory at which he had worked was closed. The final line, "Nowhere to run, ain't got nowhere to go," made it clear, he thought, that the protagonist wanted to "strip away that mythic America which was Reagan's image of America." And yet, in concert, Springsteen obscured this message by unfurling a large American flag as he sang. For this reason, and what appeared to be strong, patriotic background music, conservative George Will lauded the song in his widely syndicated newspaper column: "I have not got a clue about Springsteen's politics, but flags get waved at his concerts while he sings songs about hard times. He is no whiner, and the recitation of closed factories and other problems always seems punctuated by a grand, cheerful affirmation: 'Born in the U.S.A.'"

Ronald Reagan's handlers noticed. When the president announced his reelection bid in New Jersey, he asked Springsteen to appear with him. The singer declined, but with the Statue of Liberty at his back, the president told the crowd, "America's future rests in a thousand dreams inside our hearts. It rests in the message of hope so many young people admire: New Jersey's own Bruce Springsteen. And helping you make those dreams come true is what this job of mine is all about." The president frequently listened to Springsteen records, an aide told a reporter for the *Los Angeles Herald-Examiner*.[9]

Before long, in an editorial in *USA Today*, New Jersey Senator Bill Bradley claimed the song as the property of the Democratic Party. Chrysler offered the singer $12 million dollars to use "Born in the U.S.A." for a car commercial. L&M cigarettes, Citicorp checking accounts, VISTA volunteer internships, and the United Way made use of the song. It is not entirely clear how much responsibility Springsteen should shoulder for the contradictory interpretations of his songs or whether he has been misread with malice aforethought. "If the song was misunderstood," Springsteen maintains, "it was only misunderstood by Republicans." The meaning "is not ambiguous. You just have to listen to the verses." Yet, as we have seen, there is more to rock 'n' roll messages than the lyrics. In any event, the episode underscores the pivotal role rock 'n' roll continues to play in the lives of millions of Americans, a role that explains the zeal of corporate marketers and elected officials to appropriate the messenger to *their* message. Springsteen fans told Eric Alterman that the singer "makes me feel like I belong in this world"; his art "keeps my conscience alive"; "his music creates an internal dialogue that [helps] us discover who we are"; he has "given me solace in my grief, provided me with joy for celebrations, introduced me to lifelong friends, raised my blood pressure, increased my heart rate, added smile lines to my face, and made me dance on a folding chair and scream, 'Gooba, gooba, gooba.'"[10]

In the half century since rock 'n' roll got its name, the music has taken many forms, including R&B, romantic rock, heavy metal, punk rock, grunge rock, Christian rock, and postmodern feminist rock. More than ever, it frustrates anyone intent on giving it a rigorous, musical definition. It still has legions of fanatic fans and ferocious foes, ready to pledge more than their allegiance or antipathy to Madonna, Bono, or J.Lo. The music that changed America in the 1950s and '60s, rock 'n' roll continues to solidify youth consciousness and bring meaning and order to the lives of millions of people.

NOTES

1. "All Shook Up": Popular Music and American Culture, 1945–1955

1. "Rock 'n Roll Fight Hospitalizes Youth," *New York Times*, April 15, 1957.

2. See, e.g., "Gas Ends Rock 'n Roll Riot," *New York Times*, November 4, 1956; "Six Dallas Youths Hurt," *New York Times*, July 17, 1957; "Rock 'n Roll Stabbing," *New York Times*, May 5, 1958.

3. "Rock 'n Rollers Collect Calmly," *New York Times*, July 4, 1957; "Rock 'n Roll Teenagers Tie Up the Times Square Area," *New York Times*, February 23, 1957; "Times Square 'Rocks' for Second Day," *New York Times*, February 24, 1957.

4. "Rock 'n Roll," *Time*, July 23, 1956; "Jersey City Orders Rock-and-Roll Ban," *New York Times*, July 10, 1956; "Rock-and-Roll Gets Slowed to a Waltz," *New York Times*, July 12, 1956; "Rock 'n Roll Banned," *New York Times*, September 20, 1956.

5. Linda Martin and Kerry Segrave, *Anti-Rock: The Opposition to Rock 'n Roll* (Hamden, Conn: Archon, 1988), 29; "Rock 'n Roll," *Time*, July 23, 1956; "Boston, New Haven Ban 'Rock' Shows," *New York Times*, May 6, 1958.

6. "Rock 'n Roll," *Time*, July 23, 1956; Gertrude Samuels, "Why They Rock 'n Roll—And Should They?" *New York Times Magazine*, January 12, 1958.

7. Gertrude Samuels, "Why They Rock 'n Roll—And Should They?" *New York Times Magazine*, January 12, 1958; "Yeh-Heh-Heh-Hes, Baby," *Time*, June 18, 1956; "Rock-and-Roll Called Communicable Disease," *New York Times*, March 28, 1956.

8. Jack Lait and Lee Mortimer, *U.S.A. Confidential* (New York: Crown, 1952), 37–38.

9. James Gilbert, *A Cycle of Outrage: America's Reaction to the Juvenile Delinquent in the 1950s* (New York: Oxford University Press, 1986), 9; Warren Sussman, with the assistance of Edward Griffin, "Did Success Spoil the United States?: Dual Representations in Postwar America," in *Recasting America: Culture and Politics in the Age of the Cold War*, ed. Lary May (Chicago: Chicago University Press, 1989).

10. Douglas T. Miller and Marion Nowak, *The Fifties: The Way We Really Were* (Garden City, N.Y.: Doubleday, 1977), 22–23.

11. Gilbert, *Cycle of Outrage*, 13, 75. See also Elaine Tyler May, *Homeward Bound: American Families in the Cold War Era* (New York: Basic Books, 1988).

12. Robin Kelley, *Race Rebels: Culture, Politics, and the Black Working Class* (New York: Free Press, 1994), 181; Greil Marcus, *Mystery Train: Images of America in Rock 'n Roll Music* (New York: Dutton, 1975), 55, 121–22; Studying fads, according to Siegfried Kracauer, provides "unmediated access to the fundamental substance of the

state of things." Quoted in Russell Jacoby, *The End of Utopia: Politics and Culture in an Age of Apathy* (New York: Basic Books, 1999), 83.

13. Jeff Greenfield, *No Peace, No Place: Excavations Along the Generational Fault* (Garden City, N.Y.: Doubleday, 1973), 29.

14. Landon Y. Jones, *Great Expectations: America and the Baby Boom Generation* (New York: Coward, McCann & Geoghegan, 1980), 20.

15. Ibid., 11, 39, 68; May, *Homeward Bound*, 58, 165.

16. Laurence Redd, *Rock Is Rhythm and Blues: The Impact of Mass Media* (East Lansing: Michigan State University Press, 1974), 62; Erik Barnouw, *Tube of Plenty: The Evolution of American Television* (New York: Oxford University Press, 1975); Karal Ann Marling, *As Seen on TV: The Visual Culture of Everyday Life in the 1950s* (Cambridge: Harvard University Press, 1994). In 1950, *Life* magazine worried no one when it published a list of the people most admired by teenagers: Louisa May Alcott, Babe Ruth, Joe Dimaggio, Vera Ellen, Doris Day, Roy Rogers, Franklin Roosevelt, Abe Lincoln, Clara Barton, Florence Nightingale, and Sister Kenney.

17. Hugh Mooney, "Just Before Rock: Pop Music 1950-1953 Revisited," *Popular Music and Society* (1974): 65-108; Arnold Shaw, *The Rockin' '50s* (New York: Hawthorn, 1974), 26-114.

18. Arnold Shaw, *Honkers and Shouters: The Golden Years of Rhythm and Blues* (New York: Macmillan, 1978), xvi-xx, 349; Richard Aquila, *That Old-Time Rock & Roll: A Chronicle of an Era* (New York: Schirmer, 1989), 12-13; Charlie Gillett, *The Sound of the City: The Rise of Rock and Roll* (New York: Outerbridge & Dienstfrey, 1970), 12.

19. Miller and Nowak, *Fifties*, 183-84; Diane Ravitch, *Left Back: A Century of Failed School Reforms* (New York: Simon & Schuster, 2000), 376; Nadine Cohodas, *Spinning Blues into Gold: The Chess Brothers and the Legendary Chess Records* (New York: St. Martin's, 2000), 19.

20. Shaw, *Honkers and Shouters*, 61-75.

21. Brian Ward, *Just My Soul Responding: Rhythm and Blues, Black Consciousness, and Race Relations* (Berkeley and Los Angeles: University of California Press, 1998), 80-82.

22. Shaw, *Honkers and Shouters*, 45-49, 61-75, 305; Ward, *Just My Soul Responding*, 77-78. James Miller, *Flowers in the Dustbin: The Rise of Rock and Roll, 1947-1977* (New York: Simon & Schuster, 1999), 25-34. Female R&B vocalists, most notably Ruth Brown and Dinah Washington, celebrated their sexuality and commented sharply on the inadequacies of black men.

23. Steven Waksman, *Instruments of Desire: The Electric Guitar and the Shaping of Musical Experience* (Cambridge: Harvard University Press, 1999), 118-19; Gillett, *Sound of the City*, 154; Miller, *Flowers in the Dustbin*, 40-43.

24. Louis Cantor, *Wheelin' on Beale* (New York: Pharos, 1992), 12, 53, 144-46, 170-71; Redd, *Rock Is Rhythm and Blues*, 30; Sam Evans, "Kickin' the Blues Around," *Cash Box*, August 23, 1952.

25. Jones, *Great Expectations*, 108; Richard Peterson, "Why 1955? Explaining the Advent of Rock Music," *Popular Music* 9, no. 1 (1990): 102; James M. Curtis, *Rock Eras: Interpretations of Music and Society, 1954-1984* (Bowling Green, Ohio: Bowling Green State University Popular Press, 1987), 43.

26. Marc Eliot, *Rockonomics: The Money Behind the Music* (New York: F. Watts, 1989), 38; Ward, *Just My Soul Responding*, 22. Founded in 1952 by James Bracken Vivian, Carter Bracken, and Calvin Carter, Vee Jay Records was the most successful of the few black-owned "indies."

27. Miller and Nowak, *Fifties*, 189.

28. Ibid. 199.

29. "Kickin' the Blues Around with Sam Evans," *Cash Box*, May 31, June 28, November 29, 1952. A year earlier, *Cash Box* congratulated Evans, who had just received an award on the stage of the Chicago Opera House from Billy Eckstine and George Shearing, "for his great efforts on behalf of better interracial relations in the field of music." "In Tribute to a Columnist," November 24, 1951. *Cash Box* also cheered when a reception for the Four Aces in Nashville included two African-American DJs: "This action established a precedent in that area and quite possibly for the South.... It is said the National Association for the Advancement of Colored People contemplates national publicity." "Platter Spinner Patter," April 25, 1953.

30. Mitch Miller, "June, Moon, Swoon, and Ko Ko Mo," *New York Times Magazine*, April 24, 1955.

31. Shaw, *Rockin' '50s*, 103; Sam Evans, "Kickin' the Blues Around," *Cash Box*, December 13, 1952.

32. Paul Friedlander, *Rock and Roll: A Social History* (Boulder, Colo.: Westview Press, 1996), 22; George Lipsitz, "Land of a Thousand Dances: Youth, Minorities, and the Rise of Rock and Roll," in *Recasting America: Culture and Politics in the Age of the Cold War*, ed. Lary May (Chicago: Chicago University Press, 1989), 271. Large numbers of record buyers, Bob Rolontz and Joel Friedman reported in *Billboard*, are "of Mexican and Spanish descent." "Teen-agers Demand Music with a Beat, Spur Rhythm-Blues," *Billboard*, April 24, 1954.

33. Michael Lydon, "Chuck Berry," *Ramparts* (1969): 52; Bruce Tucker, "Tell Tchaikovsky the News: Postmodernism, Popular Culture, and the Emergence of Rock 'n Roll," *Black Music Research Journal* 8/9, no. 2 (1989): 281.

34. Laura Helper, "Whole Lot of Shakin' Going On: An Ethnography of Race Relations and Crossover Audiences for Rhythms and Blues and Rock and Roll in 1950s Memphis" (Ph.D. dissertation, Rice University, 1997), 172, 174, 186, 232, 239, 249. It is interesting that Berger recalled, incorrectly, that the audience was "mixed." For a description of the performers at the Plantation Inn, see Peter Guralnick, *Sweet Soul Music: Rhythm and Blues and the Southern Dream of Freedom* (Boston: Little, Brown, 1999), 110.

35. Cantor, *Wheelin' on Beale*, 164–67, 173, 177; Ward, *Just My Soul Responding*, 138.

36. Ward, *Just My Soul Responding*, 39; Jack Kerouac, *On the Road* (New York: Viking Compass, 1959), 180.

37. Ward, *Just My Soul Responding*, 241.

38. "Rhythm 'n Blues Ramblings," *Cash Box*, August 21, 1954; "Stop Making Dirty R&B Records," *Cash Box*, October 2, 1954.

39. John A. Jackson, *Big Beat Heat: Alan Freed and the Early Years of Rock & Roll* (New York: Schirmer, 1991), 1–54; Shaw, *Honkers and Shouters*, 512.

40. Jackson, *Big Beat Heat*, 55–71; Bill Millar, *The Drifters: The Rise and Fall of the Black Vocal Group* (London: Studio Vista, 1971), 31.

41. Jackson, *Big Beat Heat*, 72–87; Shaw, *Honkers and Shouters*, 73.

42. "Spotlight," *Billboard*, August 7, 1954.

43. The authoritative biography of Elvis is Peter Guralnick, *Last Train to Memphis: The Rise of Elvis Presley* (Boston: Little, Brown, 1994); see also Nick Tosches, *Country: The Twisted Roots of Rock 'n Roll* (New York: Da Capo, 1996), 44–46; Marcus, *Mystery Train*, 158–59. For a succinct summary of Elvis's early career see David Halberstam, *The Fifties* (New York: Villard, 1993), 456–79.

44. "A Hound Dog, to the Manor Born," *Esquire*, February 1968, 106–8, 48–52.

45. Guralnick, *Last Train to Memphis*, 47; Marcus, *Mystery Train*, 164; Gillett, *Sound of the City*, 36.

46. Guralnick, *Last Train to Memphis*, 3–8, 56–65.

47. Ibid. 3–65; Helper, "Whole Lot of Shakin' Going On," 60; Miller, *Flowers in the Dustbin*, 67–73.

48. Guralnick, *Last Train to Memphis*, 89–125; Marcus, *Mystery Train*, 174; Helper, "Whole Lot of Shakin' Going On," 158; Miller, *Flowers in the Dustbin*, 81–83; Curtis, *Rock Eras*, 28; Pete Daniel, *Lost Revolutions: The South in the 1950s* (Chapel Hill: University of North Carolina Press for Smithsonian National Museum of American History, Washington, D.C., 2000), 135.

49. Guralnick, *Last Train to Memphis*, 98–101.

50. Ibid., 111–14.

51. Helper, "Whole Lot of Shakin' Going On," 62.

52. Guralnick, *Last Train to Memphis*, 109–11.

53. Gillett, *Sound of the City*, 38.

54. Marcus, *Mystery Train*, 189–90.

55. Colin Escott with Martin Hawkins, *Good Rockin' Tonight: Sun Records and the Birth of Rock 'n Roll* (New York: St. Martin's, 1991), 84; Guralnick, *Last Train to Memphis*, 134.

56. John Swenson, *Bill Haley: The Daddy of Rock and Roll* (New York: Stein & Day, 1982); Miller, *Flowers in the Dustbin*, 87–94; "Platter Spinner Patter," *Cash Box*, May 9, 1953.

57. Richard Aquila, *That Old-Time Rock & Roll: A Chronicle of an Era* (New York: Schirmer, 1989), 8; Miller, *Flowers in the Dustbin*, 87–94.

58. Ronald Reagan told a committee of the U.S. Senate investigating juvenile delinquency that he was thrilled "at the great tribute" to schoolteachers in *Blackboard Jungle*. Audiences, he thought, reacted with "disgust for the boys on the wrong side of the fence" and "a feeling of triumph when the one boy was won over and became a leader for the right." *Hearings Before the Subcommittee to Investigate Juvenile Delinquency of the Committee of the Judiciary, United States Senate, Eighty-fourth Congress, First Session, Pursuant to Senate Resolution 62, June 15, 16, 17, 18, 1955* (Washington, 1955), 94.

59. Thomas Doherty, *Teenagers and Teenpics: The Juvenilization of American Movies in the 1950s* (Boston: Unwin Hyman, 1988), 57–58, 134–35. Johnny Green, who ran the music department at MGM, according to Doherty, thought "Rock Around the Clock" a "flash in the pan." He acquired rights to the song for *Blackboard Jungle* for $5,000 and made the monumental mistake of declining to pay another $25,000 to own it outright (204); Jones, *Great Expectations*, 61; Gilbert, *Cycle of Outrage*, 183–89.

60. Nick Tosches, *Unsung Heroes of Rock 'n Roll* (New York: Charles Scribner's Sons, 1984), 77. In *Rock Around the Clock*, manager Steve Hollis hears Haley and the Comets playing "See You Later, Alligator" and asks, "What's the outfit playing up there? . . . It isn't boogie, it isn't jive, and it isn't swing. It's kind of all of them." A dancer replies, "It's rock 'n roll, brother, and we're rocking tonight." Doherty, *Teenagers and Teenpics*, 86.

61. David Sanjek, "Can a Fujiyama Mama Be the Female Elvis?" in *Sexing the Groove: Popular Music and Gender*, ed. Sheila Whitely (London and New York: Routledge, 1997), 149; "Rock 'n Roll Carries On," *Cash Box*, August 27, 1955.

62. "Rock and Roll May Be the Great Unifying Force!" *Cash Box*, March 17, 1956.

2. "Brown-Eyed Handsome Man": Rock 'n' Roll and Race

1. For a concise account of these developments see David Halberstam, *The Fifties* (New York: Villard, 1993), 411–24, 539–63, 667–98. The seminal work on *Brown v. Board of Education* is Richard Kluger, *Simple Justice* (New York: Knopf, 1975). On the importance of this decision and its legacy see James T. Patterson, *Brown v. Board of Education: A Civil Rights Milestone and Its Troubled Legacy* (New York: Oxford University Press, 2001). For a treatment of the Montgomery Bus Boycott, see Taylor Branch, *Parting the Waters: America in the King Years, 1954–1963* (New York: Simon & Schuster, 1988).

2. "In every stage of the bus boycott," Eastland told a rally at the Montgomery Coliseum, "we have been oppressed and degraded because of black, slimy, juicy, unbearably stinking niggers.... African flesh eaters. When in the course of human events it becomes necessary to abolish the Negro race, proper methods should be used. Among these are guns, bows and arrows, slingshots, and knives.... All whites are created equal with certain rights, among these are life, liberty, and the pursuit of dead niggers." Robert A. Caro, *The Years of Lyndon Johnson: Master of the Senate* (New York: Knopf, 2002), 767.

3. "White Council vs. Rock and Roll," *Newsweek*, April 23, 1956; "Segregationist Wants Ban on Rock and Roll," *New York Times*, March 30, 1956; Brian Ward, *Just My Soul Responding: Rhythm and Blues, Black Consciousness, and Race Relations* (Berkeley and Los Angeles: University of California Press, 1998), 99–104, 225.

4. Ward, *Just My Soul Responding*, 95–96.

5. Ibid., 100, 102–3.

6. Ibid., 104–6; Peter Guralnick, *Last Train to Memphis: The Rise of Elvis Presley* (Boston: Little, Brown, 1994), 370.

7. Ward, *Just My Soul Responding*, 106–9, 168.

8. "Dominoes to Star in NAACP Benefits," *Cash Box*, September 25, 1954.

9. Ward, *Just My Soul Responding*, 130–33; for Cole's defense of his actions see "The Nat 'King' Cole Nobody Knows," *Ebony*, October 1956. Cole's political consciousness was also raised when his variety show, the first network television program to be hosted by a black performer, was canceled in 1957 after a year on the air, because NBC could not find sponsors willing to be associated with an African American. See Nat King Cole (as told to Lerone Bennett Jr.), "Why I Quit My TV Show," *Ebony*, February 1958.

10. "Letters to the Editor," *Ebony*, July 1957; Editorial, *Ebony*, March 1957; "How Serious Are Our Teenagers?" *Ebony*, October 1958; "The War on Rock 'n Roll," *Pittsburgh Courier*, October 6, 1956; "The Platters," *Ebony*, December 1956. See also "Rock 'n Roll Helping Race Relations, Platters Contend," *Down Beat*, May 30, 1956.

11. "Teen-Age Singers: Negro Youths Highest Paid in Junior Rock 'n Roll Biz," *Ebony*, November 1956; "Tweedle Dee Girl," *Ebony*, April 1956.

12. James Miller, *Flowers in the Dustbin: The Rise of Rock and Roll, 1947–1977* (New York: Simon & Schuster, 1999), 97–102.

13. "King of Rock 'n Roll: Fats Domino Hailed as New Idol of Teen-Agers," *Ebony*, February 1957.

14. "Pop Goes the Blues," *Cash Box*, February 13, 1954; Miller, *Flowers in the Dustbin*, 133; Norman Mailer, "The White Negro," in *Advertisements for Myself* (New York: Putnam, 1959), 337–58. In the 1960s, Eldridge Cleaver mocked whites who were "swinging and gyrating and shaking their dead little asses like petrified zombies trying

to regain the warmth of life, rekindle the dead limbs, the cold ass, the stone heart, the stiff mechanical disused joints with the spark of life." *Soul on Ice* (New York: McGraw-Hill, 1968), 197–98.

15. Ward, *Just My Soul Responding*, 189–90.

16. Langston Hughes, "Jazz: Its Yesterday, Today, and Its Potential Tomorrow," *New York Age*, July 28, 1956.

17. Berta Wood, "Are Negroes Ashamed of the Blues?" *Ebony*, May 1957. For responses to Wood see "Letters to the Editor," *Ebony*, July 1957. See also George E. Pitts, "Are Negroes Ashamed of Their Music?" *Pittsburgh Courier*, January 31, 1959.

18. "Musicians Argue Values of Rock and Roll," *Down Beat*, May 30, 1956.

19. "Breaking Down the Barriers," *Cash Box*, January 22, 1955; "R&B Ramblings," *Cash Box*, July 28, 1956; "Platter Spinner Patter," *Cash Box*, March 12, 1955.

20. "Breaking Down the Barriers," *Cash Box*, January 22, 1955; "American Music Becomes National Rather Than Regional," *Cash Box*, September 25, 1954. See also Ray Clark, "Rhythm and Blues Spreads Its Wings," *Cash Box*, July 28, 1956. For the link between universal values and racial tolerance see David A. Hollinger, *Postethnic America: Beyond Multiculturalism* (New York: Basic Books, 1995).

21. "Rhythm and Blues Ramblings," *Cash Box*, September 25, 1954; Ward, *Just My Sould Responding*, 128.

22. William Graebner, *Coming of Age in Buffalo: Youth and Authority in the Postwar Era* (Philadelphia: Temple University Press, 1990), 34.

23. Ward, *Just My Soul Responding*, 128–29.

24. Pete Daniel, *Lost Revolutions: The South in the 1950s* (Chapel Hill: University of North Carolina Press for Smithsonian National Museum of American History, Washington, D.C., 2000), 272; Gerald Grant, *The World We Created at Hamilton High* (Cambridge: Harvard University Press, 1988), 16. In a poll in 1957, 46 percent of upper-income and 38 percent of lower-income teenagers approved of school desegregation; 70 percent of upper-income and 50 percent of lower-income teenagers disapproved of disturbances to prevent desegregation. Jessie Bernard, "Teen-age Culture: An Overview," *Annals of the American Academy of Political and Social Science* 338 (November 1961): 1–12. Ward, *Just My Soul Responding*, 128.

25. Arnold Shaw, *The Rock Revolution* (London: Crowell-Macmillan, 1969), 34; Nik Cohen, "Classic Rock," in *The Penguin Book of Rock & Roll Writing*, ed. Charles Heylin (London: Penguin, 1993), 38.

26. Arnold Shaw, *Honkers and Shouters: The Golden Years of Rhythm and Blues* (New York: Macmillan, 1978), 32–33; Daniel, *Lost Revolution*, 122.

27. "Breaking Down the Barriers," *Cash Box*, January 22, 1955; Nadine Cohodas, *Spinning Blues into Gold: The Chess Brothers and the Legendary Chess Records* (New York: St. Martin's, 2000), 147.

28. Ward, *Just My Soul Responding*, 124.

29. Peter Guralnick, *Sweet Soul Music: Rhythm and Blues and the Southern Dream of Freedom* (Boston: Little, Brown, 1999), 14.

30. Ralph Ellison, *Living with Music: Ralph Ellison's Jazz Writings* (New York: Modern Library, 2001), 14, 25, 31; Ray Charles and David Ritz, *Brother Ray: Ray Charles' Own Story* (New York: Da Capo, 1992), 85–86, 176.

31. Ward, *Just My Soul Responding*, 45.

32. James M. Curtis, *Rock Eras: Interpretations of Music and Society, 1954–1984* (Bowling Green, Ohio: Bowling Green State University Popular Press, 1987), 65; Ward, *Just My Soul Responding*, 47.

33. Steve Perry, "Ain't No Mountain High Enough: The Politics of Crossover," in

Facing the Music, ed. Simon Frith (New York: Pantheon, 1988), 67, traces the history of the song (and quotes Greil Marcus). On the multicultural Otis see George Lipsitz, "Land of a Thousand Dances: Youth, Minorities, and the Rise of Rock and Roll," in *Recasting America: Culture and Politics in the Age of the Cold War*, ed. Lary May (Chicago: University of Chicago Press, 1989), 273–74.

34. Miller, *Flowers in the Dustbin*, 100–102.

35. Jonathan Kamin, "Taking the Roll out of Rock and Roll," *Popular Music and Society* 2 (Fall 1973): 1–17.

36. Ward, *Just My Soul Responding*, 48. To be sure, some white artists were compensated at this rate as well, though few accepted a one-time payment.

37. Chuck Berry, *The Autobiography* (New York: Harmony, 1987), 104, 110.

38. Ward, *Just My Soul Responding*, 45; John A. Jackson, *American Bandstand: Dick Clark and the Making of a Rock 'n Roll Empire* (New York: Oxford University Press, 1997), 89–92, 134–36, 181–90.

39. Ward, *Just My Soul Responding*, 48; "Rhythm 'n Blues Ramblings," *Cash Box* May 7, 1955; "WINS Will Not Play 'Copy' Records, *Cash Box*, August 7, 1955.

40. "Too Many Cover Jobs," *Cash Box*, February 26, 1955; "Rhythm 'n Blues Ramblings," *Cash Box*, September 10, 1955.

41. Jonathan Kamin, "The White R&B Audience and the Music Industry, 1952–1956," *Popular Music and Society* 6 (1978): 150–67; Jonathan Kamin, "Taking the Roll out of Rock and Roll," *Popular Music and Society* 2 (1973): 1–17; Ward, *Just My Soul Responding*, 49.

42. "Platter Spinner Patter," *Cash Box*, April 16, 1955.

43. "Rhythm 'n Blues Ramblings," *Cash Box*, February 4, 1956. According to his biographer, Armstrong "reveled in his blackness, in black language and bits of black experience that he tossed into his songs." Lawrence Bergreen, *Louis Armstrong: An Extravagant Life* (New York: Broadway Books, 1997), 333.

44. Paul Kohl, "Who Stole the Soul? Rock and Roll, Race, and Rebellion" (Ph.D. dissertation, University of Utah, 1994), 13.

45. Cohen, "Classic Rock," 38, 40; Miller, *Flowers in the Dustbin*, 108–13; Charles White, *The Life and Times of Little Richard, the Quasar of Rock* (New York: Harmony, 1984), 75; Daniel, *Lost Revolution*, 152; Dave Rogers, *Rock 'n Roll* (London: Routledge & Kegan Paul, 1982), 61–62.

46. Cohen, *Classic Rock*, 38, 40; *Rock & Roll Generation; Teen Life in the '50s* (Alexandria, Va.: Times-Life Books, 1998), 29.

47. Linda Martin and Kerry Segrave, *Anti-Rock: The Opposition to Rock 'n Roll* (Hamden, Conn.: Archon, 1988), 73–74; Ward, *Just My Soul Responding*, 52–53.

48. John A. Jackson, *Big Beat Heat: Alan Freed and the Early Years of Rock 'n Roll* (New York: Schirmer, 1991), 168; David Szatmary, *Rockin' in Time: A Social History of Rock and Roll* (Upper Saddle River, N.J.: Prentice-Hall, 2000), 21.

49. "Now Freud Gets into Teen-age R&R Act," *Billboard*, July 14, 1956.

50. Peter Guralnick, *Feel Like Going Home: Portraits in Blues and Rock 'n Roll* (New York: Outerbridge & Dienstfrey, 1971), 4.

51. Berry, *Autobiography*; Steve Waksman, *Instruments of Desire: The Electric Guitar and the Shaping of Musical Experience* (Cambridge: Harvard University Press, 1999), 158; Shaw, *Honkers and Shouters*, 64.

52. Miller, *Flowers in the Dustbin*, 103–7; Bruce Tucker, "Tell Tchaikovsky the News: Postmodernism, Popular Culture, and the Emergence of Rock 'n Roll," *Black Music Research Journal* 8/9, no. 2 (1989): 281.

53. Miller, *Flowers in the Dustbin*, 106; Herbert London, *Closing the Circle: A*

Cultural History of the Rock Revolution (Chicago: Nelson-Hall, 1984), 40–41. Berry's other "car songs" include "No Money Down" and "You Can't Catch Me."

54. Miller, *Flowers in the Dustbin*, 107. In his autobiography, Berry recounts an experience that suggested in a very different way how "white" his music seemed. In Knoxville in 1956, the proprietor of a club, misled perhaps by the photographs sent by Berry's agent, the Gale Agency, insisted that "he had no idea that 'Maybellene' was recorded by a niggra man." He refused to allow Berry to perform, and that night the singer sat in his Hertz rental car, listening to another band play his song. Berry, *Autobiography*, 136.

55. Ward, *Just My Soul Responding*, 111, 207–8. In the entry for "Chuck Berry" in the 1977 edition of *Current Biography* (57–60), "Brown-Eyed Handsome Man" is described as a song "about a black man's frustration in grasping unsuccessfully for the petty hedonism America supposedly promises everyone."

56. Ward, *Just My Soul Responding*, 207–8.

57. *Back to the Future*, the blockbuster film of the mid-1980s, provides an interesting perspective on Berry and the white cover phenomenon. Marty McFly, the hero of the movie, returns to his parents' high school in the 1950s. An early scene captures the optimism about integration and the persistent resistance to racial justice during the decade. Offered encouragement by George McFly, Marty's father, after a humiliating exchange with a customer, the black busboy in a diner expresses confidence that he will be a success. Marty discloses to the audience that the busboy will become mayor of the town. But when he gives voice to that possibility in the diner, the white manager replies, "That'll be the day." More important is the climactic scene of the film, set during a rhythm and blues concert by Marvin Berry and the Starlighters, where Marty brings the couple who will be his parents back together. When school bullies yell racial epithets at the band, George McFly decks one of them with a single punch, gaining the admiration of his future wife. When Marvin Berry is injured during the fracas, Marty replaces him, performing "Earth Angel" and "Johnny B. Goode" and doing the "duck walk." A stunned Marvin Berry calls Chuck, his cousin, and says, "You know the new sound you're looking for. Well, listen to this." This scene, as Steve Waksman has pointed out, simultaneously acknowledges and effaces the contribution of Berry as "the father of rock 'n roll," in a fantasy of racial cooperation that retains pride of place for the white male. And yet, since Marty actually proves to be a comically inept guitarist, the film may be subverting its own analysis, with a reminder about who really deserves the credit for inventing rock 'n roll. See Waksman, *Instruments of Desire*, 284–88, 366.

3: "Great Balls of Fire": Rock 'n' Roll and Sexuality

1. Stephanie Coontz, *The Way We Never Were: American Families and the Nostalgia Trap* (New York: Basic Books, 1992), 197; See also Jeffrey Moran, *Teaching Sex: The Shaping of Adolescence in the Twentieth Century* (Cambridge: Harvard University Press, 2000). For the phrase sexual "anti-inhibitor . . . the provocation to erotic vandalism," see Philip Roth, *The Dying Animal* (Boston: Houghton Mifflin, 2001), 56.

2. Simon Frith, *Sound Effects: Youth, Leisure, and the Politics of Rock and Roll* (New York: Pantheon, 1981), 239; Simon Frith and Angela McRobbie, "Rock and Sexuality" in *On Record: Rock, Pop, and the Written Word*, ed. Simon Frith and Andrew Goodwin (New York: Pantheon, 1990), 373, 388.

3. Elaine Tyler May, *Homeward Bound: American Families in the Cold War Era* (New York: Basic Books, 1988), 92–113; Frances Bruce Strain, *"But You Don't*

Understand": A Dramatic Series of Teenage Predicaments (New York: Appleton-Century-Crofts, 1950), 205–6; H. H. Remmers and D. H. Radler, *The American Teenager* (Indianapolis: Bobbs-Merrill, 1957), 91; Dwight Macdonald, "A Caste, a Culture, a Market—II," *New Yorker*, November 29, 1958, 79.

4. *Hearings Before the Subcommittee to Investigate Juvenile Delinquency of the Committee of the Judiciary, United States Senate, Eighty-Third Congress, Second Session, Pursuant to Senate Resolution* 89, April 14, 15, 1954 (Washington, 1954), 73; *Hearings Before the Subcommittee to Investigate Juvenile Delinquency of the Committee of the Judiciary, United States Senate, Eighty-fourth Congress, First Session, Pursuant to Senate Resolution* 62, May 24, 26, 31, June 9, 18, 1955 (Washington, 1955), 82; *Hearings Before the Subcommittee to Investigate Juvenile Delinquency of the Committee of the Judiciary, United States Senate, Eighty-fourth Congress, First Session, Pursuant to Senate Resolution* 62, March 11, April 28, 29, 30, 1955 (Washington, 1955), 81.

5. Strain, *"But You Don't Understand,"* 207.

6. Moran, *Teaching Sex*, 125–49.

7. "What Girls Think About Sex," *Seventeen*, July 1959. All the girls stressed the importance of seeking advice from parents. Unlike "your closest friend," Leslie asserted, "your parents are always there. They're steady." "It's up to us to let them know they can trust us," Valery added. And Susan admitted that although she had not always listened to her parents, with whom she sometimes had violent arguments, "sometimes I've found out in the end that they were correct, and I learned the hard way. Other times, I've thought I was correct and did what I thought was best. They respected that, too."

8. Coontz, *Way We Never Were*, 38–40; May, *Homeward Bound*, 117.

9. May, *Homeward Bound*, 114–34. The best biography of Kinsey is James H. Jones, *Alfred C. Kinsey: A Public/Private Life* (New York: Norton, 1997).

10. David Halberstam, *The Fifties* (New York: Villard, 1993), 272–81.

11. Douglas T. Miller and Marion Nowak, *The Fifties: The Way We Really Were* (Garden City, N.Y.: Doubleday, 1977), 293, 305. *The Cash Box* first linked Kinsey to R&B in "Platter Spinner Patter," March 29, 1952.

12. Jonathan Kamin, "Parallels in the Social Reactions to Jazz and Rock," *Black Perspective in Music* (1975): 278–97; Charlie Gillett, *The Sound of the City: The Rise of Rock and Roll* (New York: Outerbridge & Dienstfrey, 1971), 179.

13. Arnold Shaw, *Honkers and Shouters: The Golden Years of Rhythm and Blues* (New York: Macmillan, 1978), 285–86; Nick Tosches, *Unsung Heroes of Rock 'n Roll* (New York: Charles Scribner's Sons, 1984), 113; "Midnighter" Annie, "Follow-Up Keeps King Presses Rolling," *Cash Box*, August 21, 1954.

14. "Letter Asks Clean-Up of Filth Wax," *Billboard*, December 18, 1954; "DJ's Would Ban Smut and Racial Barbs on Disks," *Billboard*, February 27, 1954; Bob Rolontz, "Rhythm and Blues Notes," *Billboard*, October 9, 1954.

15. Bob Rolontz, "Rhythm and Blues Notes," *Billboard*, October 9, 1954.

16. "Stop Making DIRTY R&B Records," *Cash Box*, October 2, 1954; "Rhythm 'n Blues Ramblings," *Cash Box*, October 2, 1954; "Smutty Records Smell Up Spots," *Cash Box*, October 2, 1954.

17. Steve Schickel, "Cities Wield Heavy Broom in Air-Wave Clean-Up Campaign: Chi Teensters' 15,000 Letters Flood Stations," *Billboard*, April 2, 1955; Jane Bundy, "Obscene R&B Tunes Blasted in New England," *Billboard*, April 2, 1955; Brian Ward, *Just My Soul Responding: Rhythm and Blues, Black Consciousness, and Race Relations* (Berkeley and Los Angeles: University of California Press, 1998), 93.

18. "Second Bill to Ban Dirty Records," *Billboard*, February 13, 1954.

19. Gillett, *Sound of the City*, 25–26; *Honkers and Shouters*, 285–86.

20. Ward, *Just My Soul Responding*, 94; "Rhythm 'n Blues Ramblings," *Cash Box*, April 16, 1955. *Cash Box* applauded rock 'n' roll because "it is more melodic and the lyrics are more meaningful." "Pop Music Today Is Rock and Roll," *Cash Box*, April 20, 1957.

21. "The Question of Elvis Presley," *Cash Box*, September 1, 1956; "Ram Switches from Rock 'n Roll to Happy Music," *Cash Box*, September 8, 1956; "WMGM Intros Unusual New DJ Show," *Cash Box*, November 5, 1955; "Teenage Canteens," *Cash Box*, June 23, 1956; "Nationwide Acclaim Grows for Creation of Teenage Canteens," *Cash Box*, July 14, 1956.

22. Carl Belz, *The Story of Rock* (New York: Oxford University Press, 1972), 32; Jeff Greenfield, *No Peace, No Place: Excavations Along the Generational Fault* (Garden City, N.Y.: Doubleday, 1973), 54; Bruce Pollock, *Hipper than Our Kids: A Rock & Roll Journal of the Baby Boom Generation* (New York: Schirmer, 1993), 21.

23. Charles Heylin, ed., *The Penguin Book of Rock & Roll Writing* (London: Penguin, 1993), 47; Gillett, *Sound of the City*, 55; "Teen-Age Crush," *Time*, May 13, 1957.

24. Arnold Shaw, *The Rockin' '50s* (New York: Hawthorn, 1974), 235.

25. Ibid., 188.

26. *Rock & Roll Generation: Teen Life in the '50s* (Alexandria, Va.: Time-Life Books, 1998), 46; Arnold Shaw, *The Rock Revolution* (London: Atheneum, 1969), 38.

27. David Szatmary, *Rockin' in Time: A Social History of Rock and Roll* (Upper Saddle River, N.J.: Prentice-Hall, 2000), 24.

28. Shaw, *Rock Revolution*, 38.

29. Pat Boone, *'Twixt Twelve and Twenty* (Englewood Cliffs, N.J.: Prentice-Hall, 1958), 21–22, 29, 31, 35, 41, 68–69, 84, 88.

30. James Coleman, *The Adolescent Society: The Social Life of a Teenager and Its Impact on Education* (New York: Free Press of Glencoe, 1961), 23, 126, 205.

31. James Miller, *Flowers in the Dustbin: The Rise of Rock and Roll, 1947–1977* (New York: Simon & Schuster, 1999), 147–48.

32. John A. Jackson, *American Bandstand: Dick Clark and the Making of a Rock 'n Roll Empire* (New York: Oxford University Press, 1997), 1–50.

33. Ibid., 61–82; Shaw, *Rockin' '50s*, 176.

34. Dick Clark and Richard Robinson, *Rock, Roll & Remember* (New York: Crowell, 1976), 67, 81–82. Asked about the pin she was wearing, one girl told Clark it was "a mumble pin." "A what?" he asked. "A virgin pin," she replied, blushing. Clark, presumably, was not unhappy to have her on *American Bandstand*.

35. Ibid., 97; Miller, *Flowers in the Dustbin*, 147.

36. George Gallup and Evan Hill, "Youth: The Cool Generation," *Saturday Evening Post*, December 1961, 86; Jackson, *American Bandstand*, 71.

37. Ibid., 69–70.

38. Dick Clark, *Your Happiest Years* (New York: Rosho, 1959), 64, 125.

39. "Yeh-Heh-Heh-Hes, Baby," *Time*, June 18, 1956; "Newest Music for a New Generation: Rock 'n Roll Rolls On 'n On," *Life*, December 22, 1958.

40. Reebee Garofalo, *Rockin' Out: Popular Music in the USA* (Boston: Allyn & Bacon, 1997), 97; Pete Daniel, *Lost Revolutions: The South in the 1950s* (Chapel Hill: University of North Carolina Press for Smithsonian National Museum of American History, Washington, D.C., 2000), 153. Industry insiders were well aware of the

absence of women rock 'n roll performers. See "The Plight of the Female Singer," *Cash Box*, November 17, 1956.

41. "Teeners' Hero," *Time*, May 14, 1956; May, *Homeward Bound*, 92–93, 112.

42. Linda Ray Pratt, "Elvis, or the Ironies of a Southern Identity," and Richard Middleton, "All Shook Up?," in Kevin Quain, ed., *The Elvis Reader: Texts and Sources on the King of Rock 'n Roll*, ed. Kevin Quain (New York: St. Martin's, 1992), 9–12, 99–100.

43. Thomas R. Morgan, "Teen-Age Heroes: Mirrors of Muddled Youth," *Esquire*, March 1960, 65–71; Steve Waksman, *Instruments of Desire: The Electric Guitar and the Shaping of Musical Experience* (Cambridge: Harvard University Press, 1999), 253.

44. Miller, *Flowers in the Dustbin*, 134; "Elvis—A Different Kind of Idol," *Life*, August 27, 1956; "Beware Elvis Presley," *America*, June 23, 1956. "I'm convinced that the suggestiveness is lost on much of the teenage audience, and that their response to the stimulating rhythm, though physical, is hardly sexual," John Sharnik wrote in "The War of the Generations," *House & Garden*, October 1956.

45. Linda Martin and Kerry Segrave, *Anti-Rock: The Opposition to Rock 'n Roll* (Hamden, Conn.: Archon, 1988), 64–65.

46. Presley was taken aback by the vituperation directed at him, and by what he regarded as the hypocrisy of his critics. Appearing on the Berle show with him, Elvis told a reporter in Charlotte, North Carolina, was Debra Paget, who "wore a tight thing with feathers on the behind where they wiggle most. And I never saw anything like it. Sex? Man, she bumped and pooshed out all over the place. I'm like Little Boy Blue. And who do they say is obscene? Me!" Peter Guralnick, *Last Train to Memphis: The Rise of Elvis Presley* (Boston: Little, Brown, 1994), 288.

47. Presley's television appearances are treated authoritatively in Guralnick, *Last Train to Memphis*, 244–46, 249–50, 251, 252, 263–64, 283–85, 287, 290, 293–95, 301, 311, 337–39, 351–53, 379. For a briefer account see Miller, *Flowers in the Dustbin*, 129–37. See also Jack Gould, "Elvis Presley," *New York Times*, September 27, 1956.

48. Garofalo, *Rockin' Out*, 135–39; Szatmary, *Rockin' in Time*, 31–34, 49–51.

49. Garofalo, *Rockin' Out*, 107; Paul Friedlander, *Rock and Roll: A Social History* (Boulder, Colo.: Westview Press, 1966), 48–49.

50. This account of Lewis's career draws on Jimmy Guterman, *Rockin' My Life Away: Listening to Jerry Lee Lewis* (Nashville: Rutledge Hill Press, 1991), 29–93; Nick Tosches, *Hellfire: The Jerry Lee Lewis Story* (New York: Dell, 1982), 15–148.

51. Grace Hechinger and Fred M. Hechinger, *Teen-Age Tyranny* (New York: Morrow, 1963), 59.

4. "Yakety Yak, Don't Talk Back": Rock 'n' Roll and Generational Conflict

1. Harrison Salisbury, *The Shook-Up Generation* (New York: Harper, 1958), 136; James Gilbert, *A Cycle of Outrage: America's Reaction to the Juvenile Delinquent in the 1950s* (New York: Oxford University Press, 1986), 78; John Sharnik, "The War of the Generations," *House & Garden*, October 1956.

2. Dwight Macdonald, "A Caste, a Culture, a Market—I," *New Yorker*, November 22, 1958, 57; Thomas Doherty, *Teenagers and Teenpics: The Juvenilization of American Movies in the 1950s* (Boston: Unwin Hyman, 1988), 51; Simon Frith, *Sound Effects: Youth, Leisure, and the Politics of Rock and Roll* (New York: Pantheon, 1981), 187–89; Grace Palladino, *Teenagers: An American History* (New York: Basic Books, 1996), 81–173.

3. Macdonald, "A Caste, a Culture, a Market—I," 58.

4. Doherty, *Teenagers and Teenpics*, 44; Gilbert, *A Cycle of Outrage*, 19.

5. Gilbert, *A Cycle of Outrage*, 29, 34.

6. Salisbury, *Shook-Up Generation*, 109–17; *Hearings Before the Subcommittee to Investigate Juvenile Delinquency of the Committee of the Judiciary, United States Senate, Eighty-third Congress, First Session, Pursuant to Senate Resolution 89, November 19, 20, 23, 24, 1954* (Washington, 1954), 675; *Hearings Before the Subcommittee to Investigate Juvenile Delinquency of the Committee of the Judiciary, United States Senate, Eighty-third congress, Second Session, Pursuant to Senate Resolution 89, January 28, 29, 30, 1954* (Washington, 1954), 47; *Hearings Before the Subcommittee to Investigate Juvenile Delinquency of the Committee of the Judiciary, United States Senate, Eighty-third Congress, Second Session, Pursuant to Senate Resolution 89, April 14, 15, 1954* (Washington, 1954), 170; *Hearings Before the Subcommittee to Investigate Juvenile Delinquency of the Committee of the Judiciary, United States Senate, Eighty-third Congress, Second Session, Pursuant to Senate Resolution 89, September 24, 27, October 4, 5, 1954* (Washington, 1955), 139.

7. Sumner Ahlbum, "Are You Afraid of Your Teenager," *Cosmopolitan*, November 1957, 43; *Hearings Before the Subcommittee to Investigate Juvenile Delinquency of the Committee of the Judiciary, United States Senate, Eighty-third Congress, First Session, Pursuant to Senate Resolution 89, December 14, 1953* (Washington, 1954), 80.

8. *Hearings Before the Subcommittee to Investigate Juvenile Delinquency of the Committee of the Judiciary, United States Senate, Eighty-third congress, First Session, Pursuant to Senate Resolution 89, November 19, 20, 23, 24, 1953* (Washington, 1954), 210, 483, 485.

9. Elaine Tyler May, *Homeward Bound: American Families in the Cold War Era* (New York: Basic Books, 1988), 147–48.

10. *Hearings Before the Subcommittee to Investigate Juvenile Delinquency of the Committee of the Judiciary, United States Senate, Eighty-third Congress, First Session, Pursuant to Senate Resolution 89, November 19, 20, 23, 24, 1953* (Washington, 1954), 679–80; *Hearings Before the Subcommittee to Investigate Juvenile Delinquency of the Committee of the Judiciary, United States Senate, Eighty-fourth Congress, First Session, Pursuant to Senate Resolution 62, January 15, 16, 17, 18, 1955* (Washington, 1955), 29; James S. Coleman, *The Adolescent Society: The Social Life of a Teenager and Its Impact on Education* (New York: Free Press of Glencoe, 1961), 313. Experts found the traditionalists' recommendation that mothers stop working unrealistic as well. See, e.g., the testimony of Zollie Maynard of Florida's Department of Education in *Hearings Before the Subcommittee to Investigate Juvenile Delinquency of the Committee of the Judiciary, United States Senate, Eighty-sixth Congress, First Session, Pursuant to Senate Resolution 54, November 9, 10, 12, 16, 17, 19, 20, 1959* (Washington, 1960), 1372.

11. Gilbert, *A Cycle of Outrage*, 67; H. H. Remmers and D. H. Radler, *The American Teenager* (Indianapolis: Bobbs-Merrill, 1957), 42–43, 87–88, 96, 100; Grace Hechinger and Fred Hechinger, *Teen-Age Tyranny* (New York: Morrow, 1963), 145.

12. Enid Haupt, *The Seventeen Book of Young Living* (New York: McKay, 1957), 13–15. See also Charles H. Brown, "The Teen Type Magazine," *Annals of the American Academy of Political and Social Science* (November 1961): 13–21. *Newsweek* reported that parents in an Ohio town used the Haupt approach to thwart the teenagers' plea "all the other kids are doing it." They met secretly and drafted a code setting a curfew, the number of nights out per week they would permit, and the age at which a girl could attend dances. One of "the most devastating arguments that an American teenager can raise was erased," *Newsweek* concluded, "because all the

parents knew just exactly what all the other youngsters were doing." Cited in Douglas Miller and Marian Nowak, *The Fifties: The Way We Really Were* (Garden City, N.Y.: Doubleday, 1977), 279.

13. Edgar Z. Friedenberg, *The Vanishing Adolescent* (Boston: Beacon Press, 1959), 9, 10, 13, 15. Friedenberg, it is worth observing, was less sympathetic to girls than boys: "Girls also play a form of basketball, of course, as do paraplegics in wheel chairs and, for all I know, purple cows; but I do not know why. Even a culture which can usually convince itself that it would enjoy nothing more than the opportunity to observe scantily clad young ladies closely for two or three hours seems to find something incongruous in the spectacle and to avoid it. The emotional aura seems wrong; a girls' basketball team is likely to strike an audience as unconvincing, in the same sense that a bad play does, even if it is technically competent. Dr. Johnson might have compared a girl playing basketball to a woman preacher" (28).

14. Dwight Macdonald, "A Caste, a Culture, A Market—II," *New Yorker*, November 29, 1958, 60, 62, 69; Salisbury, *Shook Up Generation*, 16, 107, 127; Jon Savage, "The Enemy Within: Sex, Rock, and Identity," in *Facing the Music*, ed. Simon Frith (New York: Pantheon, 1988), 144; Susan J. Douglas, *Where the Girls Are: Growing Up Female with the Mass Media* (New York: Times Books, 1994), 21–22. "Since it was assumed that delinquency in Negro children was a racial rather than a human problem," Rose Cooper Thomas of the National Council of Negro Women acidly observed, "opportunity to gain experience and skill in preventing delinquency has been lost to the entire community." See *Hearings Before the Subcommittee to Investigate Juvenile Delinquency of the Committee of the Judiciary, United States Senate, Eighty-third congress, First Session, Pursuant to Senate Resolution 89*, November 19, 20, 23, 24, 1953 (Washington, 1954), 727.

15. Jeff Greenfield, *No Peace, No Place: Excavations Along the Generational Fault* (Garden City, N.Y.: Doubleday, 1973), 36.

16. Macdonald, "A Caste, a Culture, a Market—II," 101. The "good" students are described in Gerald Grant, *The World We Created at Hamilton High* (Cambridge: Harvard University Press, 1988), 14.

17. "Teen-Age Singers: Negro Youths Highest Paid in Junior Rock 'n Roll Biz," *Ebony*, November 1956; Hechinger and Hechinger, *Teen-Age Tyranny*, 131. Although he suggests that "the average '50s parent was probably more anxious about fluoridation than teenage music," Doherty acknowledges that public discourse about it was neither "calm nor reasoned" and that rock 'n' roll "had become a dramatic arena in which to play out generational conflict." Doherty, *Teenagers and Teenpics*, 81–82.

18. Herbert London, *Closing the Circle: A Cultural History of the Rock Revolution* (Chicago: Nelson-Hall, 1984), 73. Ethan Russell, *Dear Mr. Fantasy: Diary of a Decade: Our Time and Rock and Roll* (Boston: Houghton Mifflin, 1985), 23.

19. "Letter to the Editor," *Senior Scholastic*, November 15, 1956.

20. "Open Letter to Parent," *Seventeen*, November 1956.

21. "Rhythm 'n Blues Ramblings," *Cash Box*, April 7, 1956; "World Wide Reaction Supports *Cash Box* Editorial Refuting Charge That Rock & Roll Causes Juvenile Delinquency," *Cash Box*, June 9, 1956.

22. "Rhythm 'n Blues Ramblings," *Cash Box*, April 7, 1956; "Does Rock & Roll Cause Juvenile Delinquency?" *Cash Box*, April 14, 1946; Eugene Pleshette, "It's the Same Old Thing," *Cash Box*, July 28, 1956.

23. Doherty, *Teenagers and Teenpics*, 199–200.

24. "Rhythm 'n Blues Ramblings," *Cash Box*, July 14, 1956; "WOV's 'Jocko' Using Rock 'n Roll to Guide Teeners," *Cash Box*, September 22, 1956.

25. "ABC-Paramount Releases 'The Teen Commandments,'" *Cash Box*, November 8, 1958.

26. "Dick Clark Talks to Teenagers," *Seventeen*, July 1959; Dick Clark, *Your Happiest Years* (New York: Rosho, 1959), 17, 20, 60, 69, 84, 90, 92. Clark's analysis did not gain him the respect of all adults. Most of the responses to the article in *Seventeen* were critical. Clark's claims that parents envy teens, wrote L. B. of Mineral Wells, Texas, was "fiction, fiction, fiction." J.M.K. of North Hampton, New Hampshire, believed there was "already enough discord between teenagers and parents without [Clark] heaping coals on the fire." And C. A. of Cornwallis Heights, Pennsylvania, asked, "How does a grinning radio announcer and rock 'n' roll messiah suddenly burst out with the authority of a super-Freud? Isn't it high time teenagers returned to the human race and tried to develop some character and self-discipline?" See "Your Letters," *Seventeen*, September 1959.

27. Pat Boone, *'Twixt Twelve and Twenty* (Englewood Cliffs, N.J.: Prentice-Hall, 1958), 22, 24, 41, 62, 109, 117, 120.

28. Both Boone films are analyzed in Doherty, *Teenagers and Teenpics*, 188–93.

29. Ibid., 79, 93, 97.

30. Ibid., 87–90; David Ehrenstein and Bill Reed, *Rock on Film* (New York: Delilah Books, 1982), 11, 31–32.

31. Doherty, *Teenagers and Teenpics*, 97–98.

32. The preceding narrative draws on Joel Selvin, *Ricky Nelson: Idol for a Generation* (Chicago: Contemporary, 1990), 28, 41, 46, 54–55, 57, 62–67, 68. James M. Miller, *Flowers in the Dustbin: The Rise of Rock and Roll, 1947–1977* (New York: Simon & Schuster, 1999), 138–43; "Ozzie and Harriet . . . They Never Leave Home," *Look*, October 2, 1950.

33. Bob Rolontz, "The New Look in Rock and Roll," *Cash Box*, July 28, 1956; David Reisman, "Listening to Popular Music," in *On Record: Rock, Pop, and the Written Word*, ed. Simon Frith and Andrew Goodwin (New York: Pantheon, 1990), 12; Macdonald, "A Caste, a Culture, a Market—I," 57–58; Friedenberg, *Vanishing Adolescent*, 37.

34. Macdonald, "A Caste, a Culture, a Market—I," 72–73; Bill Davidson, "18,000,000 Teen-Agers Can't Be Wrong," *Collier's*, January 4, 1957, 13–25; "The Big Youth Market: How to Learn What It Thinks," *Dun's Review and Modern Industry*, December 1953, 153–56; Louis Cassels, "The Coming Boom in the Teenage Market," *Management Review*, August 1957, 6–8.

35. Macdonald, "A Caste, a Culture, a Market—I," 72–74; Eugene Gilbert, "Why Today's Teenagers Seem So Different," *Harper's Magazine*, November 1959, 76–79; Richard Gehman, "The Nine Billion Dollars in Hot Little Hands," *Cosmopolitan*, November 1957, 72–79.

36. Macdonald, "A Caste, a Culture, a Market—I," 76; Miller and Nowak, *Fifties*, 119; Hechinger and Hechinger, *Teen-Age Tyranny*, 185. In the 1960s, at least for a time, adults concluded "if you can't beat 'em, join 'em." In 1961, *Seventeen* proclaimed, "*Seventeen* is 17 . . . Isn't everybody?"

37. Doherty, *Teenagers and Teenpics*, 53.

38. "Over 7,300,000 Teenage Disk Buyers in U.S.A.," *Cash Box*, December 12, 1953; "Teen-Age Market!" *Cash Box*, January 28, 1956; "Rhythm 'n Blues Ramblings," *Cash Box*, March 3, 1956; "There's More to the Teenager Market than Meets the Eye," *Cash Box*, December 1, 1956; "Teenage Market Points Way to New Prosperity Heights!" *Cash Box*, June 8, 1957.

39. Doherty, *Teenagers and Teenpics*, 54–61.

40. Arthur R. Hammer, "Fad Also Rocks Cash Registers," *New York Times*, February 23, 1957; "General Electric Promotes Teenage R&R Cookery," *Cash Box*, September 28, 1957.

41. Dwight Macdonald, "A Caste, a Culture, a Market—II," 100; "Thar's Gold in Them Side Burns," *Billboard*, August 25, 1956; "Lip Rouge to Rock 'n' Roll," *Billboard*, September 29, 1956.

42. Two years earlier, Miller had defended lyrics of "questionable dignity" in the songs he promoted: "Maybe it is drivel. But a pop song doesn't make a claim on anyone's life, and the lyrics aren't there at the expense of something else. The lyrics of great operas sound silly too, if you separate them from the music." See Dean Jennings, "The Shaggy Genius of Pop Music," *Saturday Evening Post*, April 21, 1956, 42–43.

43. "Mitch Miller Speech at DJ Convention," *Cash Box*, March 22, 1958; "Answers to Mitch Miller Speech," *Cash Box*, March 22, 1958; "'Teen Buyers Grow Up,' Warns Miller," *Billboard*, September 8, 1956; Macdonald, "A Caste, a Culture, a Market—II," 91, 96–98. To "wean the teenagers away from rock 'n' roll," a campaign "to establish the polka and 'commercial corn' dance music as the next national craze" was mounted. Most teenagers dismissed it as "strictly square." See Doherty, *Teenagers and Teenpics*, 56–57.

44. Macdonald, "A Caste, a Culture, a Market—II," 69; Hechinger and Hechinger, 16–17, 32.

45. Landon Y. Jones, *Great Expectations: America and the Baby Boom Generation* (New York: Coward, McCann & Geohegan, 1980), 86; Hechinger and Hechinger, 135, 195, 214. Eugene Gilbert attributed the increase in conservatism and conformity to life in the shadow of atomic bombs: "To lose one's identity within the pattern of one's contemporaries, to seek the haven of a steady job rather than personal achievement, to prize material possessions above abstract principles—these may be the best available safety rafts in an insecure world." "Why Today's Teen-Agers Seem So Different," *Harper's Magazine*, November 1959, 79.

46. Jones, *Great Expectations*,76; Friedenberg, *Vanishing Adolescent*, 7–8.

47. Hechinger and Hechinger, 237, 243.

5. "Roll Over Beethoven, Tell Tchaikovsky the News": Rock 'n' Roll and the Pop Culture Wars

1. "R&B Ramblings," *Cash Box*, January 5, 1957; Steve Chapple and Reebee Garofalo, *Rock 'n Roll Is Here to Pay: The History and Politics of the Music Industry* (Chicago: Nelson-Hall, 1978), 13–20; Susan J. Douglas, *Listening In: Radio and the American Imagination* (New York: Times Books, 1999), 227.

2. Matthew A. Killmeier, "Voices Between the Tracks: Disc Jockeys, Radio, and Popular Music, 1955–1960," *Journal of Communication Inquiry* (October 2001): 353–74.

3. Thomas Doherty, *Teenagers and Teenpics: The Juvenilization of American Movies in the 1950s* (Boston: Unwin Hyman, 1988), 71–83.

4. Kerry Segrave, *Payola in the Music Industry: A History, 1880–1991* (Jefferson, N.C.: McFarland, 1994), 83.

5. Chapple and Garofalo, *Rock 'n Roll Is Here to Pay*, 43–47.

6. Ibid., 46, 77–78; "The Changing Nature of the Publishing Business," *Cash Box*, February 8, 1958; "Buying Masters," *Cash Box*, March 8, 1958. Rock 'n roll records were not nearly as easy or inexpensive to make as critics charged. Marion Keisker of Sun Records recalled that "each record was sweated out with hours of do it again and hold onto that little thing there." Albin J. Zak III, *The Poetics of Rock: Cutting*

Tracks, Making Records (Berkeley and Los Angeles: University of California Press, 2001), 131.

7. Philip H. Ennis, *The Seventh Stream: The Emergence of Rock 'n Roll in American Popular Music* (Hanover, N.H.: University of Press of New England, 1992), 108–9. Russell Sanjek, *American Popular Music and Its Business: The First Four Hundred Years, Volume III, from 1900 to 1984* (New York: Oxford University Press, 1988), 215–90; Chapple and Garofalo, *Rock 'n Roll Is Here to Pay*, 64–65; Marc Eliot, *Rockonomics: The Money Behind the Music* (New York: F. Watts, 1989), 22–26.

8. Eliot, *Rockonomics*, 42.

9. "Music Ops' Leaders Prepare for Forthcoming Legislative Battle," *Cash Box*, February 28, 1953; Paul Ackerman, "Tin Pan Alley Days Fade on Pop Music Broader Horizons," *Billboard*, October 5, 1955; Chapple and Garofalo, *Rock 'n Roll Is Here to Pay*, 64–66.

10. *Hearings Before the Subcommittee on Communications of the Committee on Interstate and Foreign Commerce, United States Senate, Eighty-fifth Congress, Second Session, Pursuant to an Amendment to the Communications Act of 1934* (Washington, 1958; hereafter cited as *Hearings*), 1; Sanjek, *American Popular Music and Its Business*, 423–24.

11. *Hearings*, 7.

12. Ibid., 24–27.

13. Ibid., 107–11, 114–15, 118–19, 132–33, 136–40.

14. Sanjek, *American Popular Music and Its Business*, 429; "Communists, Traitors, and Music Men," *Cash Box*, March 29, 1958.

15. Sanjek, *American Popular Music and Its Business*, 427.

16. *Hearings*, 547–53.

17. Ibid., 389–91, 406–7, 420–23, 471.

18. Sanjek, *American Popular Music and Its Business*, 430.

19. *Hearings*, 29–30, 35.

20. Ibid., 10–11, 26–27, 75, 121, 152.

21. Sanjek, *American Popular Music and Its Business*, 430–31.

22. "Hungry DJ's a Growing Headache," *Billboard*, December 23, 1950; Segrave, *Payola in the Music Industry*, 80.

23. Killmeier, "Voices Between the Tracks," 363; Segrave, *Payola in the Music Industry*, 80. At the height of the scandal, Kevin Sweeney, president of the Radio Advertising Bureau, estimated that payola influenced less than 1 percent of the music played. "FCC & FTC Move Against Payola," *Cash Box*, December 12, 1959.

24. Segrave, *Payola in the Music Industry*, 79–80, 84, 85–86.

25. Killmeier, "Voices Between the Tracks," 364.

26. Segrave, *Payola in the Music Industry*, 80, 82, 85; "What's All This Nonsense About Frankensteins and Disc Jockeys?", *Cash Box*, August 18, 1951.

27. Segrave, *Payola in the Music Industry*, 84–85.

28. Chapple and Garofalo, *Rock 'n Roll Is Here to Pay*, 57–60.

29. Mildred Hall, "Payola Hit at BMI Inquiry; Chairman Calls for Proof," *Billboard*, March 24, 1958; Segrave, *Payola in the Music Industry*, 80.

30. David Halberstam, *The Fifties* (New York: Villard, 1993), 643–66.

31. "Subcommittee Hooks Set for Payola Probe," *Billboard*, December 7, 1959; Mildred Hall, "Exhaustive Probe for Whole Music Industry on Way," *Billboard*, December 21, 1959; Chapple and Garofalo, *Rock 'n Roll Is Here to Pay*, 66.

32. Jack Gould, "TV: Assessing Effects of Life Under the Table," *New York Times*,

November 20, 1959; "Lame, Halt, and Blind," *Billboard*, November 30, 1959.

33. Segrave, *Payola in the Music Industry*, 105.

34. Ibid., 105–7.

35. Ibid., 105, 107–8, 150–53.

36. Ibid., 107, 117; "FCC & FTC Move Against 'Payola,'" *Cash Box*, December 12, 1959.

37. Segrave, *Payola in the Music Industry*, 135, 139–42; Sanjek, *American Popular Music and Its Business*, 449–51.

38. Segrave, *Payola in the Music Industry*, 116–17, 123–24, 134, 153–54.

39. For an account of Freed's role in the "riot" see John A. Jackson, *Big Beat Heat: Alan Freed and the Early Years of Rock and Roll* (New York: Schirmer, 1991), 190–206.

40. The preceding narrative draws on ibid., 243–327.

41. The preceding narrative draws on John A. Jackson, *American Bandstand: Dick Clark and the Making of a Rock 'n Roll Empire* (New York: Oxford University Press, 1997), 156–96; Segrave, *Payola in the Music Industry*, 110, 154–55.

42. "Nobody Blew the Whistle," *Newsweek*, May 9, 1960.

43. Jackson, *Big Beat Heat*, 278–85.

44. *Responsibilities of Broadcasting Licensees and Station Personnel. Hearings Before a Subcommittee of the Committee on Interstate and Foreign commerce, House of Representatives, Eighty-sixth Congress, Second Session, on Payola and Other Deceptive Practices in the Broadcasting Field* (Washington, 1960; hereafter cited as *Responsibilities*), 1025–1054.

45. Ibid., 1095–1112.

46. Ibid., 830–895.

47. Ibid., 1113–45.

48. Ibid., 945–96.

49. Ibid., 997–1025; Jackson, *American Bandstand*, 182.

50. Jackson, *American Bandstand*, 181–82.

51. *Responsibilities*, 1167–85, 1189–90, 1200, 1202, 1335.

52. Jackson, *American Bandstand*, 186–87; *Responsibilities*, 1350–51.

53. Ibid., 1200, 1201, 1204, 1214.

54. Ibid., 1312, 1316–18, 1322–23, 1326, 1332.

55. Ibid., 770, 1342; "FCC & FTC Move Against 'Payola,'" *Cash Box*, December 12, 1959; Segrave, *Payola in the Music Industry*, 116, 125, 126, 136, 155. In 1962, Pravda congratulated WINS in New York City "for dropping rock 'n roll, that contaminator of American Youth." Arnold Shaw, *The Rock Revolution* (London: Atheneum, 1969), 187.

56. Segrave, *Payola in the Music Industry*, 137.

6. "The Day the Music Died": Rock 'n' Roll's Lull and Revival

1. Alice Echols, *Shaky Ground: The '60s and Its Aftershocks* (New York: Columbia University Press, 2002), 24.

2. The preceding narrative draws on Charles White, *The Life and Times of Little Richard, the Quasar of Rock* (New York: Harmony, 1984), 88–102, 113–15; Reebee Garofalo, *Rockin' Out: Popular Music in the USA* (Boston: Allyn & Bacon, 1997), 106–8; "Gone Signs Little Richard," *Cash Box*, June 20, 1959.

3. My account draws on Nick Tosches, *Hellfire: The Jerry Lee Lewis Story* (New

York: Dell, 1982), 151–71; Jimmy Guterman, *Rockin' My Life Away: Listening to Jerry Lee Lewis* (Nashville: Rutledge Hill Press, 1991), 88–109; Colin Escott with Martin Hawkins, *Good Rockin' Tonight: Sun Records and the Birth of Rock 'n Roll* (New York: St. Martin's, 1991), 201.

4. The preceding narrative draws on Howard A. DeWitt, *Chuck Berry: Rock 'n Roll Music* (Ann Arbor: Pierian Press, 1985), 83–97, 109; *Chuck Berry, the Autobiography* (New York: Harmony, 1987), 199–209; Brian Ward, *Just My Soul Responding: Rhythm and Blues, Black Consciousness, and Race Relations* (Berkeley and Los Angeles: University of California Press, 1998), 111–12.

5. Peter Guralnick, *Last Train to Memphis: The Rise of Elvis Presley* (Boston: Little, Brown, 1994), 384–85.

6. Brian Tucker, "Tell Tchaikovsky the News: Postmodernism, Popular Culture, and the Emergence of Rock 'n Roll," *Black Music Research Journal* 8/9, no. 2 (1989), 292–93.

7. Guralnick, *Last Train to Memphis*, 443, 445–46, 456, 460–65.

8. Greil Marcus, *Mystery Train: Images of America in Rock 'n Roll Music*, 3d ed. (New York: Dutton, 1990), 169; Tosches, *Hellfire*, 168.

9. James Miller, *Flowers in the Dustbin: The Rise of Rock and Roll, 1947–1977* (New York: Simon & Schuster, 1999), 168–73; Marcus, *Mystery Train*, 167; Garofalo, *Rockin' Out*, 138.

10. Ellis Amburn, *Buddy Holly: A Biography* (New York: St. Martin's, 1995), 224–25.

11. Beverly Mendheim, *Ritchie Valens: The First Latino Rocker* (Tempe, Ariz. Bilingual Press, 1987); David Reyes and Tom Waldman, *Land of a Thousand Dances: Chicano Rock 'n Roll from Southern California* (Albuquerque: University of New Mexico Press, 1998), 37–38; George Lipsitz, "Land of a Thousand Dances: Youth, Minorities, and the Rise of Rock and Roll," in *Recasting America: Culture and Politics in the Age of the Cold War*, ed., Lary May (Chicago: University of Chicago Press, 1989), 275–76.

12. Amburn, *Buddy Holly*, especially 170, 209–10, 243–48; Garofalo, *Rockin' Out*, 142–43; Richard Aquila, *That Old-Time Rock & Roll: A Chronicle of an Era, 1954–1963* (Urbana: University of Illinois Press, 2000), 242–43.

13. Amburn, *Buddy Holly*, 144–45, 291–300.

14. Alan Clayson, *Only the Lonely: Roy Orbison's Life and Legacy* (New York: St. Martin's, 1989).

15. Marcus, *Mystery Train*, 170; David Szatmary, *Rockin' in Time: A Social History of Rock and Roll* (Englewood Cliffs, N.J.: Prentice-Hall, 1987), 83.

16. Garofalo, *Rockin' Out*, 201; Marc Eliot, *Rockonomics: The Money Behind the Music* (New York: F. Watts, 1989), 86–87.

17. Charlie Gillett, *The Sound of the City: The Rise of Rock and Roll* (New York: Outerbridge & Dienstfrey, 1970), 127; Garofalo, *Rockin' Out*, 160–64.

18. Thomas Doherty, *Teenagers and Teenpics: The Juvenilization of American Movies in the 1950s* (Boston: Unwin Hyman, 1988), 213.

19. Garofalo, *Rockin' Out*, 163–64.

20. Ibid., 186–91; Steve Chapple and Rebee Garofalo, *Rock 'n Roll Is Here to Pay: The History and Politics of the Music Industry* (Chicago: Nelson-Hall, 1977), 50.

21. Peter Guralnick, *Sweet Soul Music: Rhythm and Blues and the Southern Dream of Freedom* (Boston: Little, Brown, 1999), 7.

22. This sketch of Gordy draws on Garofalo, *Rockin' Out*, 191–96; Ward, *Just My Soul Responding*, 258–74; Echols, 169–72.

23. Guralnick, *Sweet Soul Music*, 3–4.

24. Ibid., 61–70, 97–103, 152–76, 233, 332–52.

25. Taylor Branch, *Pillar of Fire: America in the King Years, 1963–1965* (New York: Simon & Schuster, 1998), 419.

26. Szatmary, *Rockin' in Time*, 88; Garofalo, *Rockin' Out*, 202.

27. Arnold Shaw, *The Rock Revolution* (London: Atheneum, 1969), 88.

28. Allen J. Matusow, *The Unraveling of America: A History of Liberalism in the 1960s* (New York: Harper & Row, 1984), 294–95.

29. Hunter Davies, *The Beatles: The Authorized Biography* (New York: McGraw-Hill, 1968), 195–96.

30. For rock 'n' roll in the '60s and '70s see John Orman, *The Politics of Rock Music* (Chicago: Nelson-Hall, 1984). For the phrase "teen breakout from jailhouse America" see Matusow, *Unraveling of America*, 306.

Epilogue: "Born in the USA"

1. "Age of Aquarius," *Newsweek*, August 25, 1969; "A Whole New Minority Group," *Newsweek*, September 1, 1969.

2. "The Message of History's Biggest Happening," *Time*, August 29, 1969; "Nightmare in the Catskills," *New York Times*, August 18, 1969.

3. Rock 'n' roll was even cited to explain the action of American soldiers in the Vietnam War. "Introjected into the technology" wrote Herman Rapaport, "the libidinal impulses of rock became the lure by which some men killed with pleasure, the lure of 'heavy metal.' ... Putting the weapon on 'automatic fire' was called putting it on 'rock and roll.'" "Vietnam: The Thousand Plateaus," in *The '60s Without Apology*, ed. Sonya Sayres, Anders Stephanson, Stanley Aronowitz, and Fredric Jameson (Minneapolis: University of Minnesota Press, 1988), 137–47.

4. "The Message of History's Biggest Happening," *Time*, August 29, 1969.

5. Eric Alterman, *It Ain't No Sin to Be Glad You're Alive* (Boston: Little, Brown, 1999), 17–18, 54–55. See also Jim Cullen, *Born in the U.S.A.: Bruce Springsteen and the American Tradition* (New York: HarperCollins, 1997).

6. Alterman, *It Ain't No Sin*, 64–67, 72–76. For another deeply personal reaction to Springsteen, see Jefferson Cowie, "Fandom Faith and Bruce Springsteen," *Dissent* (Winter 2001): 112–17.

7. Cullen, *Born in the U.S.A.*, 232–34; Alterman, *It Ain't No Sin*, 103, 118–20, 127, 137–38.

8. Alterman, *It Ain't No Sin*, 95.

9. Ibid., 150–51, 156–68; Cullen, *Born in the U.S.A.*, 1–5, 233–35.

10. Alterman, *It Ain't No Sin*, 156–68, 175, 239–40.

INDEX